Social Democracy and European Integration

What kind of Europe do social democratic parties prefer? What is the origin of their preferences? Are they shaped by interests, institutions or ideas? If so, how? Why do social democratic political parties respond differently to the crucial question of the future of the European Union? While many social democratic parties initially opposed European integration either in principle or because of the form it took, gradually they came to lend their full, though often critical, support to it. Despite this evolution, important differences between them have remained.

This book examines the preferences of social democratic parties in Germany, France, the UK, Sweden and Greece towards European integration, in comparative perspective. Using a variety of sources, including interviews with key party officials, the contributors explore what kind of Europe these parties want, and seek to explain the formation and evolution of these preferences over time. They examine the interplay of national peculiarities and cross-national factors and their impact on preferences on European integration. In addition to highlighting the role of party leaders, they reveal that, far from being united on European integration, these parties disagree with each other in part because they have retreated – to varying degrees – from key social democratic principles.

Making an important contribution to the scholarship on preference formation and the research that links the European Union with the nation state, this book will be of interest to students and scholars of the EU, comparative politics and political parties.

Dionyssis G. Dimitrakopoulos is Senior Lecturer in Politics at Birkbeck College, University of London, UK.

Routledge Advances in European Politics

Social Democracy and European Integration

The politics of preference formation

**Edited by
Dionyssis G. Dimitrakopoulos**

Routledge
Taylor & Francis Group

LONDON AND NEW YORK

First published 2011
by Routledge
2 Park Square, Milton Park, Abingdon, Oxfordshire OX14 4RN

Simultaneously published in the USA and Canada
by Routledge
711 Third Avenue, New York, NY 10017

First issued in paperback 2016

Routledge is an imprint of the Taylor & Francis Group, an informa business.

Typeset in Times New Roman by
Florence Production Ltd, Stoodleigh, Devon

British Library Cataloguing in Publication Data
A catalogue record for this book is available from the British Library

Library of Congress Cataloging in Publication Data
 Social democracy and European integration: the politics of preference formation/
 edited by Dionyssis Dimitrakopoulos.
   p.cm. – (Routledge advances in european politics)
 Includes bibliographical references and indes.
 1. Socialist parties – European Union countries. 2. Europe – Economic
 integration – Political aspects. 3. European Union countries – Politics and
 government. I. Dimitrakopoulos, Dionyssis G., 1969–
 JN50.S615 2010
 324.2'172094–dc22   2010006942

ISBN 13 : 978-1-138-99621-2 (pbk)
ISBN 13 : 978-0-415-55985-0 (hbk)

Contents

Contributors

Dionyssis G. Dimitrakopoulos is Senior Lecturer in Politics at Birkbeck College, University of London. He has held a Marie Curie Post-Doctoral Fellowship at Oxford (Dept. of Politics & International Relations and Nuffield College) and the National Bank of Greece Senior Fellowship at the LSE (Hellenic Observatory/European Institute). His research and teaching focus mainly on the politics of European integration. He is the author of *The Power of the Centre: Central Governments and the Macro-implementation of EU Public Policy* (Manchester University Press, 2008) and several articles that have appeared, *inter alia*, in *Political Studies*, the *Journal of Public Policy*, the *European Journal of Political Research*, the *Journal of Common Market Studies*, the *Journal of European Pubic Policy*, the *European Law Journal*, *Government and Opposition* and the *European Journal of International Relations*.

Christoph Egle is Assistant Professor at Ludwig-Maximilians University in Munich. He received his Ph.D. from the University of Heidelberg in 2007. His main research interests are comparative public policy, political parties, and German and French politics. He is co-author of *Social Democracy in Power: The Capacity to Reform* (Routledge, 2008) and editor of several books on public policy in Germany. His work has appeared in numerous books and journals in German, English and French.

Karl Magnus Johansson is currently Associate Professor of Political Science at Södertörn University, Sweden. He will be moving to the University of Uppsala in January 2011. His primary research interests are European integration, Europeanization, foreign policy analysis, political parties, and transnationalism. His publications include *Transnational Party Alliances: Analysing the Hard-Won Alliance between Conservatives and Christian Democrats in the European Parliament* (Lund University Press, 1997), *European Political Parties between Cooperation and Integration* (edited jointly with Peter A. Zervakis, Nomos, 2002), and the edited volume *Sverige i EU* (SNS Förlag, 2002, 2nd edition). His work has appeared in several journals including the *European Journal of Political Research*, the *Journal of Common Market Studies*, the *Journal of European Public Policy*, *Party Politics* and *West European Politics*.

Hussein Kassim is Professor in Politics at the University of East Anglia. He taught previously at Birkbeck College, University of London, the University of Nottingham, and the University of Oxford, and has held visiting positions at Columbia University, New York University, Harvard University, Sciences Po in Paris, and ARENA, University of Oslo. He writes mainly on the interaction between the EU and the member states, EU institutions and EU competition policy. His publications include *Air Transport and the European Union* (co-authored with Handley Stevens, Palgrave, 2010), *The National Coordination of EU Policy* (two co-edited volumes, Oxford University Press, 2000 and 2001), *The EU and National Industrial Policy* (edited jointly with Anand Menon, Routledge, 1996) and articles published, *inter alia*, in the *Journal of Common Market Studies*, the *Journal of European Public Policy*, *West European Politics* and *Revue Française de Science Politique*. He is currently principal investigator on a major ESRC-funded research project on the European Commission.

Philippe Marlière is Professor of French and European Politics at University College London. In 2007, he held the Marcel Liebman Chair at the Université Libre de Bruxelles. His research focuses on French Socialism and European Social Democracy. His main publications include *La social-démocratie domestiquée. La voie blairiste* (Aden, 2008), *La mémoire socialiste. Sociologie du souvenir politique en milieu partisan* (L'Harmattan, 2007) and *Social Democratic Parties in the European Union. History, Organisation, Policies* (edited jointly with Robert Ladrech, Macmillan, 1999).

Argyris G. Passas is Assistant Professor in Public Administration and European Integration at Panteion University of Social and Political Sciences, Athens where he directs the Centre for Policy and Institutional Analysis. He has previously worked in the European Parliament, headed the National Centre for Public Administration (1996–2001) and served on several government expert committees on issues regarding the EU and public administration. His research and teaching focus on the European integration, public administration and public policy. His most recent publications include *National Administration and European Integration: The Greek Experience* (edited jointly with Th. Tsekos, Papazissis, Athens, 2009, in Greek) and *National Parliaments in the European Union's Political System. The "European Perplexity" of the Greek Parliament* (Papazissis, Athens, in press 2010, in Greek).

Göran von Sydow is researcher at the Swedish Institute for European Policy Studies, Stockholm and teaches courses on European integration in the Department of Political Science, University of Stockholm. He has studied at the doctoral programme at the European University Institute, the University of Stockholm and Sciences Po in Paris. He has published on political parties, European integration and, more recently, several articles on the Swedish EU Presidency of 2009.

Acknowledgements

This book stems from discussions on the social democratic family and the process of European integration that I have had with Argyris G. Passas and Philippe Marlière, occasionally over a glass of wine in Athens or a pint in Bloomsbury – during the operation of the Convention on the Future of Europe. Having observed the often truly remarkable differences between the preferences of several members of this political family on the central, indeed defining – issue of the future of the European Union, I asked the Leverhulme Trust for financial support. Without the Leverhulme Trust's international network grant F/07 112/M, this book would not have seen the light of day. The grant covered part of the seven (initially eight) contributors' research costs, as well as the costs associated with an authors' workshop and a conference held at Birkbeck College, University of London on 8–9 December 2006 and 20–21 April 2007, respectively. The University Association for Contemporary European Studies also covered part of the costs associated with the second event through a small conference grant (0730). Birkbeck hosted the two events with its typical mixture of grace and efficiency.

Collective processes of this kind inevitably generate a whole host of 'debts'. The contributors are grateful to our interviewees who agreed to be interviewed for the purposes of this project. My own main debt of gratitude is owed to the contributors to this volume, not only for their contributions, but also for dealing graciously and efficiently with an impatient editor's numerous demands. I owe a particular debt of gratitude to Argyris and Philippe for nourishing, at the crucial early stages, the idea upon which this book is based. I am also grateful to Kevin Featherstone, Anand Menon and Paul Taggart who offered helpful comments in their capacity as discussants at the two events. Of course, the usual disclaimer applies. Last but not least, thanks are also due to the anonymous referees and Heidi Bagtazo's team at Routledge for their patience and efficiency.

Bloomsbury, February 2010

Abbreviations

CAP	Common Agricultural Policy
CERES	*Centre d'Etudes, de Recherche et d'Education Socialistes*
CFSP	Common Foreign and Security Policy
CSPEC	Confederation of Socialist Parties of the European Community
EC	European Communities
ECB	European Central Bank
ECJ	European Court of Justice
ECSC	European Coal and Steel Community
EDC	European Defence Community
EEA	European Economic Area
EEC	European Economic Community
EFTA	European Free Trade Area
EK	*Enossi Kentrou* (Centre Union)
EMS	European Monetary System
ERM	Exchange Rate Mechanism
ETUC	European Trade Union Confederation
EU	European Union
GS	*Gauche Socialiste*
IGC	Intergovernmental Conference
IMF	International Monetary Fund
IMP	Integrated Mediterranean Programmes
KPD	*Kommunistische Partei Deutschlands*
LO	*Landsorganisationen i Sverige* (Swedish Trade Union Confederation)
MDC	*Mouvement des Citoyens*
NATO	North Atlantic Treaty Organisation
NEC	National Executive Committee
NPA	*Nouveau Parti Anticapitaliste*
NPS	*Nouveau Parti Socialiste*
OECD	Organisation for Economic Co-operation and Development
OEEC	Organisation for European Economic Co-operation
PASOK	*Panelinio Sosialistiko Kinima* (Panhellenic Socialist Movement)

PCF	*Parti Communiste Français*
PES	Party of European Socialists
PG	*Parti de Gauche*
PLP	Parliamentary Labour Party
PS	*Parti Socialiste*
QMV	Qualified Majority Voting
SAMAK	*Arbettarrörelsens nordiske samarbejdskommitté* (Joint Committee of the Nordic Social Democratic Labour Movement)
SAP	*Sveriges socialdemokratiska arbetarparti* (Swedish Social Democratic Party)
SDP	Social Democratic Party
SEA	Single European Act
SED	*Sozialistische Einheitspartei Deutschlands*
SFIO	*Section Française de l'Internationale Socialiste*
SGP	Stability and Growth Pact
SPD	*Sozialdemokratische Partei Deutschlands*
TCO	*Tjänstemännens Centralorganisation* (Swedish Confederation of Professional Employees)
TUC	Trades Union Congress
UMP	*Union pour un Mouvement Populaire*
WEU	Western European Union

1 Introduction

Social democracy, European integration and preference formation

Dionyssis G. Dimitrakopoulos

Die einzige Form, in der Europa als politisch handlungsfähige Einheit entstehen kann, ist die soziale Demokratie.

(Glotz 1985, 50)

The decision to proceed with integration or to oppose it rests on the perception of interests and on the articulation of specific values on the part of existing political actors.

(Haas [1958] 2003, 13)

Introduction[1]

The social democrats' relationship with, and involvement in, European integration has been turbulent over the years (Newman 1983; Featherstone 1988; Griffiths 1993; Haahr 1993; Delwit 1995).[2] Although several social democratic parties have in the past opposed either the principle or the individual manifestations of European integration, they have (over time) come to lend their – often critical – support to it (Marks and Wilson 2000). However, acknowledging this basic fact tells only part of the 'story' of this major political family's stance on a singularly important political and economic phenomenon in post-war Europe. Their declarations of support for European integration does not necessarily reflect a single set of motives, nor does it automatically indicate that they hold the same views with regard to the future of the EU. Indeed, even a cursory reading of the proposals that social democrats submitted to the Convention on the Future of Europe indicates significant differences between them. For example, although they are members of the same political family, some espouse the notion of a 'federal Europe', while others oppose it. Some support the enhancement of the EU's redistributive capacity, whereas others object to it. Some want the EU to counterbalance US hegemony, while others oppose this idea. Equally telling was their disarray ahead of the 2009 European elections, i.e. the first EU-wide electoral contest since the onset of a financial and economic crisis that vindicated those among them who opposed (instead of embracing) neo-liberalism. This begs the basic question that this project seeks to answer: what accounts for social democratic party preferences on European integration?

There are additional reasons why it is worth exploring the origin of preferences of social democratic parties – i.e. mass (rather than class) parties with a strong working-class anchoring (in terms of membership and electorate), a 'governmental vocation', close relationships with centralised and representative trade union organisations, an 'inter-classist' (in terms of their sociological and electoral basis) and national profile, a dominant position on the left of the political spectrum, and support for parliamentary democracy and the mixed economy (Marlière 1999, 4–5) – with regard to the development of European integration. European integration was, to a large extent, the product of their domestic political rivals.[3] It relied on instruments (markets) that they distrusted. It begun to materialise at a time when social democrats were redefining their ideological basis and it challenged many of their concrete achievements, or at least a particular understanding of them. It seemed – at least initially, to favour groups (such as industrialists and farmers) who were not particularly (or at least not necessarily) well disposed towards the social democratic project.[4] Although many opposed its specific form or even rejected it *in toto*, social democratic parties subsequently came to support it.[5] Despite this evolution, important differences between them have remained (Marks and Wilson 2000, 442–8). Both their content and, more importantly, their origins deserve to be analysed in a comparative perspective.

Market-making was the primary focus of European integration from the 1950s to the 1970s. Although the partial reconciliation with the market was a central theme in the redefinition of social democracy after 1945,[6] some of these parties often reacted in a reserved or even hostile manner to European integration, precisely because of its reliance on market-making. Instead, they highlighted the need to build the 'Europe of peoples'. Moreover, cardinal and more traditional aspects of their standard ideological platform – including internationalism, solidarity and the 'democratisation of the economy' – remained intact and legitimised sustained criticisms of European integration.

After having fought for the democratisation of national political systems, social democrats had, after World War II, the opportunity to engage more vigorously in the pursuit of socio-economic objectives, but these remained focused on the national level (Eley 2002; Judt 1996, 32).[7] Although internationalism and solidarity remained central features of the social democrats' ideological basis, in reality integration often appeared to some of them (at least initially) to amount to an assault on their concrete national achievements. How did they seek to reconcile the two, and, more importantly, what accounts for the differences between them?

Many social democratic parties discovered that European integration, far from being simply a constraint, represented a new means for the pursuit of their reformist agenda. This seems to have affected their decision – in principle – to support it, but it also meant that they had to design and then pursue a 'social democratic Europe'.

Preferences, preference formation and the study of European integration

How do political actors come to know what they want? How are their preferences[8] formed? How do they reach decisions about the ranking of possible futures? Why do they give priority to some political outcomes over others (Druckman and Lupia 2000, 2; Frieden 1999, 41; Lake and Powell 1999, 9; Moravcsik 1997, 513)? As Aaron Wildavsky reminds us, 'although it is eminently reasonable to study . . . how people try to get what they want through political activity, it is also *unreasonable* to neglect the study of why people want what they want' (Wildavsky 1987, 3, emphasis in the original). This statement applies to many sub-fields of political science, but it is particularly relevant to the study of European integration, of which this project is part. Indeed, the origin of preferences of political actors with regard to European integration has remained remarkably under-researched. Political scientists have focused on either the operation of the EU and its predecessors or their development over time. In that context, intellectual effort has been invested overwhelmingly in the analysis of the way in which political actors interact with each other in an effort to achieve their objectives, both in 'normal' EU policy-making and the intergovernmental conferences that reform the EU treaties.

This emphasis is unsurprising. It can be construed as a reflection of the corresponding political debate pitching the supporters of 'more Europe' against their opponents. 'Building Europe' was a key political target, and the question of having more or less of it (i.e. more or less integration) was at the heart of the debate on the post-World War II development of the continent. Although the objective of European integration had a key political component, the gradual construction and subsequent operation of the European Communities and the European Union relied on technocracy, depoliticisation and the quest for the 'common European interest'.[9] The importance of key value judgements was more often than not obscured or downplayed.[10] The emphasis on the 'common European interest' was, in part, due to the need to defeat narrowly defined egotistical attitudes nourished by each country's history. That the EU has become a successful example of regional integration is, to a large extent, the result of this political strategy.

However, Joschka Fischer's famous speech at Humboldt University in May 2000 crystallised the new focus of the political debate on European integration against the backdrop of the end of the Cold War and the prospect (and now reality) of enlargement to the East: what *kind* of Europe do we want (Fischer 2000)? The exigencies of the choice between 'Europe as an area' and 'Europe as an actor' go well beyond the EU's embedded emphasis on technocratic (and seemingly 'neutral') arrangements. The new debate calls for explicit value judgements.[11] More importantly, citizens do not appear willing to grant their leaders the degree of autonomy afforded to them during the post-war 'permissive consensus', as politicians are coming to realise. The value-laden debates regarding the ratification of the Constitutional Treaty in several member states demonstrated the increased relevance of domestic perceptions and realities, on the one hand, and the distinction between the political Left and Right on the other. Although, in terms of political practice, this distinction often seems to be blurred or even irrelevant, it remains germane for two reasons. First, it reflects real differences of political principles. Second, it is at the heart of the citizens' *référentiel* and often informs their understanding of the current shape and practice of the EU, as well as the implications of future alternatives (Gabel and Anderson 2004, 30–1). Exploring the historical origins of the preferences of key actors is a *conditio sine qua non*, both for understanding their current views and for assessing how far they are prepared to go in terms of the reform of the EU.

In the context of the study of European integration, Andrew Moravcsik (1993; 1998) was the first scholar to problematise preferences and preference formation. Inspired by a rationalist account of the formation and operation of international regimes, he put forward a model of preference formation that focuses on governments.[12] This model of preference formation has been criticised on conceptual and empirical grounds, with scholars illustrating the importance of ideological as well as institutional factors in preference formation (Aspinwall 2000; 2002; Dimitrakopoulos and Kassim 2004b; 2004c). Moreover, comparativists have argued that the EU political space is defined on the basis of two dimensions, namely more versus less integration, and Left versus Right (Hix 1999; Hooghe and Marks 1999). Given its focus, Moravcsik's model is understandably not useful for the analysis of the origin of *party* preferences,[13] but it raises – albeit indirectly – a question of cardinal importance. If, as he argues, the main objective of politicians is to maintain (or gain) power, elections are crucial. They are the mechanism by which voters choose the party (or parties) that will govern. This begs the question as to *how* competing political parties define their preferences in the run-up to electoral contests and beyond (e.g. when they are in power). Voters are asked to choose between competing political platforms, but how are these platforms constructed? What do we know about the origin of party preferences in general, and the preferences of social democratic parties on European integration in particular?

Competing rationalities and the impact of membership

The literature on the origin of party preferences (and change therein) reflects broader trends in the analysis of political phenomena in that it is couched in two kinds of rationality. On the one hand, the Downsian perspective stresses the importance of vote maximisation: "politicians . . . are motivated by the desire for power, prestige and income . . . their primary objective is to be elected. This in turn implies that each party seeks to receive more votes than any other" (Downs 1957, 30–1). This line of reasoning has been further elaborated. 'Hard decisions' have been ascribed to *office-seeking* (aimed at increasing the party's control of executive office benefits), *policy-seeking* (the effort to maximise the impact on public policy) and *vote-seeking*[14] (Strøm and Müller 1999, 5–9). As democracy is, ultimately, a competitive game, electoral considerations can be deemed to affect party preferences as well as strategies (see *infra*).

Despite their importance, electoral considerations are not the only factor accounting for party preferences and change therein (Harmel *et al.* 1995). At the other extreme of the continuum, a different kind of rationality has been utilised. Ideational accounts of politics stress the importance of the cognitive and the normative aspects of ideas. In this context, social democratic party preferences have been ascribed to different 'programmatic beliefs', that is distinctive versions of social democracy that, once institutionalised, offered different solutions to major political and economic problems that these countries faced (Berman 1998). In addition, ideology affects both the choice of policy spaces that a party seeks to occupy and its position within these spaces (Budge 1994).

Finally, institutionalist accounts can be located between rationalist and ideational analyses. Political parties are – like other organisations – internally differentiated arenas. Institutional issues have featured prominently in the study of the internal operation of parties – none more so than the 'iron law of oligarchy', which raised the issue of a party's internal operation and the role of leadership (Michels [1911] 1989). The relationship between party leadership (a minority of directors) and party members (the majority of the directed) can be expected to affect, not only a party's strategy, but also its preferences. Although existing work highlights the importance of the institutional environment in which a party operates, it has focused overwhelmingly on the impact of institutions on party *strategies* rather than preferences (see, for example, Strøm, Budge and Laver 1994).

In the particular domain of the study of party politics and the EU, several issues have attracted attention (Ladrech 2002; Mair 2001; 2007). As regards preferences and preference formation, two specific elements have attracted considerable attention, namely: (a) the origin of party families' broad preferences on the issue of European integration, and (b) the switch to a positive ('pro-European') stance (and the related matter of Euroscepticism[15]). The key conclusion of the first body of literature links ideology and a party family's stance on European integration (Marks and Wilson 2000; Hooghe, Marks and Wilson 2002; Marks, Wilson and Ray 2002; Marks *et al.* 2006; Marks *et al.* 2007; Rohrschneider and Whitefield 2007; Hellström 2008). Indeed, as Marks and Wilson (2000, 433) put it, 'the new issue of European integration is assimilated into pre-existing ideologies of party leaders, activists and constituencies that reflect long-standing commitments on fundamental domestic issues.' The transformation from a cautious (or even hostile) to a positive attitude has been ascribed to several factors. The first can be labelled the *instrumental view* of integration (Camiller 1989, 11; Sassoon 1996, 734; Marlière 2001, 6; Marks and Wilson 2000, 447). Integration has come to be seen by social democrats as the means to achieve the regulation of markets (albeit at the supranational level) or the modernisation of the domestic economy. This was part of their programmatic renewal[16] that took place during the 1980s and early 1990s and – coupled with the significant policy and institutional developments that followed the adoption of the Single European Act (SEA) and subsequent reforms of the treaties – casts doubt[17] on the continuing accuracy of earlier claims that highlight the influence of distinct national contexts as a key determinant of these parties' attitude vis-à-vis European integration (Featherstone 1988, 304; Gaffney 1996a, 9–10). The instrumental view has been challenged by the *obfuscation thesis*, according to which support for integration has been used by social democrats in an effort 'to compensate for failure and retrenchment at the national level'. Seen from that angle, European integration is a vehicle for the mobilisation of support[18] by social democratic parties 'despite the absence of substantive social democratic policy output' (Bailey 2005, 14).[19] Finally, the *dependence thesis* links continued membership and active engagement with a fear of national exclusion: the willingness of other member states to proceed creates the risk of costly exclusion from decision-making regarding issues (such as the shape of the market and the institutional framework) that concern the reluctant partners (Haahr 1993, 263).

This literature deserves credit, both for raising and dealing with a complex and multifaceted issue, and for doing so on the basis of a variety of qualitative and quantitative methods, but it has a fundamental problem that this research project and book seek to help overcome. It reflects the nature of political debates, where the question of having more or less 'Europe' (i.e. integration) has dominated until the late 1990s, but this has obscured major differences *between* parties of the social democratic family. Indeed, even the literature that explicitly discusses differences *within* party families (Marks and Wilson 2000, 442ff.; Featherstone 1988; Gaffney 1996b) does not go beyond the social democrats' decision to support or oppose European integration. These differences are both more evident and – since Joschka Fischer's speech (2000) at Humboldt University – more salient. Although these parties have adopted a positive stance on European integration, they do not pursue the same objectives, nor are these objectives necessarily stable over time, as the cases examined in this volume clearly demonstrate. In other words, while they have come to support membership of the European Union, they do not necessarily (and certainly not always) share the same preferences with regards to its future – i.e. the same *kind* of EU. Indeed, the leaders of the members of the Confederation of the Socialist Parties of the EC declared in 1993 that

> the ever increasing internationalisation of the economy and interdependence of our societies at every level means that it is increasingly difficult to respond on a national level to the new challenges which arise. Democratic control of the future remains possible, provided that those elements of sovereignty which can no longer be exercised in a purely national framework are pooled.
>
> (cited in Notermans 2001b, 6)

However, their subsequent rhetoric and praxis have revealed a much more diverse picture marked by disagreement and conflict between these parties.[20]

Why is that so? What accounts for these differences? This issue is worthy of examination and particularly salient in the aftermath of the financial and economic crisis that commenced in 2008, i.e. at a time when the limits of unfettered financial markets have become obvious even to the most ardent supporter of neo-liberalism. Indeed, if European integration proceeds on the basis of the struggle between neo-liberals and supporters of regulated capitalism[21] (Hooghe and Marks 1999; Ross 1992), the combination of the economic crisis and the 2009 European elections presented social democrats with an excellent opportunity, but their divisions and many of the reforms that they introduced in their ideology, discourse and praxis during the previous two decades led them to a major defeat. Their divisions were so deep that they (a) tellingly failed (unlike their main opponents) to answer reformist calls (Hix 2008) to name a common candidate for the presidency of the European Commission and (b) ended up defeated by a Centre-Right that – if its rhetoric is to be believed – had stolen their 'clothes'. In short, their differences are consequential too, and this is an additional reason why they are worthy of systematic investigation.

Three sets of variables can be used in an effort to identify an actor's preferences with regard to European integration, namely the *scope* of integration – that is, the functional areas that are covered by integration (Taylor 1975, 343) – its *aims* and, finally, the *institutions* that give precise meaning to it. These issues have remained at the centre of political and academic debates on European integration since the 1950s. The key criterion used for the definition of each set of options is the policy-making autonomy of the state. Should it be exercised unilaterally, or should it be shared and, if so, to what extent and how? The autonomy of the state is a defining issue, both for social democracy and European integration, in different but complementary ways. First, the importance that social democratic parties ascribe to the nation state and the degree of policy-making autonomy that it ought to maintain vis-à-vis societal actors – the primacy of politics in Sheri Berman's apposite formulation (2006) – is at the heart of the entire social democratic project. Before World War II, the debate regarding the relationship between class and nation had been affected by the presence (and the break-up) of multinational empires (Bauer 2000; Delwit 1995, chapter 1). After the end of World War II, the autonomy of the market and the impact of the international environment took centre stage in the debate on the relative autonomy of the state (Poulantzas 1968; Krasner 1978; Nordlinger 1981). Second, the autonomy of the state is the defining characteristic of theoretical and political debates regarding the process of integration (Haas [1958] 2003; Moravcsik 1998). While functionalists and neo-functionalists saw integration as an answer to the exigencies of post-war Europe – and therefore advocated placing the state within a broader institutional framework – proponents of liberal intergovernmentalism construed integration as a mechanism that enhances the autonomy of national executives (Moravcsik

1994). Social democratic parties mirrored this debate at different points in time (see the chapters by Marlière, Kassim, Dimitrakopoulos and Passas, as well as Johansson and von Sydow in this volume). This debate has been conducted with regard to three central issues. These are discussed in the next section.

What kind of Europe? An outline of the explanandum

The scope of integration

Should integration be limited to some sectors (and if so, which ones?) or should it, at least in principle, be expanded to all policy sectors? Although we now know that the EU is involved (in one way or another) in virtually all policy sectors, the expansion of its activity has been a politically contentious issue both for the Left and the Right. Therefore, it must be problematised. Two distinct positions can be identified as part of a continuum. In principle, integration, could be limited to a small number of policy areas or, alternatively, extensive.[22]

The aims of integration[23]

Why should integration be pursued?[24] Post-war integration in Europe was a political project that utilised the economy as an instrument. Although the distinction between economic and political integration is unhelpful, because the boundaries between them are artificial – after all, economic integration is achieved or opposed via political decisions – ignoring it would obscure the duality of the process that has unfolded since 1945. Although economic integration has now reached a much more advanced stage in its development, the two facets are closely intertwined. Thus, instead of being separated, they ought to be placed on a continuum. Moreover, they highlight the major challenges that social democratic parties faced after the war, both of which entail the use of political power. The autonomy of the market (and the economy as a whole) and the establishment of a new political order in Europe are two of these major issues.

Integration can be pursued either as one of a number of instruments for the achievement of social democratic objectives or as an objective in its own right.[25] Either way, the social democrats had to choose between two abstract models, namely Europe construed as an *area*, and Europe construed as an *actor*. This distinction embodies two different sets of aims spanning the full range of options regarding economic and political integration.[26] They also reflect different views about the position and the role of the state. To what extent should the state share competences with the institutions of the EU? What objectives should be pursued? Should integration be limited to the establishment of a free trade area, or should it be a more ambitious project?

While scholars of economic integration distinguish between negative and positive integration, a much more illuminating, and therefore relevant, distinction between market-making and market-correcting policy interventions[27] 'marks the frontline of ideological conflict between anti-interventionist (e.g. neoliberal) and interventionist (e.g. social democratic or Keynesian) theorists, political parties and interest groups' (Scharpf 1999, 45–6).

Market-making (like negative integration) entails the removal of tariffs, quantitative restrictions and other obstacles to trade and competition.[28] *Market correction* goes further because it entails the establishment and active use of the capacity to intervene in the economy in an effort to achieve a 'level playing field' where economic actors can compete and, to a lesser extent, to remove the negative effects of market-making.[29] Crucially, while the opponents of intervention accept intervention only to the extent that it serves market-making purposes, proponents of intervention consider it a condition for market-making (Scharpf 1999, 46). A common market combines market-making and market-correcting measures.

More advanced levels of integration entail not only a more pronounced political commitment to capacity building, but an increased degree of joint decision-making as well. This is why neo-liberals consider the common market as the completion of most legitimate aspirations of economic integration and view further positive integration[30] as 'unnecessary and dangerous', while supporters of intervention see it as a constraint (Scharpf 1999, 49). *Economic and monetary union* – the next step in the process – exacerbates these divisions. It entails the adoption of a single currency as well as 'common policies with regard to economic matters in order to eliminate the frictions and disruptions resulting from divergent national interventions in the common market' (Scharpf 1999, 47). This raises two major issues[31] for social democrats, namely the emerging organisation's redistributive capacity and the extent of political involvement in economic decision-making. The enhancement of the EU's redistributive capacity entails the establishment of the means[32] to promote redistribution across geographical areas, sections of the population and sectors of the economy (i.e. regional, social and industrial policies), but the policy challenge takes a new form, which can be dissociated from the exigencies of market-making and market correction. Whereas, in earlier stages of economic integration, redistribution had been utilised as a side payment (in an effort to facilitate agreement), in subsequent stages it is more likely to either be valued in its own right – as it reflects the importance of economic and social cohesion – or at least become a political problem, because the common market and economic and monetary union create constraints that undermine the capability of national political systems to pursue democratically legitimised policy objectives (Scharpf 1999, 49).

The significant enhancement of the redistributive capacity of the EU brings it closer to political union. *Political union* is based on a sense of solidarity and – in addition to a fully fledged redistributive capacity – it entails common policies in the areas of foreign affairs, security and defence, taxation, justice and home affairs that are made and implemented by a new supranational set of institutions.

The institutions of integration

How should the aforementioned aims be pursued? What kinds of institutional arrangement should integration entail, and what should the position of the state be therein? The answers to these questions are important, not only because institutions shape political outcomes (including the content and direction of integration) but also because they reflect substantive preferences.[33]

Two models[34] can be envisaged as part of a continuum, namely a traditional *intergovernmental organisation* with a light secretariat, such as those found in several traditional international organisations, and, at the other extreme, a *supranational organisation* built on the federal model. Whereas the former allows individual member states to retain a significant degree of autonomy in decision-making (as the secretariat does not have the right of initiative, and decisions are taken unanimously), the latter entails the complete overhaul of political decision-making.

The principle of unity in diversity permeates the vertical and the horizontal division of powers in federal systems. There is 'predominantly a division of powers between general and regional authorities, each of which, in its own sphere is co-ordinate with the others and independent of them' (Wheare 1946, 32–3), coupled with the principle of *Bundestreue* (federal comity) that is enshrined in the constitution and enforced by the supreme court of the federation. In the bicameral system of a fully-fledged federation, states are represented in the upper chamber, while the lower chamber is composed of directly elected members. The federal executive either mirrors the balance of power in the lower chamber (as it does in Germany), or it is directly elected by the people and is separated from other branches (as it is in the USA). Finally, decisions to amend the constitution of the federation require large majorities but not unanimity.

Where do preferences come from? What accounts for their content (defined both in terms of the acceptance of European integration in principle and in terms of its specific aspects and manifestations)? The next section presents the independent variables, i.e. alternative sources of party preferences. Three sets of explanatory factors can be envisaged. They focus on the broad (and internally differentiated) categories of interest-based, institutionalist and, finally, ideational accounts that permeate the study of politics.

Where do preferences come from?

Faced with this question, we had two options. First, we could opt for the focused discussion of one (set of) variable(s). Second, we could seek to discuss a broad set of potential explanatory factors and examine whether and how they could help explain party preferences at certain points in time. We opted for the latter in the belief that it was more likely to lead to empirically rich (and theoretically driven) 'thick' descriptions of the kind that would (a) do more justice to the complex realities in which we are interested and (b) include a discussion of change over time. In that sense, the discussion that follows ought to be understood as an invitation to the authors of the country-specific chapters to consider these explanatory factors (and the interplay between them) in their analysis of individual parties.

Interests[35]

Qui bono? (who benefits?) is a question that interest-based accounts of politics discuss as, 'what people want depends on where they sit, as theorists have argued long before the time of Bentley and Marx' (Gourevitch 1986, 56). There are many ways to conceptualise this most prevalent explanatory variable in the study of politics.

The broad notion of *economic interests* can be discussed with reference to the national economy and, more specifically, a country's relative economic development. In the more affluent economies of the European North, integration is often portrayed as a factor that can (or does) undermine landmark social democratic achievements, whereas, in the European South, there are calls for the enhancement of the EU's redistributive capacity, but neither these critiques nor social democratic praxis are consistent over time. Thus, it is important to explore the impact of the national economy as a whole on the preferences of social democrats on European integration. The nature of the domestic economy also reveals the distribution of power and possible attitudes of domestic groups. For example, agricultural economies of the South are more likely than those of the North to adopt a protectionist stance.

In the context of increasingly interdependent economies and pluralist democratic regimes, the impact of economic interests on party preferences should be discussed with reference to coalitions of actors. This strategy has been successfully used for the explanation of national responses to changes in international economic conditions,[36] as well as the development of European integration (Moravcsik 1998, 3). The question of the need for coalitions is a key feature of the birth of social democracy (Bernstein [1899] 1969; Przeworski 1985, 24; Gay [1952] 1979). To what extent can preferences with regard to European integration be explained on the basis of domestic economic coalitions?

The second strand in interest-based accounts focuses on the interests of politicians. To make government policy, politicians must win votes and gain access to power. Thus, interests can be conceptualised in the Downsian perspective, i.e. in terms of *vote maximisation*, but the direction of causality is not unique (Ray 2003). Parties develop preferences on the basis of the wishes of either their traditional or potential voters – or, conversely, are affected by them – but the salience of individual issues varies considerably (Steenbergen and Scott 2004). To what extent does the salience that the electorate attaches to 'Europe' affect a party's preferences on European integration?

Preference formation construed in terms of vote maximisation can also be affected by the presence of competitors in the same political space (Johansson and Raunio 2001). To what extent has the presence (or absence) of competition from other left-wing parties affected the preferences of a given social democratic party on European integration (Criddle 1969)? Euroscepticism is another important aspect of this issue (Taggart 1998; Taggart and Szczerbiak 2008a; 2008b). How does the presence of a strong Eurosceptic strand or party in domestic politics affect the formation of social democratic party preferences on European integration? Does it cover both policy and institutional aspects of integration?

Interests – this time defined more loosely – can also shape preferences by inducing opposition parties to oppose (or even denounce) decisions of the party in power (or the EU), because this is what opposition parties do. This *effet d'opposition* (Delwit 1995, 258) often reflects more perceptions of interests than actual beliefs. Nevertheless, politicians' public declarations can harness public support for positions that subsequently become party preferences, in part as a consequence of (expected) vote maximisation.

Interests can also affect preferences in a more abstract way. *Policy legacies* shape expectations and provide a powerful source of inertia, because they create constituencies that oppose change both within a party and in the electoral arena. This is, in part, shaped by the specific characteristics of a party's history.[37]

The impact of policy legacies on preferences also raises the issue of *party cohesion*,[38] that is, the extent to which party members (and office holders) rally around party positions (Sjöblom 1968, 183). 'Catch-all parties' (Kirchheimer 1966) typically have wider political horizons because they aspire to increase their share of the vote and gain access to power. This, in turn, means that previously coherent political parties are also internally politicised arenas where different factions compete for supremacy. Has this trend affected preference formation on European integration? If so, how? To what extent is European integration a politically salient issue *within* a given social democratic party, and how does this affect its preferences on European integration? Also, given that European integration is, more often than not, just one of a number of politically salient matters in elections or when a party is in government, to what extent has it provided the basis for intra-party cleavages? What impact do these cleavages have on the priority that social democratic parties attach to European integration?[39] Given the multiplicity of policy challenges that any modern party has to face, is European integration seen as a primary issue of systemic importance, or is it construed in instrumental terms (and why)?

More generally, does *party type* affect party preferences on European integration? Elite parties, such as the French *Parti Socialiste* (PS), have a loose relationship with their electorate and have, in the past, comprised personalities with widely diverging views. In contrast, mass parties tend to mobilise large parts of the electorate essentially on the basis of ideology (Krouwel 2006, 254–5).[40]

Finally, interests may affect party preferences on European integration through the perceptions generated by each country's specific *geopolitical position*. Geopolitical considerations[41] may affect primary national preferences (Moravcsik 1998, 27) in the sense that integration may be the means for a country to deal with 'security externalities', but does this influence extend to party preferences as well? Delwit's argument (1995, 255) is subtle, but it needs to be discussed further: a country's geopolitical position guides – but does not determine – attitudes towards integration. A country of reduced political, economic and strategic importance is likely to have a more positive attitude *vis-à-vis* European integration. Of particular importance here is the end of the Cold War, not only because it led to the establishment of a mono-polar world order, but also because it eliminated one of the two actual 'models' that served as reference points for social democrats in Europe. Moreover, the end of the Cold War has created or exacerbated various security threats that figure prominently in the debate on the future of Europe, especially since 9 September 2001. This is a key factor that has reinvigorated the interest in the distinction between Europe defined as an area and Europe defined as an actor.

Institutions

Institutions affect the operation and behaviour of political parties in two senses. First, they create the framework in which parties compete for resources and votes. Electoral systems, constitutional arrangements (such as the structure and power of the executive, the shape of the legislature) and involvement in international and regional organisations are prominent examples. Second, parties are internally differentiated arenas where competing factions play the internal political game, which is regulated by rules that distribute power and resources between the relevant actors (leaders, members etc.), thus making the adoption of some policies more likely than others (Steinmo, Thelen and Longstreth 1992). The analysis of preference formation requires that both sets of issues be explored.

The first issue concerns party policy-making. How is party policy made? What are the sources of input (e.g. leader, party members, party conferences, think tanks), and how are competing demands aggregated? More specifically, what is the role of the *party leadership*? How autonomous is it (see Raunio 2002; Poguntke *et al.* 2007)? Is decision-making centralised (as the iron law of oligarchy would suggest) or is decentralised? Are there internal checks and balances, or is the party leader *primus solus*?[42] A related question concerns a party's *relationship to civil society*. For example, the Labour party was created by trade unions, and they have maintained, until recently, a significant role in party policy. To what extent has this fact affected the party's positions and action on European integration?

Party cohesion has been mentioned earlier as a substantive issue. It is also an institutional issue in the sense that parties utilise institutions – such as whips in parliament and party conferences – that are meant to promote cohesion, or at least the definition and co-ordinated expression of agreed party positions. Do these mechanisms affect preference formation on European integration, and if so how? Does the party leadership deal with dissent in an accommodating or in a confrontational manner (Aylott 1997; Johansson and Raunio 2001, 245)? In more general terms, *party organisation* evolves over time, like any other institutional arena. To what extent – and how – does this change affect preference formation? Two facets of this issue deserve particular attention, namely the organisation of party leadership and a party's relationship with its constituents, including its favoured groups.[43]

One important aspect of party cohesion concerns the *relationship between party and government*. When the party leader is also the head of government, the party is more likely to adopt a coherent view. When different individuals hold these posts, the potential for strife between them is greater. For example, acting as the conscience of a government, a social democratic party may push a government to maximalist positions in the area of social policy, and it may 'pull' it to minimalist positions on institutional issues (Ladrech 2002, 398). One important facet of the relationship between party and government is the pattern of presidentialisation, which entails (a) the concentration of power to the head of government and (b) growing autonomy from her party (Poguntke and Webb 2005b). If there is evidence of presidentialisation, to what extent did it affect social democratic party preferences on European integration?

Preference formation is also affected by the broader institutional context in which a party operates. At the most general level, the *constitution* of a country distributes formal power between actors and levels of government (and, therefore, it reflects the balance of power in a given society). Thus, it facilitates some forms of political action and forecloses others, but it also mirrors the normative underpinning of government.[44] The *electoral system* is another major part of this context. Electoral systems affect, not only the shape of party systems (Duverger 1950; 1951), but also the strategies pursued by political parties. Although the exigencies of party competition in PR may promote the adoption of ideologically 'pure' manifestos, less proportional systems promote ideologically diluted manifestos, at least for the parties that compete for office.[45] Moreover, 'first-past-the-post' systems lead to two-party systems, where the two major parties can be expected to oppose each other's views.

The *structure and the operation of national executives* may also affect party preferences. When the Cabinet operates in a collegiate manner, it provides an additional arena for substantive policy debates where the prime minister is *primus inter pares*. In contrast, when the Cabinet is a rubber-stamping body that operates under the authority of the prime minister as *primus solus*, substantive policy debates are more likely to take place elsewhere (e.g. in party conferences). Moreover, coalition governments impose constraints that single-party governments do not have to face (Johansson and Raunio 2001).

The *national parliament* is another contributing factor. When parliament plays an autonomous role, it provides an important arena for intra-party policy debates (especially when a party is in government) and party competition. In contrast, when the national parliament is weak, other fora (such as party conferences) perform this role.

In more general terms, electoral systems and other institutions – such as the power of parliament – often reflect and reinforce cardinal aspects of *national political cultures*. In consociational democracies, the logic of compromise is deeply embedded in institutional practices and political behaviour. On the other hand, the Westminster model promotes confrontation, adversarialism and the logic of zero-sum games. To what extent does political culture affect preference formation on European integration? One important aspect of political cultures concerns *populism* (Hayward 1996; Taggart 2000). Given the complexity of its origins, institutions and policies, the EU often lends itself to populist attacks. How does populism on the Left and the Right affect social democratic party preferences on European integration?

Finally, institutional influences on preference formation may also stem from participation in the process of integration. EU-level transnational party families may act as fora for the socialisation of party officials in a manner that affects political choices (Johansson 2002b; Ladrech 2000, 399). How do social democratic parties interact with/fit into the Party of European Socialists (PES)?[46] *Isomorphic pressures* transcend institutional fields, such as transnational party federations, and may lead to the adoption of similar structures and policies, either because these are widely regarded as legitimate or successful models (mimetic isomorphism) or – in the case of normative isomorphism – because they are couched in knowledge and experience that are diffused by networks of professional officials with common training (DiMaggio and Powell 1991).

European integration has also affected party preferences in a more specific sense. In the 'thin' institutional context of the European Communities of the 1950s, party preference formation was much more of an intellectual exercise than it has been since the SEA of 1986. The *acquis communautaire* is a key difference between the two eras. For example, whereas majority decision-making at the European level and the autonomy of the European Commission were central but abstract institutional innovations introduced in the 1950s, more than five decades later political parties (among other actors) have a more concrete idea as to what they truly entail. Given the extent to which the EU has changed over time, it is not unreasonable to expect political parties' preferences to reflect (or to have been constructed with reference to) this change – which creates constraints as well as opportunities (Merkel and Ostheim 2004b; Marks and Wilson 2000) – in line with the literature on feedback effects (Pierson 1993). Even if one were to focus on issues close to core social democratic concerns, concrete examples would abound: from the enhancement of the EU's redistributive capacity since 1986, to the possibility of re-regulation at the European level in the context of the single market, the protection of the environment, the relationship between deepening and widening, and the capacity of individual actors (such as powerful member states or institutions of the EU) to shape political outcomes. To what extent has the development of the EU (especially since the mid 1980s) affected the formation of party preferences on European integration? Do individual cases mirror the modernisation, obfuscation or dependence theses (see *supra*)?

Ideas

Ideational variables have been conceptualised in many ways (Berman 2001; Goldstein and Keohane 1993), varying from culture and ideology to programmatic beliefs and policy paradigms. These variables affect political outcomes (including preferences) in two ways. First, they act as cognitive maps that allow political actors to make sense of the context in which they operate. Second, they provide normative templates that enable actors to choose between appropriate and inappropriate options. They legitimise some forms of political action but not others.

Programmatic beliefs are ideas that are abstract, systematic and co-ordinated, marked by integrated assertions, theories and goals, on the basis of which programmes of action are formulated through the provision of relatively clear and distinctive links between theory and practice (Berman 1998, 21). The social democratic ideological platform has always been a fundamental part of its appeal, but it has not led to a single and unified set of programmatic beliefs. Different programmatic beliefs lead political actors to provide different political answers to the same challenges (Berman 1998). To what extent did distinctive programmatic beliefs influence these parties' stance on European integration? Three issues are of critical importance here, namely the relationship between *internationalism* (coupled with *solidarity*) and the nation state;[47] the dominant conception of democracy espoused by social democratic parties; and, finally, the notion of social cohesion.

The debate on the relationship between socialism (as a class concept) and the nation predates the establishment of the European Communities in the 1950s (Bauer 2000; Delwit 1995, chapter 1), but few social democratic parties resolved this issue before World War II. The anti-statist characteristics of European integration reinvigorated this debate after 1945. How did these parties reconcile social democracy's instinctive internationalism[48] with the exigencies of European integration? To what extent has the belief in the need for market intervention shaped social democratic preferences on European integration? Why did the need for market intervention at the national level prevail over solidarity with other Europeans and the social democrats' emphasis on internationalism? Moreover, to what extent can ideological considerations explain the fact that some social democratic parties have, at various times, adopted a zero-sum perspective on the relationship between the nation state and European integration, while others have not? How did they conceptualise democracy at the national level, and which conception of democracy did they develop for the EC/EU? As social democratic parties by definition adhere to parliamentary democracy (Esping-Andersen 1985, 6–7; Przeworski 1985, chapter 1), to what extent did their views on representation and accountability at the national level shape their views on democracy at the

European level? Why have some of these parties consistently supported the 'parliamentarisation' of the EU, while others have opposed it? Finally, how do they conceptualise the notion of social cohesion[49] at the national level, and why do some support the enhancement of the EU's redistributive capacity, while others oppose it?

A *policy paradigm* is 'a framework of ideas and standards that specifies not only the goals of policy and the kind of instruments that can be used to attain them, but also the very nature of the problems' that policy is meant to address: 'Like a *Gestalt*, this framework is embedded in the very terminology through which policy makers communicate about their work, and it is influential precisely because so much of it is taken for granted and unamenable to scrutiny as a whole' (Hall 1993, 279).

Social democratic parties have relied on Keynesianism for many decades, but the advent of neo-liberalism has challenged their cohesion. To what extent has their choice of economic policy paradigm affected their preferences on European integration?

Finally, historical experience shapes the *référentiel* (Muller 1995) deployed by policy makers, politicians and voters. Since the late 1940s, the debate regarding European integration has been affected by views on Europe's relationship with the USA. In that context – and, especially, in the area of security and defence policy – the dichotomy between Atlanticism and Europeanism has come to occupy an important position. To what extent has this dichotomy affected a party's preferences on European integration?

Structure and organisation of the book

There are five reasons why this book covers the entire post-war period.[50] First, political problems, alternative solutions and our understanding of them are time-sensitive. As Tilly reminds us, '*when* things happen within a sequence affects *how* they happen' (1984, 14; emphasis in the original). The pool of available alternatives, the political opportunity structure and an actor's assessment of the opportunities afforded by this structure evolve over time. Second, preferences are neither fixed, nor exogenous. Rather, they can change over time (which is why they ought to be problematised). Third, experience in government is, in many respects, a reality test (Glyn 2001). The opportunities to pursue party preferences are much greater when a party is in power. When a party is in opposition, there is greater scope for policy deliberation and programmatic renewal. As all of the parties that are covered by this research project and volume have been both in power and in opposition, only a historical perspective can do justice to this *alternance* and its effects. Fourth, although many of the aforementioned explanatory factors have remained relevant throughout the six decades that followed the establishment of the European Coal and Steel Community, their salience has varied over time.[51] Finally, European integration has evolved since the 1950s in terms of membership, institutional architecture and scope. As a result, parties have sought to define their preferences, at least in part, in relation to an evolving organisation. To the extent that they are responsive organisations, parties are also expected to revisit, update and inform their preferences, partly on the basis of the changing context in which they operate. This is why it is more fruitful to consider the entire post-war period, as opposed to just one part of it.

This volume covers the social democratic parties of five countries, namely Germany, France, the UK, Greece and Sweden. Given the impossibility of covering the social democratic family in its entirety, the aim was to cover a group of cases that combine (a) founding member states with states that joined subsequently, (b) small and large countries and (c) countries of the European North and South, while keeping the scale of the project to manageable levels as the resources at our disposal were finite. One additional consideration was the inclusion of countries (and, therefore, parties) with a fairly lengthy[52] experience of membership of the EU, so as to facilitate the examination of several independent variables (such as socialisation and the implications of the development of the EU) whose impact on party preferences unfolds and, therefore, can only be examined over a long period of time.[53]

The chapters contain theoretically guided historical accounts of preference formation in five social democratic parties. The authors utilise process-tracing and discuss the impact of interests, institutions and ideas and the interplay between them on preference formation throughout the period under consideration. The chapters were written on the basis of a broad range of sources, including several interviews[54] with key current and former party office holders (many with experience in government), formal documents (such as party manifestos), existing literature[55] and other sources (such as material found in the press). The presentation of the cases follows the development of the EU, starting with two parties that operate in two founding member states (Germany and France), followed by parties from countries that joined in the 1970s (UK), 1980s (Greece) and 1990s (Sweden).

Notes

1 I should like to thank Christoph Egle, Karl Magnus Johansson, Philippe Marlière, Anand Menon, Argyris G. Passas, Paul Taggart and the participants at the workshop and conference on Social democracy and European integration, held at Birkbeck on 8–9 December 2006 and 20–21 April 2007, for helpful comments on previous drafts of this chapter. The usual disclaimer applies.
2 In addition to the literature that compares two or more cases, there is a large body of literature (including in other European languages) that focuses on individual parties (for book-length treatments, see, for example, Criddle 1969; Lemaire-Prosche 1990; Robins 1979; Stroh 2004).
3 The notion of the 'founding fathers' is typically associated with eminent figures such as Schuman, Monnet, Pleven, Spaak, Beyen, Mansholt, Adenauer and De Gasperi, only two of whom (Spaak and Mansholt) were socialists (Featherstone 1988, 5).
4 For example, Kurt Schumacher, leader of the SPD when the Schuman Plan was launched, denounced it as building a Europe that would be '*konservativ, klerikal, kapitalistisch und kartellistisch*' (Sassoon 1996, 218).

5 This was so despite its perceived contribution to the emergence of what many saw as the new (neo-liberal) *pensée unique* (Ladrech 2000, 32).

6 For example, the German SPD distanced itself from Marxism in 1959 by adopting a radically reformed *Grundsatzprogramm* (basic programme) in the historic party congress held in Bad Godesberg (SPD 1959). Unlike the early attempts of Eduard Bernstein and his followers, this new revisionism has been embraced by the leadership and a majority of the supporters of these parties (Sassoon 1996, chapter 10), though in some cases reform took more time.

7 The establishment of the National Health Service in Britain is a good example.

8 It is important to distinguish clearly between *preferences* as defined here and *strategies*, i.e. the 'particular transient bargaining positions, negotiating demands' used by governments in their attempt to realise their preferences (Moravcsik 1997, 519; see also Frieden 1999; Lake and Powell 1999). The difference between the two can be illustrated by means of an example. A social democratic party may enter a coalition government in order to promote the reform of the welfare state along neo-liberal lines. The decision to enter a coalition government is the strategy, whereas the reform of the welfare state along neo-liberal lines indicates the party's preferences. In other words, 'preferences are by definition independent of strategic calculations' (Moravcsik 1998, 21).

9 The central position of the 'neutral' Commission, the institutionalised emphasis on consensual decision-making, and the explicit attempt to downplay the ideological content of key choices were at the heart of this effort.

10 This was in part due to the structure of the EU – the need to secure unanimous agreement and the institutionalisation of consensus-seeking means that agreements are often deliberately ambiguous, with detailed arguments about substance and ideological implications coming later.

11 The debate on the inclusion of references to God in the Treaty is a good example.

12 He construes the state as a unitary, rational and purposive actor that represents a sub-set of domestic societies; 'groups articulate preferences; governments aggregate them' (Moravcsik 1993, 480; 483). Although governments act purposively in the international arena, they do so on the basis of domestically defined goals. Their preferences are 'exogenous to a specific international policy environment' (Moravcsik 1998, 24). The national interest emerges as a result of domestic political conflict. '[S]ocietal groups compete for political influence, national and transnational coalitions form, and new policy alternatives are recognized by governments' (Moravcsik 1993, 481). In that model, the government is decisively constrained by civil society, because the main objective of a government is to maintain itself in power (Moravcsik 1993, 482).

13 This was not his objective. After all, his focus on national governments is understandable as they are major actors in the reform of EU treaties.

14 The distinction between a vote-maximising and a vote-seeking party stems from the system in which parties operate. Vote-maximising is particularly applicable to two-party systems (Strøm and Müller 1999, 8).

15 On Euroscepticism, see Taggart and Szczerbiak (2008a; 2008b).

16 The gradual reduction of the importance of ideology has been combined with the increasing emphasis on the nation state and the national interest, to the detriment of internationalism (Delwit 1995, 256).

17 After all, Featherstone's claim has preceded the 'turn to Europe' performed by some of these parties.

18 This mirrors Delwit's (1995, 258) finding: when they are in opposition, these parties modify their views.

19 There is correlation between economic conditions and attitudes towards integration, but the intensity of this correlation has changed over time (Delwit 1995, 253).

20 A good example is their attitude vis-à-vis monetary union (Notermans 2001a).

21 These too are internally differentiated groups (Hooghe and Marks 1999; Hix 1999).

22 This is an important distinction because it sheds light on two facets of the relation-ship between the social democrats and the nation state. First, it is an indication of their real attachment to internationalism. Second, it illustrates the importance that they attach to concrete achievements made at the national level. This, in turn, implies the extent to which integration is conceptualised as a zero-sum game.

23 This is akin to Paul Taylor's definition of the *level* of integration, i.e. the way in which the functional areas that are covered by the integration project are organised and, in particular, 'the extent to which they are ruled from new centres which can act independently of governments' (Taylor 1975, 343).

24 This question does not assume a positive attitude vis-à-vis the principle of integration. By raising the issue of the aims of this project, this question is meant to facilitate the exploration of the *critiques* used by some social democratic parties against either the principle or specific stages of this process.

25 This highlights the need to consider the *salience* of integration within each party in two senses. First, European integration might have to compete with other platforms for the pursuit of a party's objectives. Second, integration might challenge the party's unity (see *infra*).

26 A clear distinction between economic and political integration is unhelpful because it obscures the fact that even an elementary form of the former (i.e. a free trade area) is couched in a political decision. This is why this section focuses on the most salient aspects of the two, namely the ambition and the scope of joint decision-making. These are the issues that social democratic parties had to deal with in post-war Europe. Moreover, negative and positive integration do not refer to economic processes but to 'government policy aimed at enlarging the economic space beyond existing national boundaries' (Scharpf 1999, 45).

27 Although the theory of economic integration typically identifies neat stages such as a free trade area, a customs union, a common or single market and economic and monetary union, it obscures the political nature of the decision to enter each stage, despite the fact that these decisions entail increasingly *joint* decision-making. For example, the common external tariff is *not* the only difference between a free trade area and a customs union. The existence of the common tariff implies that political decisions are at the heart of its creation (e.g. how high the rates will be) as well as its actual operation (e.g. who negotiates trade agreements with third parties).

28 It can also be limited to specific sectors of the economy.

29 For example, this may be achieved through the regulation of working conditions or pollution control (Scharpf 1999, 45; Héritier 1999, 28) through 'flanking policies'.

30 Another aspect of economic integration that divides neo-liberals from the propon-ents of regulated capitalism is competition policy. Like all forms of regulation, it can be restrictive or enabling. Whereas neo-liberals construe competition as the means to ensure 'a level playing field', proponents of regulated capitalism see it as the means to actively pursue broader objectives, such as the introduction of new technologies and the nurturing of new industries while they are in their infancy.

31 Together, these two issues reflect the centrality of the autonomy of markets (and the economy as a whole), which is a central theme in the post-war social democratic critique of capitalism (SPD 1959).

32 A bigger common budget is a good example.

33 For example, resistance to the federal model can be construed as both an indication of resistance to a common foreign and security policy and support for NATO as the main locus of Europe's collective security.

34 Of course, alternative models can be found between these two extremes, not least because politicians defy neat academic typologies and remain determined (or compelled) to pick and mix elements of various models. Nevertheless, one category deserves to be mentioned separately because it is based (much more than others) on the key criterion used here, namely the autonomy of the state. A *confederation* is a federation with a weak centre. In that model,

> (a) sub-units may legally exit, (b) the center only exercises authority delegated by sub-units, (c) the center is subject to sub-unit veto on many issues, (d) center decisions only bind sub-units but not citizens directly, (e) the center lacks an independent fiscal or electoral base, *and/or* (f) the sub-units do not cede authority permanently to the center. Confederations are often based on agreements for specific tasks, and the common government may be completely exercised by delegates of the sub-unit governments.
>
> (Føllesdal 2003)

35 The discussion of the role of interests in party preference formation provides an excellent opportunity for the assessment of the aforementioned 'obfuscation thesis'. If that thesis is correct, there must be a correlation between public opinion (and electoral trends) on the one hand, and party positions on the other.

36 Different socio-economic groups join together to support particular policies and alliances (Gourevitch 1986, chapter 3).

37 For example, the traditional link that many social democratic parties maintain with trade unions is part of the political opportunity structure in which these parties' preferences are formed, even if these unions do not have the electoral leverage that they once had.

38 Moreover, party preferences on European integration can be affected by the autonomy and cohesion of a sub-set of its members, namely the parliamentary party (Sjöblom 1968, 264–5).

39 For example, do parties organise special conferences on European integration?

40 One could add the cartel party, which relies on collusion and state resources to ensure its survival (Katz and Mair 1995).

41 For example, German unification and Greece's relations with Turkey concern primarily (but by no means exclusively) German and Greek political parties.

42 A related question concerns the impact of membership on the distribution of power *within* parties (Carter, Luther and Poguntke 2007).

43 The emphasis here is not on the balance of power between competing factions or ideological platforms within a party. Rather, the main issue here concerns the evolution of a party's internal *institutional configuration.*

44 For example, federalism reflects diversity and distrust towards the centralisation of power.

45 Of course, in both cases government actions (i.e. a party's revealed preferences) are likely to differ from their manifesto commitments. In the context of PR, compromises must be found between parties in government, whereas, in first-past-the-post systems, concrete meaning has to be given to abstract electoral pledges.

46 Recent discussions within the PES on Iraq, the Constitutional and Lisbon Treaties and the Bolkestein directive indicate important differences between the parties that are covered by this research project. This is why their interactions with the PES should be problematised.

47 For example, whereas some social democratic parties adopted an Atlanticist stance on the issue of security policy in Europe, others opted for a nationalist, a Europeanist or a neutral stance.

48 Acting at the level of the Socialist International as early as 1951, social democrats recognised that 'democratic socialism is international because it recognises that

no nation can solve all its economic and social problems in isolation' (cited in Featherstone 1988, 1).

49 The dominant conception of solidarity has changed over time, and this is exemplified by the evolution of redistribution. Whereas in the past it had a predominantly national focus, in the post-national era – which is characterised by the presence of the EU – it has a more pronounced intra- and extra-European dimension.

50 PASOK may seem to be an exception (as it was founded in 1974), but, in reality, it is not. Many of the internal characteristics and programmatic beliefs of this party reflect the country's experience since the end of the Greek civil war in the late 1940s.

51 For example, the impact of competition from communist parties has changed over time (Delwit 1995, 261).

52 That is, at least a decade.

53 This is one of several reasons why central and eastern European parties have not been included in this research project (on the preferences of these parties on European integration, see Marks *et al*. (2006); Rohrschneider and Whitefield (2007; 2010)).

54 Each chapter includes an appendix with the list of interviewees that corresponds to it. With one exception, these lists are comprehensive. The presentation of the material that stems from interviews reflects the authors' agreements with their interviewees regarding unanimity.

55 Translations used throughout this volume are the contributors' own.

2 The SPD's preferences on European integration

Always one step behind?

Christoph Egle

Introduction[1]

The issue of European integration in the political life of the Federal Republic of Germany is dominated by two specific features. First, German political parties – whether of the Left or the Right – are quite pro-European in their attitudes. Second, Germany – along with France – has been a crucial engine of European integration since the early 1950s (Bulmer, Jeffery and Paterson 2000; Lees 2002; Müller-Brandeck-Bocquet *et al.* 2002). The catchphrase '*Europapolitik als Staatsraison*' ('European policy as a reason of state') describes very well this common denominator in German (foreign) policy (Müller-Brandeck-Bocquet 2006). In contrast to many other countries where (a) the 'question of Europe' has been contentious in party competition, and (b) the respective social democratic parties have often adopted Eurosceptic attitudes, only minor party political differences can be detected in Germany. Finally, the German Social Democratic Party (SPD) can be portrayed as 'one of the strongest and most influential political parties supporting integration within the European Community, particularly amongst socialist parties' (Featherstone 1988, 163). Against this background, this chapter not only seeks to answer the question regarding the origin of the SPD's particular preferences on European integration, but also attempts to explore the reasons for that bipartisan consensus. In this regard, two further questions arise. First, is there any considerable social democratic impact on Germany's European policy since World War II? Second, under what circumstances did the SPD's political preferences on European integration differ from those held by the Christian Democratic Union (CDU), the SPD's main (bourgeois) competitor? In fact, the SPD twice deviated from the aforementioned bipartisan consensus, namely during the early 1950s, when the SPD vehemently opposed European integration, and the mid 1990s, when it was divided on the question of European Monetary Union (EMU). In both cases, the German Social Democrats swung back to the Europeanist line after some time.

Hence, this begs the question of what explains these changes in the party's preferences. In his seminal book on the SPD and European integration, William Paterson (1974, ix) concluded, 'that domestic factors within the West

German political system were more important in shaping the attitudes of the party to West European institutions than the form which the institutions took'.

Does this description still hold for the time since the 1980s, and what about factors beyond the (domestic) German context? These issues shall be analysed in the remainder of this chapter. The first section explores the political preferences of the SPD towards European integration and the SPD's impact on Germany's European policy since 1945. Subsequent sections discuss the extent to which these preferences have been influenced by ideas, economic and other interests, and institutional factors. The basic argument presented here is that the German Social Democrats have exerted only limited influence on Germany's European policy, and, although the SPD has the strongest pro-European tradition among all German political parties, it often seemed to be one step behind its Christian Democratic rival (CDU). The main reason for that observation is the 'shadow of German history' and, as a consequence, the fact that European integration is predominantly seen as a 'peace project'. This historical legacy has continuously overshadowed potential party political differences – with the considerable exception of the very early post-war years. In addition, it was in the SPD's interests in terms of both vote- and office-seeking to stick to the German consensus on European policy.

The transformation of the SPD's attitudes towards European integration: scepticism, pragmatism and unfulfilled ambitions

The SPD had argued in favour of the economic and political integration of Europe since its Heidelberg Programme of 1925 (Paterson 1974, 2). With its famous claim to build the 'United States of Europe', the SPD was the first political party in Germany to learn the lesson that catastrophic events such as World War I can only be prevented by a common European idea. Another reason for that early Europeanist claim was to confront emerging left-wing and right-wing totalitarianism with a distinct peaceful and democratic vision. In addition, the SPD was part of (and a key actor in) the international labour movement and, therefore, it was in principle characterised by an internationalist attitude.

The subsequent horror of Nazi Germany in the 1930s and 1940s confirmed the perception within the party that the nation state had become obsolete and a danger to international peace (Moeller 1996, 34). Many social democrats there-fore envisaged a democratic, socialist and demilitarised Germany within a socialist European federation as a blueprint for a post-Hitler world (Featherstone 1988, 143). Furthermore, it was expected that the SPD would have a 'natural' right to political leadership in Germany after the end of Nazi rule (Paterson 1974, 2ff.). However, when the first *Bundestag* elections were held in West Germany in 1949, the newly founded CDU won by a narrow margin, and Konrad Adenauer became the first chancellor. This incident strongly affected the SPD's attitudes towards European integration in the early 1950s.

The analysis of the SPD's manifestos sheds light on the development of its preferences on Europe since 1949. Figure 2.1 relies on data provided by the 'Manifesto Research Project' and shows the percentage of all political statements within each party's manifestos indicating a positive attitude towards European integration.[2] The picture that emerges from the comparison of the main parties can be summarised as follows. During the entire post-war period, the CDU/Christian Social Union (CSU) appears to be the party with the strongest pro-European attitude. SPD manifestos contained stronger pro-European positions than those of other parties represented in the German *Bundestag* only in the early 1950s and in the mid-1970s. Since the 1990s, the parties covering the spectrum to the right of the SPD (i.e. CDU/CSU and the FDP) were more pro-European than the SPD; since the mid-1990s, the parties covering the spectrum to the left of the SPD (Greens and PDS) have been more pro-European, too.

Despite its enduring pro-European tradition, illustrated by the aforementioned famous claim of the Heidelberg Programme, the SPD has – on the basis of these data – had only a low profile on European policy since 1949. However, it is surprising that, at the beginning of the 1950s, the SPD had expressed stronger pro-European positions in its manifestos than the CDU, even though the SPD vehemently criticised the pro-integration policies pursued by the CDU-led Adenauer government during that period (see below). Therefore, the development of the SPD's political positions should be examined in greater detail. In this regard, five periods can be identified on

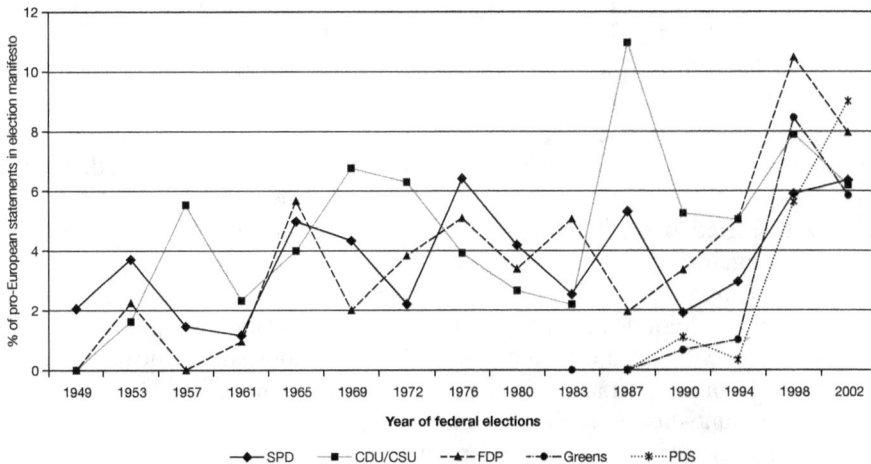

Figure 2.1 Positive attitudes towards European integration in the manifestos of German political parties

Source: Author's calculation on the basis of the data (covering the period until 1998) found in Budge *et al.* (2001) on CD-ROM; the data for 2002 have been kindly provided by Andrea Volkens.

the basis of the SPD's changing political preferences and its participation in government:

1   European scepticism in the early post-war years (1945–55);
2   the pragmatic turn in preparation for government (1955–66);
3   the SPD in power: *Ostpolitik* and economic crisis management (1966–82);
4   in search of a political profile as an opposition party (1982–98);
5   the unfulfilled aspirations of a governing party (1998–2009).

European scepticism in the early post-war years

After Germany's capitulation in 1945, the country was divided into four zones of occupation. One year later, in the Soviet zone of occupation, the SPD was forced to merge with the Communist Party (KPD) to form a new party, the *Sozialistische Einheitspartei Deutschlands* (SED) (Socialist Unity Party). This event revealed that the four Allied powers could not agree on a common strategy for Germany. As a result, Germany's future was inevitably determined by the emerging East–West conflict. The creation of a West German state, made up of the occupation zones of the Western Allies, initially encountered resistance from France. France would only accept a West German state if the Saarland remained under French control. Moreover, the French insisted on putting the Ruhr Valley's heavy industry (coal and steel) under international control (the 'International Authority of the Ruhr').

Both the division of Germany and the French attempts to exercise control over its eastern neighbour were key reasons for the SPD's initially negative approach towards West European integration (Featherstone 1988, 140–50; Hrbek 1972; 1993; Lodge 1976, 5–25; Paterson 1974, 1–139). Kurt Schumacher, leader of the SPD and its *Bundestagsfraktion* (parliamentary party) until his death in 1952, played a decisive role in shaping and expressing this position. Indeed, there is consensus among historians that the SPD's positions on foreign and European issues were determined by Schumacher during that time (Edinger 1965, 112ff.; Paterson 1974, 7ff.). His extraordinary status within the party rested upon his strong moral authority, which derived from his resistance against the Nazi regime and the torture he had endured as a prisoner in the concentration camp at Dachau. In addition, at that time, intra-party democracy and joint decision-making had not yet developed as much as it did later on in the SPD's history. Schumacher's most important political objective was to overcome Germany's division as quickly as possible. Owing to his well-known anti-fascist stance, he could rely on a more patriotic and even nationalistic argument than those deployed by many conservatives. Although European integration had both Schumacher's and the party's support in principle, it was regarded as possible only with a unified Germany (Lodge 1976, 7). Schumacher's initial idea was a democratic, socialist and neutral Germany, siding neither with the USA nor the USSR (Paterson 1974, 10). Only by following such a 'third way' would Europe be able to survive, whereas taking one side or the other would inevitably lead to its end. But, in contrast to his main political rival, Chancellor Adenauer, Schumacher misunderstood both the realities of the East–West conflict and the SPD's electoral prospects. Under his leadership, the party bitterly opposed the establishment of three important bodies of European co-operation that paved the way for European integration, namely the Council of Europe, the European Coal and Steel Community and the European Defence Community.

As early as 1948, the SPD had opposed the planned establishment of the Council of Europe (Hrbek 1972, 86ff.; Lodge 1976, 9ff.; Paterson 1974, 33ff.). One crucial reason for the SPD's position was the proposal to grant associate status to the Federal Republic of Germany as well as the Saarland in the Council of Europe. Indeed, the Saarland was not meant to become part of the Federal Republic of Germany, which was established a year later. Although Konrad Adenauer, chairman of the Parliamentary Assembly convened in 1948 to draw up a German constitution, agreed with that proposal, Schumacher regarded it as an unacceptable capitulation to an alleged French attempt to resolve the 'Saar question' in favour of France, preventing the possible future accession of the Saarland to the Federal Republic. As no solution to the 'Saar question' could be found at that time, the SPD even considered whether to send delegates to the Council of Europe – but in the end it did (Lodge 1976, 10).

The SPD equally opposed the Schuman Plan for the establishment of the European Coal and Steel Community (Hrbek 1972, 102–26; Paterson 1974, 49ff.). Given the good relationship between the conservative governing parties of France and Germany, the SPD rejected the plan and denounced it as a conservative–catholic–capitalist project (Paterson 1974, 52). It also feared that France would try to exercise economic control over Germany. Moreover, the ECSC project would jeopardise the SPD's intention to nationalise the coal and steel industries. In order to preserve the prospect of the future reform of the ECSC along more socialist lines, the SPD demanded that Britain and the Scandinavian countries participate in it. The party also supported the involvement of trade unions and the establishment of comprehensive democratic control mechanisms. After Jean Monnet had supported an extensive form of co-determination, the German trade unions approved the establishment of the ECSC, while the SPD remained sceptical.[3] Nonetheless, SPD MPs participated in negotiations on the establishment of the ECSC. At the regional level (*Bundesländer*), the ECSC project had more support within the SPD. After the establishment of the ECSC, SPD delegates took up their seats in its Common Assembly, where they were able to establish contacts with some pro-European socialists from other countries. Along with the SPD delegates in the Council of Europe, they contributed to the subsequent change of the SPD's European policy (Hrbek 1993, 77; Paterson 1974, 117). In particular, Herbert Wehner, who established a good personal relationship with Jean Monnet and Dutch social democrat Alfred Mozer (a native German), did not share Schumacher's uncompromising opposition to West European integration.

After Schumacher's death, Wehner became one of the most influential officials within the SPD (and later the legendary leader of the SPD's *Bundestagsfraktion* from 1969 to 1983) and had an enduring impact on the party's European policy from the mid-1950s onwards.

Prior to this change, the SPD had vehemently opposed the plan for a European Defence Community. Like the majority of Germans at the beginning of 1950, the SPD was sceptical about the re-armament of West Germany. The French proposal (Pleven Plan) to create a pan-European defence force, which would include West German soldiers (without the establishment of a German army), strengthened Schumacher's belief that France was pressing ahead with European integration only because it wanted to assert its own national interests (Paterson 1974, 76). In addition, the SPD pointed out that the deployment of armed forces would require the amendment of the *Grundgesetz*, and new elections should be held, because the question of re-armament had not been foreseen at the time of the general election of 1949. In such a situation, Soviet leader Josef Stalin released his contentious note (in March 1952), offering German re-unification but on the conditions of German neutrality and disarmament. As a reaction to Stalin's offer, the SPD – like the CDU and the Western Allies – called for free elections in the German Democratic Republic (GDR). The USSR rejected that proposal, and the SPD felt that its views – that German unity was still possible, but a military integration of the FRG in Western Europe would make a swift re-unification impossible – had been vindicated. Whereas Chancellor Adenauer swiftly denounced Stalin's note as a mere tactical manoeuvre, many within the SPD considered it a missed chance for re-unification (Paterson 1974, 86). In fact, many German social democrats still believe that Adenauer was not really interested in German unification (Bahr 1996, 58–62).[4]

Although the SPD remained opposed to the establishment of the EDC after Schumacher's death in 1952, more pragmatic politicians were beginning to gain influence within the party. Nevertheless, following the *Bundestag's* approval of Germany's participation in the EDC, the SPD appealed against that decision to the Constitutional Court.[5] However, on 17 June 1953, Adenauer's claim that Stalin was not worth negotiating with seemed to be confirmed, as Soviet Red Army troops violently suppressed a national uprising in East Berlin. As a consequence, the aim to bind Germany closely to Western Europe in order to resist the Soviet threat gained support within the electorate. In the *Bundestag* election held three months after the uprising in the GDR, the conservative CDU/CSU won more than 45 per cent of the votes (up 14 per cent), whereas the SPD stagnated at fewer than 30 per cent.

This electoral defeat was a wake-up call for the SPD to change its policy. As Ernst Reuter, then mayor of West Berlin, pointed out, the SPD could not merely highlight what it disapproves of in European affairs. Rather, it ought to make clear what it stood for (Paterson 1974, 98ff.). In any case, a new situation had emerged after the rejection of the EDC plan by the French National Assembly. As the issues of political and military integration could now be addressed separately, the SPD found it easier to support the former (Lodge 1976, 18; Paterson 1974, 107). The party thought at this point that *military* integration in Western Europe would harm Soviet interests and therefore would make re-unification difficult, if not impossible. *Political* integration in Western Europe, on the other hand, would not exclude the possible future re-unification of the country (Hrbek 1993, 75).

Another consequence of the French *non* to the EDC was the renegotiation of the *Deutschlandvertrag* and the adoption of the Paris Agreements in 1954. The Paris Agreements restored most of West Germany's sovereignty (by ending the occupation status), paved the way for the country's accession to the North Atlantic Treaty Organisation (NATO) and the Western European Union (WEU), and finally offered a solution to the unresolved 'Saar question'. As regards the latter, the Paris Agreements initially provided for a European status, which was rejected by the people of the Saarland in a referendum held on 23 October 1955. After the necessary renegotiation with France, the Saar finally became part of the Federal Republic of Germany on 1 January 1957. With the institutional separation of military questions (NATO) from the project of European *political* integration and the resolution of the Saar problem, two major building blocks of the SPD's resistance to West European integration had become obsolete.

The pragmatic turn in the party's quest for evidence of its Regierungsfähigkeit[6]

During the mid-1950s, the SPD began to evolve towards support for European integration. The change within the SPD first appeared in its support for the creation of the European Economic Community (EEC) and EURATOM. Although the SPD initially claimed to reject the establishment of the EEC, it finally approved it. Jean Monnet personally convinced Herbert Wehner to do so just a few days before the final vote in the *Bundestag* (interview with former SPD official). With regard to the EEC, the SPD went as far as to demand the inclusion of provisions for common monetary, economic and investment policies in the treaties of Rome and – acting in an effort to strengthen Europe vis-à-vis the two superpowers – argued for the inclusion of the UK, Austria and the Scandinavian countries (Moeller 1996, 37). The party's support for the European Atomic Energy Community was due to its belief that EURATOM could guarantee the civil use of nuclear energy and prevent nuclear armament (Lodge 1976, 21).

If the election defeat in 1953 led many to question the SPD's uncompromising opposition (see *supra*), the new poor result in the *Bundestag* election of 1957 provided the final impetus for major reform within the party. The CDU/CSU even won an absolute majority of the votes in 1957, while the SPD got only just over 30 per cent. The Social Democrats were forced to realise that a future participation in government required a major revision of their outdated party ideology. Indeed, with the adoption of a new party programme in 1959 (the landmark *Godesberger Programm*), the SPD abandoned Marxism, accepted the free market economy and laid the foundations for becoming a modern *Volkspartei* (catch-all party). By the same token, a key speech by Herbert Wehner at the German *Bundestag* on 30 June 1960 was a watershed in the SPD's foreign policy. Wehner argued that there were no more major differences between the policies of the CDU-led Adenauer government and the SPD in foreign and European matters. He also set out the broad lines for a common, bipartisan foreign policy (Wehner 1960). His explicit statement that the FRG was an uncompromising, loyal partner with regards to all international treaties – irrespective of which party was in power – reflected his overarching aim to prove the SPD's *Regierungsfähigkeit*. Indeed, the Bad Godesberg programme and the acceptance of Adenauer's long-standing argument that German re-unification could only rely on a tight *Westbindung* (political and military attachment to the West) were decisive milestones for the subsequent establishment of coalition governments with the CDU/CSU (from 1966 to 1969) and the FDP (from 1969 to 1982). Even if vote-seeking played a role after the disappointing electoral results of 1953 und 1957, office-seeking was a dominant factor in that shift towards the preferences of bourgeois parties.

The question of German re-unification – until then one of the major reasons why the SPD was hesitant about European integration – lost much of its importance with the construction of the Berlin Wall in 1961. As that event caused major tensions, the four Allied powers were subsequently interested in preserving the status quo. Indeed, 'nobody wanted to fight a war for Germany' (interview with former SPD politician). German unification appeared to be unrealistic in the short term, and the perceived trade-off between German unity and West European integration faded away. As a result, these developments fostered the SPD's pragmatic turn on further Western European integration (Friedrich 1975; Lodge 1976, 37–89; Paterson 1974, 141–55; 1975, 181–7). In addition, the pro-European course of the SPD was strengthened by the economic success of the ECSC. Consistent with previous claims, the SPD continued to call for the enlargement of the European Economic Community and it severely criticised French president Charles de Gaulle, who twice vetoed (in 1963 and again in 1967) the UK's applications to join the EEC (Paterson 1974, 141ff.). The SPD also argued for enhanced parliamentary control of the European institutions and, in 1965, proposed the direct election of the German representatives to the European Parliament (Moeller 1996, 38).

The SPD in government: Ostpolitik and economic crisis management

Despite that pragmatic turn, the SPD still had to wait until 1966 to participate in the federal government. After the split of the Christian Democratic/ liberal coalition, CDU/CSU and SPD formed a 'grand coalition', and SPD leader Willy Brandt became vice-chancellor and foreign minister. The SPD's pro-European course was consolidated after entering government, although Willy Brandt as the SPD's leading Cabinet minister was more interested in implementing his *Ostpolitik* than in a possible deepening of West European integration (Featherstone 1988, 153ff.; Paterson 1975). As a reaction to the fact that German division could not be overcome in the short term, Willy Brandt – until 1966 the mayor of West Berlin – and his close aid Egon Bahr developed the idea of *Wandel durch Annäherung* (change through *rapprochement*) in order to achieve the democratisation of (and liberalisation in) the GDR. The first steps entailed the establishment of better relations between West and East Germany, especially by facilitating personal visits between families from West and East Berlin. As Egon Bahr put it, 'if we cannot do away with the Berlin Wall, we have to make it penetrable. That was the basic consideration' (Bahr 1996, 161).[7]

With its *Ostpolitik*, the SPD for the first time had the means to deal with the issue of German unity, although re-unification could not be expected in the near future. Henceforth, German and European interests could be considered as two sides of the same coin. *Ostpolitik* was developed by the SPD predominantly on the basis of German interests, but it was also stated that *Entspannungspolitik* (policy of *détente*) served European interests as well, as it contributed to stability and peace across Europe – and providing peace has been the main objective of Germany's European policy since 1949 (interview with former senior SPD official).

After Willy Brandt had become chancellor in 1969, the SPD-led government was able to achieve further improvements in the relationship with East Germany, as well as a number of political objectives in its European policy, such as the enhancement of the powers of the European Parliament. In addition, Brandt played an important role in enlargement negotiations; indeed, it has been argued that he convinced the Danish government to join the EEC (Lodge 1976, 40) and that he helped convince French President Pompidou not to veto the UK's accession after de Gaulle had resigned (interview with former SPD politician). Besides the first enlargement of the EC, the democratisation of Spain, Portugal and Greece and the subsequent accession of these countries were important events for the establishment of a new understanding of European policy within the SPD; thus the vision of the European Community as an 'agent of democratisation' for the first time took concrete form (interview with former SPD official). Although the EC's role as a promoter of democracy was widely acknowledged within the SPD, its ordinary members did not have a specific conception of the finality of European integration (Lodge 1976, 42).

Despite Brandt's achievements concerning the enlargement of the European Community, his overall position on European policy remained unclear during his tenure as chancellor. Although he repeatedly argued for the deepening of European integration, he hardly ever tried to realise those ideas (Lodge 1976, 40ff.; Moeller 1996, 38). Brandt's rhetoric on European integration was often seen as 'flowery language' (interview with former SPD official), although his general Europeanist attitude was taken for granted. Brandt's vague attitude towards further integration and his unclear political weighting between West and East were expressed in 1974 in his proposal on 'differentiated integration' (Paterson 1975, 183). In the same year, the revelation that a close aide to Brandt (Günther Guillaume) was an intelligence agent of East Germany's secret service led him to resign (for further reasons for his resignation, see Paterson 1975). However, he remained leader of the SPD until 1987, while the former finance minister, Helmut Schmidt, succeeded him as chancellor.

Although Brandt's succession by Schmidt did not result in a major shift in Germany's European policy, gradual changes can be observed. Whereas both Willy Brandt and his foreign minister, Walter Scheel (FDP), had embodied the policy of *détente* and *Ostpolitik*, those policies were of minor importance for the new government of Helmut Schmidt and new Foreign Minister Hans-Dietrich Genscher (FDP).[8] In fact, Schmidt's term in office was mainly characterised by economic crisis management after the oil price shock of 1973–4 and the ambition to strengthen Germany's and Europe's weight in world politics and the economy, especially as the US hegemony seemed to be in decline – economically, but also morally owing to the Vietnam war (Müller-Brandeck-Bocquet 2006, 472).

Although Schmidt was said to be sceptical about further transfers of competences to supranational institutions, his government left an important European political legacy: in 1979, the European Monetary System (EMS) was established, following an initiative by Schmidt and French president Valéry Giscard d'Estaing (Ludlow 1982; Schmidt 1990, 219–41). As Schmidt himself noted, the establishment of the EMS followed his preferred method of close negotiations with other heads of government based on trust (Stroh 2004, 78). As Schmidt and Giscard had prepared the EMS by factoring out their national bureaucracies (and their parties), potential resistance from the German *Bundesbank* could be circumvented. This arrangement for monetary co-operation was initially met with opposition from the CDU/CSU, because the party feared a weakening of the stability of the Deutschmark. However, with the European Exchange Rate Mechanism now part of the EMS, exchange rate variability and inflation could be reduced, and monetary stability achieved. Moreover, the EMS paved the way for the subsequent establishment of Economic and Monetary Union. In the end, the economic integration of Western Europe was more significantly furthered by Schmidt's pragmatic crisis management than by Brandt's visionary rhetoric. Following a functionalist argument, short-term crisis management established new institutions, enabling subsequent steps in the process of integration that could not be foreseen at that point in time. Although it is too simplistic to call Brandt an idealist and Helmut Schmidt a down-to-earth pragmatist (Featherstone 1988, 155), it is clear that they followed different approaches. Whereas Brandt was more interested in long-term visions concerning Europe's common future, Schmidt focused on economic problems that had to be resolved immediately.[9]

Another important step concerning European integration during the Schmidt government was the first direct election of the European Parliament in 1979, a long-term objective of the SPD. Although the Schmidt government did not undertake additional efforts to promote further 'parliamentarisation' of Europe (Lodge 1976, 46), Willy Brandt was the SPD's top candidate for that first European election, thus ensuring that European affairs attracted more attention within the SPD – though only for a short time, as the SPD soon afterwards was forced to return to the opposition benches.

In search of a political profile as an opposition party

As a result of differences in economic policy, the SPD/FDP coalition broke apart in 1982. The FDP Cabinet members resigned, and Chancellor Schmidt lost a vote of confidence when challenged by the CDU/CSU along with the FDP. The CDU/CSU under Helmut Kohl formed a new coalition government with the FDP that was confirmed in the *Bundestag* election in 1983. In this election, the Greens entered the *Bundestag* for the first time. As a reaction to the success of the Greens, the SPD swung to the left, particularly in those policy domains in which the Greens were especially interested (Meyer 1997). During the 1980s, the SPD therefore argued against (nuclear) armament and so shifted away from the course of foreign and security policy that the Schmidt-led government had pursued. Especially for the party's rank-and-file, European integration was of secondary importance in comparison with peace and anti-nuclear arms issues (Featherstone 1988, 163). The SPD nevertheless supported the enhancement of the role of the European Parliament and the improved democratic participation of European citizens in EC affairs, as it had done in the past. Given that the SEA was meant to complete the internal market, the SPD feared the dominance of capital and an impetus for deregulation, which would put social standards under pressure (Stroh 2004, 80ff.). Accordingly, the SPD, together with the trade unions, warned of market liberal rollback disguised by the EC and driven by conservative parties that were governing most of the member states during the 1980s (Moeller 1996, 41). However, as the SPD was in opposition, it could not exert much influence over Germany's European policy at that point in time (Featherstone 1988, 166).

Nevertheless, in the context of making a new party programme in the late 1980s, some attempts were made to enrich the European project with social democratic claims. In particular, Heidemarie Wieczorek-Zeul, a leading figure in the party's left wing and member of the European Parliament from 1979 to 1987, then European affairs spokesperson of the SPD's parliamentary party from 1987 to 1998,[10] campaigned for her concept of *Europäisierungsstrategie* (Stroh 2004, 80–9). She suggested some kind of common European economic government to deal with the constraints of globalisation, especially integrating financial markets. Yet, she was unsucessful in anchoring that attempt to the new *Berliner Programm* that replaced the Bad Godesberg Programme in 1989. The party's leadership was sceptical about publicly supporting policies that were judged to be completely unrealistic owing to diverging interests in most other member states. Moreover, the challenges of globalisation did not attract much attention within the SPD until the early 1990s (interview with SPD politician). Therefore, references to European issues remained quite vague in the SPD's basic programme.[11]

Besides the failure to develop a distinctive social democratic profile in European policy, the SPD had almost abandoned its belief in German re-unification during the 1980s, especially within the young generation. When the Berlin Wall collapsed in 1989, and the astonishingly quick re-unification of Germany was accompanied by the deepening of European integration – thus confirming the widespread belief that German unification and European integration were indeed two sides of the same coin – it was the Kohl government that led the action, whereas the SPD seemed to be in disarray. At that crucial point in time, the SPD experienced once more that foreign and European policy is above all the executive's business, as the Kohl government controlled the agenda and seized this historic opportunity, whereas the Social Democrats were divided on the question of how to deal with the 'German question'. As Oskar Lafontaine, the SPD's candidate for the chancellorship in the 1990 general election, was reserved vis-à-vis re-unification, the bitter defeat of the SPD in the elections that were held two months after re-unification came as no surprise.

Concerning the Maastricht Treaty, the SPD once more experienced that, as an opposition party, it could not shift Germany's European policy, as the Treaty was negotiated only by governments. As a consequence, the *Ministerpräsident* of the Saarland, Oskar Lafontaine, threatened not to approve the Maastricht Treaty in the *Bundesrat*, where SPD-led *Länder* governments had a majority at that time. In fact, the consent of the *Bundesrat* to the Maastricht Treaty was associated with amendments to the *Grundgesetz* that provided the *Länder* with significant additional competences with regard to European affairs (Stroh 2004, 405–47). Through this strategy, the SPD sought to strengthen its influence on European policy. However, blocking the Maastricht Treaty was never a realistic option, as the party would have been isolated in Europe, and this would have produced detrimental effects in terms of office- and vote-seeking as well (interview with former SPD official). As the SPD finally approved the Maastricht Treaty, particularly in terms of *Staatsraison*, internal differences within the party soon emerged concerning monetary union. It seemed as though the SPD had not fully realised what it approved when it supported the ratification of the Maastricht Treaty.

In fact, after the electoral victory of Helmut Kohl and his government in 1994, the SPD began (a) questioning the previous inter-party consensus on European affairs and (a) warily criticising the planned monetary union (Notermans 2001c, 85ff.; Reinhardt 1997). Hence, EMU evolved into the first contentious issue in European policy among the political parties since the early 1950s. As monetary policy in Europe was already dominated by the Deutschmark, the Kohl government's support for a European single currency was founded on political rather than economic factors (Knodt and Staeck 1999, 9). The Kohl government's readiness to give up the Deutschmark demonstrated that (a) it was serious about its support for European integration, and (b) there would never be a German *Sonderweg* again. Indeed, EMU has been often seen as a price Germany had to pay in order to get French approval for German re-unification (Notermans 2001c, 83). As the German population felt attached to the Deutschmark as a strong currency, Kohl and his government promised that the euro would be 'as strong as the Deutschmark'. Therefore, the German government proposed a stability pact that was eventually adopted at the European level.

However, in the mid-1990s, it became apparent that only a few member states would be able to fulfil the convergence criteria by 1997. Yet, if only a few countries (excluding, for example, the southern European countries) participated in monetary union, the non-members of the euro zone would be put under pressure to devalue their currencies. This would have had negative consequences for Germany's exporting industries. Against this backdrop, senior SPD officials, notably Oskar Lafontaine and Gerhard Schröder, demanded the postponement of the introduction of the euro, although officially the party remained supportive of Europe's single currency. Nevertheless, as approximately 80 per cent of the German population argued for the mainten-ance of the Deutschmark (Reinhardt 1997, 81), the SPD saw a chance to (a) win elections on this basis and (b) put the government under pressure.[12] In the Baden-Württemberg election of 1996, the SPD went on the offensive and called for a postponement of monetary union, despite the fact that this was by no means an election topic for a *Land* election. This approach was condemned as populist both by the media and the electorate and compromised the SPD's credibility, as it had previously approved the Maastricht Treaty. Whereas the SPD's MEPs strongly rejected this vote-seeking populism, the federal leadership of the party – with Oskar Lafontaine at the helm since 1995 – seemed to wait and see if that strategy would pay off. In the end, the SPD lost a large number of votes in that Baden-Württemberg *Land* election. As a result, the party abandoned its anti-euro strategy. This change was also fostered by the fact that the political mood vis-à-vis Kohl and his government was so negative in the 1998 election year that the CDU/CSU could be defeated on the basis of less risky topics, such as the demand for the inclusion of employment and social policy considerations into EMU (Ostheim 2003, 352; Sloam 2003, 68). Besides, a failure or a postponement of the introduction of the euro would have led to an 'escape to the Deutschmark' in the financial markets, which would have caused the revaluation of the German currency, to the detriment of German exports. Therefore, the SPD agreed to support EMU in the *Bundestag* vote in 1998, despite the wishes of the majority of the Germans (Eckstein and Pappi 1999).

The unfulfilled aspirations of a governing party

After the change of government from the CDU/CSU–FDP to the SPD–Greens ('Red–Green') coalition in 1998, it was expected that Germany's European policy would change (Ostheim 2003, 351). Already, prior to becoming chancellor, Gerhard Schröder had insisted that under his chancellorship Germany would approach European policy differently than it did under Helmut Kohl.[13] According to Schröder, Germany could no longer afford its chequebook diplomacy (*Scheckbuchdiplomatie*), and he called for a reduction of Germany's net contributions to the European Union's budget. Schröder's populist rhetoric that German money should no longer be 'burned' in Brussels was judged as 'catastrophic' by social democrat MEPs (interview with SPD politician). Though Schröder's claim was inspired mainly by vote-seeking considerations, there was growing awareness within the party and the parliamentary party that German payments to the EU should be limited, and domestic policy objectives had to take priority.

Moreover, SPD leader and new Finance Minister Oskar Lafontaine called for a reversal of the 'neo-liberal' trend in EU policy-making. The conditions for that attempt were as favourable as never before, as, in thirteen of the fifteen EU member states, social democratic parties either participated in or led the government, and therefore social democratic governments had a double majority (55 per cent of the members representing at least 65 per cent of the EU's citizens) in the European Council (Merkel and Ostheim 2004a, 146).

Indeed, at the beginning of Schröder's tenure, a change in domestic policy and European policy occurred. In particular, Lafontaine's attempt to exert influence on the monetary policy of the European Central Bank and to impose on it the obligation to consider growth and employment objectives was remarkable. Lafontaine was supported by his French colleague, Dominique Strauss-Kahn. Together with Strauss-Kahn, Lafontaine vigorously demanded a co-ordinated macroeconomic policy (Lafontaine and Strauss-Kahn 1999). Their proposal, however, failed, as their European colleagues were not interested in coming into conflict with the ECB. Given that the newly introduced euro first of all needed to become stable in the financial markets, Lafontaine's attempt to question the independence of its 'guardian', i.e. the ECB, was seen as counter-productive (Notermans 2001c, 92ff.; Ostheim 2003; Sloam 2003, 72). When the two proponents of this strategy resigned from their offices – Lafontaine quit his job as finance minister and as SPD leader in March 1999, Strauss-Kahn six months later in September – their proposal was not seriously pursued any more, although it found a certain expression in the 'macroeconomic dialogue' of the 'Cologne process'. In the context of this macroeconomic dialogue, European monetary, budgetary, fiscal and wage policy should be co-ordinated. Yet, following the above-mentioned resignations and the change of fiscal policy in Germany,[14] which had been initiated in the meantime, the Cologne process did not produce any significant effect (Ostheim 2003, 356). In the end, the German government even had to withdraw the proposal for a major reduction in its net EU contributions. As it was holding the EU presidency, Germany in fact had to play the role of an 'honest broker' when the Agenda 2000 was adopted. This role was hard to reconcile with the overt pursuit of national interests (Müller-Brandeck-Bocquet 2002, 172ff.)

With the limited exception of the employment policy guidelines, no major changes towards more social democratic policies at EU level followed (Ostheim 2006). The subsequent dilution of the Stability and Growth Pact matched social democratic preferences for an active business cycle policy only in a superficial way. Budgetary interests of the 'deficit-sinners', notably Germany and France, which were independent from any party political influence, were more decisive. The same applies to the transitional restrictions on labour movement introduced after the eastern enlargement in May 2004 and the removal of the 'country of origin' principle from the Services Directive. Schröder's government considered in both cases concerns about wage dumping – highlighted by (German) trade unions – and so pursued a classic social democratic course. However, as a result of both provisions, employment opportunities for employees from the less wealthy countries have been diminished. Therefore, Schröder in fact asserted both provisions in order to protect especially the interests of *German* employees. In turn, Schröder's willingness to vehemently intervene in favour of the interests of German automobile and chemical industries was at the expense of EU environmental policy aims (Ostheim 2003, 361ff.; Jacob and Volkery 2007, 440).

Besides these incidents, driven by national interest considerations, the Schröder-led Red–Green coalition government nevertheless gave some important impetus to European integration. The speech on the finality of European integration by the (Green) foreign minister, Joschka Fischer, at Humboldt University in Berlin in May 2000 (Fischer 2000) was a significant impulse for the launch of the process that led to the European Constitutional Treaty (Laffan 2006).[15] The SPD broadly endorsed Fischer's suggestions, and, in a key motion adopted one year later, the party called for a European constitution and more federal structures for the EU as well, but, while the 'European enthusiasts' within the SPD and its MEPs endorsed Fischer's proposals, other social democrats were more hesitant (interview with former SPD official). However, the idea of a European constitution was not completely new, and, after the Nice summit that failed to provide substantive solutions to the EU's problems, 'everyone knew that some kind of institutional reform had to happen' (interview with SPD politician).

More remarkably, the SPD supported (a) the strict separation of competences between the EU and the member states, according to the principle of subsidiarity, and (b) the renationalisation of some already 'Europeanised' policy domains (SPD 2001, 52ff.). By doing so, the SPD once more adopted a political position that had been expressed by the Christian Democrats since the early 1990s, especially by the Bavarian CSU (Jeffery and Paterson 2003, 72). With those demands, the SPD responded as well to the desires of many *Bundesländer*, whose political positions had recently evolved from a 'letting us in' approach[16] towards a request of 'keeping Europe out' (Thielemann 2004, 364).[17]

In more general terms, Germany's leading role concerning the future institutional setting of the EU (Müller-Brandeck-Bocquet 2002) was not determined exclusively by the SPD. At least as important was the influence of the German *Bundesländer* and Foreign Minister Fischer. In contrast to Schröder's occasionally critical statements about the EU, Fischer consistently held pro-integrationist views (ibid., 171). In October 2002, he even replaced the SPD's member in the Convention on the Future of Europe, Peter Glotz, an intellectual who had helped shape the SPD's European policy for many years. This again showed that the making of the European Constitution was of particular importance for Fischer, but less so for the SPD. However, both the European Convention and the subsequent Intergovernmental Conference (IGC) did not attract major attention in Germany. These issues were obscured (from 2003 onwards) by severe domestic conflicts that arose in regard to the implementation of welfare state reforms introduced by the so-called 'Agenda 2010' (Zohlnhöfer and Egle 2007). As these welfare reforms proved to be rather unpopular with the electorate, the SPD had to anticipate a bitter defeat in the European elections in 2004[18] and therefore tried once more – like in the context of the *Bundestag* election in 2002 – to benefit from the popularity of its decision not to participate in the Iraq war and, consequently, campaigned for 'Europe as a peace power' (Niedermayer 2005). However, this strategy to shift attention away from domestic problems did not pay off, and, with only 21.5 per cent of the votes, the SPD scored its worst ever result in a nation-wide election (ibid.).

As regards the amendment of the Constitutional Treaty that became necessary as a consequence of the French and Dutch referenda in 2005, German European policy was again determined by a strong bipartisan con-sensus, especially as the CDU/CSU and the SPD formed a 'grand coalition' in late 2005. Both parties supported the Lisbon Treaty, as they had done with the Constitutional Treaty. In fact, the German EU presidency in the first half of the year 2007 did well in dealing with the thorny issue of the 'failed' Constitutional Treaty. By fostering a compromise between the member states, the German government paved the way for the subsequent adoption of the Lisbon Treaty. However, this success was first of all attributed to the leadership capacity of Chancellor Angela Merkel (CDU), whereas Foreign Minister Steinmeier (SPD) seemed to have played only a secondary role – at least in the public perception. The Lisbon Treaty was ratified (without receiving much public attention) by the *Bundestag* and the *Bundesrat* with a vast two-thirds majority, once the required constitutional amendments had been approved.

Although the CDU/CSU and the SPD agreed on the issue of the European Constitution (as well as the Lisbon Treaty), they disagreed on the question of Turkey's accession to the EU. The Schröder government had argued vehemently in favour of opening accession negotiations with Turkey, on the basis of the aim to stabilise democratic institutions that would make Turkey a model country combining Islam and democracy. In addition, geo-strategic security considerations, economic interests and finally the integration of Turkish citizens in Germany were mentioned. However, the CDU/CSU had attacked this position as an effort to restore the Red–Green coalition's relationship with the Bush government, which had been seriously damaged as a result of the German 'no' to the Iraq war (Ostheim 2007, 495). The Schröder government officially rejected that reproach, but the fact that Germany is highly dependent on US and NATO facilities to maintain its growing military deployments overseas is a strong indication that pressure from the Bush administration may have played a decisive role (interview with former SPD official). In any case, this decision was made against the wishes of the majority of the German population. The majority of SPD members and supporters are thought to be rather sceptical about it, too (interview with SPD politician). Therefore, this issue seems to disprove the argument that decisions on European affairs are driven by domestic issues in the first place.

Concerning the question of how to deal with the financial crisis that commenced in 2008, the SPD called for a tight re-regulation of European and global financial markets (but in a very general sense) and asked for better European co-ordination in economic policy. Bashing market liberalism was first of all considered to be an adequate vote-seeking strategy for the European elections in June 2009. In this context, Minister of Finance Peer Steinbrück (SPD) stood out in the public debate by identifying countries such as Liechtenstein and Switzerland, but also EU member states such as Luxembourg and Austria, as tax havens, provoking some diplomatic quarrels with these neighbours.

More continuity than change

Taking the whole period from the end of World War II until today into consideration, the SPD's European policy displays more continuity than change. In general terms, the SPD has always supported European integration, as well as enlargement. In addition, the SPD has consistently demanded the strengthening and democratisation of supranational institutions, notably the European Parliament. However, as a governing party, the SPD dealt effectively with intergovernmental institutions, too. Only as an opposition party did the SPD twice diverge from the remarkably stable bipartisan consensus in Germany's European policy: first, in the early 1950s, when the unresolved 'German question' contradicted West European integration in the view of the SPD, and, second, in the mid-1990s, when parts of the SPD argued for a postponement of EMU. However, only the evolution from an outright rejection to an affirmation of West European integration in the 1950s constitutes a paradigm shift for the party, as the later criticism against EMU was just an intermezzo. In both cases, the SPD resumed the political positions of the CDU/CSU, albeit after a delay. What accounts for this trend?

Explaining the SPD's preferences on European integration: the role of ideas, interests and political institutions

In order to explain political parties' preferences on European integration, a number of different theoretical approaches are discussed in the corresponding literature (for a detailed overview, see the introductory chapter). On the basis of these concepts, the remainder of this chapter will discuss the impact of interests, institutions and ideas on preference formation in the SPD. Three main sources of influence can be identified:

1 the over-arching importance of the 'burden' of German history, evoking strong Europeanist beliefs among both politicians and voters;
2 economic, party political and geopolitical interests, where the 'German question' was a particularly crucial point until the 1960s;
3 political institutions, such as the specific nature of the SPD's party organisation, its internal decision-making processes and, finally, the constraints imposed by German federalism.

Ideas, norms and beliefs: Europeanism as a reason of state

Given the SPD's Heidelberg Programme of 1925, German social democracy had affirmed its support for European integration long before the 'European project' emerged in the 1950s. Both the early and the post-war efforts of the SPD were motivated by the basic concern for peace and the conviction that only ever closer European co-operation and integration would prevent further catastrophes such as the two disastrous world wars. Although the SPD had put forward that idea already after World War I, it became commonplace in (West) Germany after 1949. In addition, after Germany's descent to Nazi barbarism, the only possible way to overcome Germany's 'historical shame' and to bring Germany back into the 'civilised world' was to make sure that no war would ever again start from German soil. That commitment became a credo of German post-war political elites and voters, whether from the right or the left of the political spectrum. As a consequence, European policy in Germany was from the beginning construed as a 'peace project', although its concrete implementation started from the economy.[19] However, as other countries (especially France) still were sceptical about Germany, the newly founded Federal Republic had to prove its credibility as a now peaceful nation by willingly transferring sovereignty to supranational institutions. As a matter of fact, German foreign policy was – and had to be – European right from the beginning.[20] In sum, the long-standing party political consensus in European affairs is predominantly a result of that burden of German history and cannot be explained only in terms of institutional constraints (i.e. German federalism and the necessity to form government coalitions), as Lees (2002) put it. Although Lees rightly argues that party competition in Germany has never supported a potential surge of Euroscepticism, the historical rationale behind that observation was decisive. To be sure, institutional and numerous other variables influenced the SPD's preferences on European integration as well (see below), but all that happened within the frame of *Europapolitik als Staatsraison*.

That said, what remains to be explained in the following is the extent to which institutional variables and different kinds of interest (geo-strategic, economic, vote- and office-seeking) supported that basic belief, and under what circumstances contradictions can be observed. In addition, it must be acknowledged that the notion of European integration as a 'peace project' changed over time. Whereas it was dominant in the 1950s, it became weaker once peace and stability in Europe could be taken for granted. Therefore, it might be no accident that economic issues attracted more attention within the SPD especially since the 1980s. Nevertheless, the SPD's approval of the Maastricht Treaty and its consent to EMU were still strongly influenced by the long-standing norm that 'Germany cannot be governed against Europe', as one interviewee put it (interview with SPD politician).

Finally, after re-unification, Germany's former 'exceptionalism' in foreign policy became obsolete, altering also the perception of the political elite about how to deal with 'German' and 'European' interests. As a consequence, it was Chancellor Schröder in particular who argued more self-confidently in favour of Germany's national interests than his predecessor ever did (Hellmann 2007). Whereas European policy was not of particular concern for Schröder (at least until he became chancellor), European integration has always been a question of 'war and peace' for Kohl (Keßler 2002), who was politically socialised in the early post-war years.

Another ideational factor that accounts for the SPD's support for European integration and enlargement in particular is the notion that the EC/EU is an 'agent of democratisation'. As the German example demonstrates, after World War II, economic and political co-operation with democratic neighbouring states might contribute to the successful consolidation of fragile political systems. This argument was first deployed within the SPD with regard to the southern enlargement (Greece, Spain, Portugal), especially as the SPD had established good relations with Spanish and Portuguese social democrats. It was also mentioned in regard to the accession of central and east European post-communist states in 2004, as well as the possible future accession of Turkey.

Geopolitical, economic and party political interests

As the previous section has demonstrated, ideas matter in preference formation and, owing to the reasons mentioned above, perhaps more so in Germany. Nevertheless, it would be a mistake to think that economic considerations, vote- or office-seeking are irrelevant. In addition, the need to overcome German division was a major geopolitical consideration that determined the SPD's changing positions towards European integration.

Geopolitics: the German question

The main reason for the SPD's critical stance towards European integration in the early 1950s was the unresolved 'German question'. In fact, only this major issue could (and did) overshadow the aforementioned pro-European tradition of German social democracy. Although counterfactual arguments are difficult to prove, the SPD would not have rejected the first steps towards European integration if there had been no division between West and East Germany, and if the Saarland had already been integrated into the new German state (interview with former SPD official).

In fact, only after (a) the Saarland had joined the Federal Republic and (b) the failure of the European Defence Community had led to the belief that political integration in Western Europe did not contradict the objective of re-unification did the SPD manage to develop a pragmatic course in European affairs. This pragmatism was strengthened by the fact that, after the construction of the Berlin Wall, the Soviet Union had to be made responsible for the German division rather than integration of Western Europe. In addition, since that point in time, re-unification could no longer be expected to materialise in the short term. Against this backdrop, the SPD developed its concept of *Ostpolitik*, which enabled it to pursue pragmatic policies towards Western Europe as well as a *rapprochement* to the Eastern bloc and the GDR. Moreover, this concept fitted nicely into the aforementioned idea that European policy was identical with the pursuit of peace, as *Ostpolitik* explicitly aimed at alleviating tensions between the two blocs.

With regard to the presumed trade-off between the 'German question' and European integration, it was a tragic mistake of the SPD to resist European integration in order to achieve German unity at a point in time when re-unification was in fact out of reach. In turn, when German unification suddenly happened in 1990, large sections of the party were sceptical about it. Thus, it is Christian Democracy (the Adenauer and the Kohl governments) that displayed a better 'historical instinct' on these issues.

Economic interests

European integration has had a major economic facet from the beginning, but, nevertheless, it has been pursued by German politicians mostly in terms of the ideational reasons mentioned above. As one MP put it (and in Marxist terms) 'in German politics, Europe is a phenomenon of the cultural superstructure, not of the economic base' (interview with SPD politician). That said, economic interests were instrumental in building Europe. That is particularly true in the case of the SPD, as the Christian Democratic Union has always had stronger ties to business and employer interests and therefore was more engaged in everyday economic policy-making on the European level than the SPD (interview with former SPD official).

In any case, some economic considerations shaping the SPD's preferences towards Europe can be mentioned. For example, in addition to the 'German question', the insistence on socialist aims was another reason for the initial post-war rejection of European integration. For the same reason, the SPD supported the accession of Scandinavian countries and above all Britain, in an effort to balance the conservative–capitalist Franco–German couple. Following the economic success of the ECSC and owing to the fact that this project was also supported by German trade unions, the reasons for that rejection later became irrelevant.

Subsequently, given Germany's growing economic strength and the success of its exporting industries, it was the Federal Republic in particular that benefited from the establishment of a single European market. Against this backdrop, the crisis management of Chancellor Schmidt (who sought to stabilise the European market and thus German external trade) might be explained primarily in terms of economic interests. From a functionalist point of view, the introduction of the EMS contributed to the deepening of Europe's political integration, though that was not its primary aim. The sceptical position of the SPD in the 1980s and 1990s towards the completion of the internal market can also be traced back to (particularly social democratic) economic concerns. Because of the comparatively high wage level and social standards in Germany, the SPD feared that its electorate would suffer from increased (cheaper) competition. As a consequence, the left wing within the SPD has repeatedly called for re-regulation at the EU level as a response to the loss of autonomy resulting from globalisation. However, a corresponding initiative by then SPD leader and Minister of Finance Lafontaine failed, not only because of diverging (economic) interests within the EU member states, but also because of conflict *within* the party about the right course in economic and social policy (Egle and Henkes 2004, 125–8).

Finally, Chancellor Schröder's initial attempts to reduce Germany's net contributions to the EU budget originated, in addition to electoral considerations, in fiscal concerns. Given the costs of German re-unification, the Federal Republic was, in the 1990s, much more constrained than it was in the 1980s (Sloam 2003, 63). Yet, this claim ought to be nuanced because of the constraints that Schröder's government soon experienced when it took over the EU presidency in 1999 (ibid., 75).

Vote- and office-seeking interests, party competition

The structure of German party competition has almost continuously produced pro-European incentives, given that a possible defection from the European consensus would have undermined the aforementioned *Staatsraison*. Usurprisingly, the SPD's attempt to be more 'national' than the CDU in the early 1950s proved unsuccessful as early as the general election of 1953, although the SPD's insistence on German re-unification appealed particularly to refugees from the occupied (eastern) territories (Paterson 1974, 14). Against this backdrop, vote-seeking considerations challenged the party's policy, especially in foreign and European affairs. However, the logic of office-seeking was the crucial factor for the SPD's subsequent U-turn – besides the changing context of the 'German question' (see *supra*). As the SPD was certainly not popular enough to gain a majority in the *Bundestag*, only by explicitly stating that it shared the foreign and European policy of the Adenauer government could it present itself as a potential coalition partner to the CDU and participate in government at all. A similar pattern was observed at the beginning of the 1990s, when the SPD supported the Maastricht Treaty without enthusiasm. A rejection would have harmed the SPD's reputation as a political party that was ready to take over government responsibility. Furthermore, it was also assumed that the SPD could not have won any election by blocking the Maastricht Treaty (interview with SPD politician).

In turn, the call of the Baden-Württemberg's regional SPD in 1996 to postpone EMU was a clear-cut vote-seeking strategy without any policy substance. The decision regarding the introduction of the euro could not have been delayed, even if the SPD had won that state election, which was extremely unlikely (interview with former SPD official). Finally, this anti-euro strategy was abandoned shortly after it had failed. That state election was perhaps the only expression of the *effet d'opposition* in Germany's European policy. Whereas the aim to confront the goverment with a different point of view as a matter of principle might have also played a role in Schumacher's decision to distance himself and the party from the Adenauer government in the early 1950s, there were nevertheless more reasons to do so then than there were in the case of EMU.

Another (unsuccessful) vote-seeking strategy of the SPD – especially of Chancellor Schröder – was the claim to reduce Germany's net contributions to the EU budget and the attempt to turn the European elections of 2004 into a belated plebiscite on the non-participation of Germany in the Iraq war. Although the references to a *Friedensmacht Europa* (Europe as a peaceful power) in that election campaign fitted very well with the aforementioned notion of Europe as a peace project, voters clearly acknowledged that the government just wanted to benefit from its stance on the Iraq war and shift attention away from its domestic problems concerning the implementation of unpopular labour market reforms.

Hence, the SPD's coalition partners had some pro-European impact on the party. Both in the social–liberal and the Red–Green coalitions, the junior coalition partner provided the minister of foreign affairs (Genscher and Fischer, respectively), who – admittedly with different focal points – continuously pursued a pro-integrationist stance. That was particularly the case in regard to the discussion about the European Constitution that was launched by Joschka Fischer's speech at Humboldt University in 2000. As a former MEP stated, 'we [the SPD] could not fall behind the Greens, a party that had rejected the Maastricht Treaty just a few years ago' (interview with former SPD politician).

Institutions: intra-party decision-making and federalism

Finally, it is important to examine to what extent the SPD's European policy was influenced by its party organisation and some particular features of German federalism.

Intra-party decision-making

As a consequence of the bipartisan consensus, issues of European policy almost never played a decisive role in German party competition and nor, therefore, in the SPD's internal party politics. As a former senior policy adviser to the SPD's parliamentary party put it, 'European policy by nature is an issue of the political and societal elite and for *bourgeois* parties, not for social democracy', as the working-class basis of the SPD would not have the same approach to European issues as the better-educated middle and upper classes (interview with former SPD official). In fact, European policy was continuously subordinated within the party. Ordinary party members rarely played a significant role and were mostly indifferent (Featherstone 1988, 165). A few exceptions were the SPD's rejection of the specific form of European integration in the early 1950s, the first European elections in 1979, when Willy Brandt led the SPD's list of candidates, and finally the debate on EMU in the 1990s.

Consequently, it is no surprise that intra-party decision-making was dominated by only a handful of individuals – for example the SPD leader or some leading MPs. What is more, as European policy is (still) construed as part of foreign policy, it is first of all 'made' by the executive (the government), and not by parliament. The chancellery has always been the 'final authority' in European policy when the SPD was in power (interviews with former SPD officials and politicians). When the SPD was in opposition, however, the parliamentary party and some MPs could influence the party's preferences to a considerable extent. In fact, social democratic members of the parliamentary assemblies of the early European institutions were socialised in a 'European' way and contributed to the SPD's change of course in the 1950s (Lodge 1976, 21; Moeller 1996, 36). As regards the SPD's earlier intransigent claim for German unity, it has to be noted that 40 per cent of the first post-war SPD *Bundestagsfraktion* (1949–53) consisted of refugees from the eastern parts of Germany (Paterson 1974, 6) and therefore had a bigger interest in a quick re-unification; in contrast, the CDU was dominated by West German MPs.

As regards the role of the leadership, Kurt Schumacher was certainly an especially significant figure, a 'monocratic leader par excellence' (Paterson 1974, 11). However, Willy Brandt (whose visionary rhetoric was deprived of major concrete results), Helmut Schmidt (whose pragmatic problem-solving was not accompanied by 'Euro-slogans') and Gerhard Schröder (who emphasised the German national interest) in their own way also determined the European policy of the SPD. This empirical finding is consistent with the theoretical notion that the political position of an agenda-setter is decisive when confronted with a 'collective' agent with low internal cohesion (Tsebelis 2002). A textbook-like example of the decisive role of an agenda-setter could be also observed in the case of the policy change after Lafontaine's resignation from his government and party offices.

Decision-making on European issues is a highly complicated process within the party, as it has to be co-ordinated between the party's executive committee (*Bundesvorstand*), the parliamentary party, its MEPs and finally the heads of *Länder* governments (*Ministerpräsidenten*). When the SPD was a governing party, all these bodies were more or less factored out by the decisive role of the chancellor. The parliamentary party is better equipped and more important than the executive committee, whereas the SPD's members of the European Parliament are said to (a) 'play their own role' and (b) be only loosely connected to the party's executive committee and the parliamentary party in the *Bundestag* (interview with former SPD official). Therefore, a comprehensive strategy on European issues could only seldom be defined, whereas the expression of contradictory positions, even on crucial issues as in the case of EMU, could not be prevented.

Federalism

As stated above, European policy is perceived as foreign policy and is therefore part of the executive's domain. In the German case, however, things are more complicated, as the *Länder* are involved in policy-making. Both the *Bund* and the *Länder* are affected by a transfer of competences towards the European level, and the approval of the *Länder* meeting in the second chamber, the *Bundesrat*, is required for the enactment of the corresponding laws.

An important case in that respect was the approval of the Maastricht Treaty, as the SPD had the majority in the *Bundesrat* at that time. In order to strenghthen the SPD's impact on European policy – given that it was in opposition until 1998 – SPD-led *Länder* governments urged the Kohl government to give the *Länder* many more competences in regard to European issues. In fact, since an amendment to the *Grundgesetz* (Art. 23) in 1992, the approval of the *Bundesrat* is required for all major decisions on European issues. That said, the SPD's approval of the Maastricht Treaty was used as an instrument to extend the competences of the *Länder*. However, the attempt to strengthen social democratic influence on Germany's European policy was not particularly successful, as *Länder* governments typically follow their own (fiscal) interests, independently of party political orientation. The extension of the competences of the *Länder* was judged by one interviewee as 'the major sin in German European policy', because since then nobody really knows who is responsible for policy (interview with former SPD official).

In sum, federalism in principle could have been employed to shift the party's European policy owing to the competences of *Länder* governments, but, in reality, institutional fragmentation made it even more difficult for the SPD to formulate a comprehensive social democratic strategy. That claim was confirmed by the experience of the European Convention as well, when the *Länder* pushed for a clear-cut division of competences between the European and the national level. This claim was picked up by the SPD, but not even a party's member of the Convention claimed that the SPD pursued any particular social democratic ambitions (interview with SPD politician).

Conclusion

Whereas the switch of other social democratic parties to a positive view of European integration took a long time to emerge, the SPD had already, since the early twentieth century, advocated the political and economic integration of Europe. Only at the beginning of the 1950s, the party rejected the first steps taken by the Adenauer government. In the aftermath, the SPD changed course and approached the European policy of the CDU. The deepening of European integration and, in particular, enlargement to new member states has always been supported by the SPD. In fact, Germany's European policy, apart from a few exceptions, has been dominated by bipartisan consensus. Therefore, a dominant 'social democratic' European policy could rarely be found. Among other reasons, this was owing to the fact that the SPD was in opposition when major breakthroughs occurred – for instance, the path-breaking decisions in the early 1950s and during the 'change of epochs' in 1989–90.

In turn, when the SPD first entered government at the end of the 1960s, it concentrated above all on its *Ostpolitik*, which was much more an affair of the party's heart than West European integration. From the mid 1970s onwards, the Schmidt government was primarily concerned with economic crisis management. Nevertheless, the introduction of the EMS, which could be largely ascribed to the Schmidt government, was an important step towards further integration, paving the way for the subsequent establishment of EMU. The party's criticism of the European single currency in the mid-1990s, driven by short-term vote-seeking interests, remained an intermezzo. After the SPD had regained power in 1998, it did not manage to initiate a 'social democratic project' on the European level, despite initial attempts. Nevertheless, the Schröder government put forward the idea of a European Constitutional Treaty. In sum, when SPD-led governments played a formative role in European integration, it was not necessarily because of ambitious (social democratic) European goals. It was much more a consequence of the aforementioned *Europapolitik als Staatsraison* and the sheer 'size' of the Federal Republic of Germany, which almost automatically required it to play a leading role within the EU. That said, some arguments put forward in the literature concerning the questions of when and why social democratic parties became more positive towards European integration (for a discussion see Dimitrakopoulos' introductory chapter) have to be put into perspective in the case of Germany and the SPD.

As regards the 'instrumental view', it has to be acknowledged that European integration was in fact pursued by German social democracy in terms of instrumental reasons, but not in order to modernise the state or the economy; rather, securing peace was the primary objective. That was already the case in the inter-war period. In addition, after World War II, Germany's single means to overcome the burden of German history and to gain back credibility was to abstain from any kind of 'national' foreign policy and, as a consequence, to foster European integration. Therefore, whereas economic considerations clearly supported European integration, they have not been the driving power of the SPD's European policy. Nevertheless, instrumentalism could be detected in the cases of the economic crisis management by the Schmidt government (EMS) and the (failed) attempts to employ the EC/EU as a countervailing power to the constraints of globalisation.

The 'obfuscation thesis', however, must be rejected. The SPD has never appealed to the EC/EU in order to deflect attention from a problem that could not be resolved at the national level. In contrast, what happened from time to time is that the SPD – like the CDU and other German parties – sometimes blamed the EC/EU for particular European policies in order to gain votes. For example, that was the case concerning EMU and the claim to reduce Germany's net contributions to the EU budget.

Finally, the 'dependence thesis' does not fit in with the German case. Since 1949, German governments never took a decision in European affairs in order to avoid being excluded by 'pioneer' countries. Quite the opposite: Germany itself was from the beginning – and in most cases together with France – one of the pacemakers of European integration.

The evolution of the SPD's preferences towards European integration can be described as follows: Given a strong pro-European tradition established even before World War II, the SPD had to deal with a trade-off between its Europeanist beliefs and the need to overcome German division as soon as possible after 1945. During the very early post-war years, 'German interests' proved to be stronger than the claim for European integration, whereas the leadership of Kurt Schumacher played a decisive role. In the aftermath, the SPD learned the lesson that vote- and office-seeking interests required support for West European integration. In addition, the geopolitical context had changed, as German re-unification became unrealistic in the short term. Accepting this fact, the SPD developed a concept (*Ostpolitik*) of how to reconcile the claim for German unity with pragmatic European policy. For the first time since 1945, political interests, geo-strategic concerns and the basic claim for peace could be combined within the framework of European integration. That said, the SPD's European policy seems to confirm a thesis put forward by Dimitrakopoulos (2005) – although developed in a different context – that norms or basic beliefs become particularly effective when they correspond with the agent's interests. In turn, when a policy that is primarily driven by interests violates that basic concern, it cannot be pursued for a long time, as the case of criticism against EMU has proved.

Appendix: list of interviewees

Egon Bahr, former Cabinet minister, state secretary and SPD *Bundesgeschäftsführer* (Secretary General), Berlin, 27 March 2007.

Hans-Eberhard Dingels, former adviser to the SPD's Executive Committee (head of unit for international affairs), Bonn, 16 March 2007.

Klaus Hänsch, former president of the European Parliament and member of the Convention on the Future of Europe, Düsseldorf, 2 April 2007.

Andreas Helle, adviser to the SPD's Executive Committee and former adviser to the chairman of the Party of European Socialists, Berlin, 23 March 2007.

Helga Köhnen, former European affairs adviser to the SPD's parliamentary party, Cologne, 2 April 2007.

Rudolf Scharping, former Cabinet minister and chairman of the SPD and its parliamentary party, Frankfurt am Main, 7 May 2007.

Angelica Schwall-Düren, Member of the *Bundestag*, vice chair of the SPD's parliamentary party and its co-ordinator for EU affairs, member of the SPD's Executive Committee and head of the SPD's Committee on EU affairs, Berlin, 28 March 2007.

Klaus Suchanek, former European affairs adviser to the SPD's Executive Committee, Berlin, 26 March 2007.

Hans-Jochen Vogel, former Cabinet minister and chairman of the SPD and its parliamentary party, Munich, 14 March 2007.

Notes

1 I am grateful to the current and former officeholders who granted me very useful interviews that inform this paper. Thanks are also due to Dionyssis G. Dimitrakopoulos and the participants at the workshop and conference on Social democracy and European integration held at Birkbeck on 8–9 December 2006 and 20–21 April 2007 for their constructive comments on previous drafts of this chapter. The usual disclaimer applies.

2 For a detailed description of this method, its validity and reliability, see Budge, Robertson and Hearl (1987) and Volkens (2001). Pro-European statements in the manifestos reflect 'favourable mention of European Community/European Union in general; desirability of expanding the European Community/European Union and/or increasing its competences; desirability of the manifesto country joining or remaining a member' (Budge *et al.* 2001, Appendix III). Negative statements on these topics could hardly be found in the manifestos of German parties. The parties only differ in terms of how much space they devote to a positive reference to European integration in their manifestos.

3 The establishment of the ECSC was the only case in which German trade unions followed a more European and integrationist approach than the SPD. In most other cases, it was the party that tried to convince the trade unions to get more involved with European issues (interview with former SPD politician).

4 In the eyes of a former Cabinet minister, Adenauer was a 'Rhenish separatist' who was much more interested in establishing strong ties to Catholic France than in gaining back East Germany (interview).

5 Article 24(2) of the *Grundgesetz* stipulates that Germany may enter a system of mutual collective security in order to maintain peace. However, the SPD claimed that, with the establishment of the EDC, the risk of war increased (Paterson 1974, 81). However, the Constitutional Court refused to make a decision about the constitutionality of the treaty that established the EDC. This is so because the ratification of an international treaty ought to take place prior to the Constitutional Court's ruling on the treaty's compatibility with the German Constitution.

6 Ability to govern.

7 All translations are the author's own.
8 The former foreign minister, vice-chancellor and leader of the FDP, Walter Scheel, was elected president of the Federal Republic almost at the same time as Schmidt became the new German chancellor. Hans-Dietrich Genscher succeeded Scheel both in the party and the government.
9 In hindsight, Schmidt stated that both he and Giscard wanted tangible and necessary progress as opposed to empty promises (Schmidt 1990, 241).
10 After the *Bundestag* election of 1998, she joined the Schröder-led government as minister for economic co-operation and development.
11 In this regard, the SPD's new basic programme adopted in October 2007 (*Hamburger Programm*) differs from the 1989 *Berliner Programm*, as these claims have now been endorsed, although in a very general and superficial sense: 'The European Union must become our answer to globalisation' (SPD 2007, 14).
12 In the mid-1990s, other parties, notably the Bavarian Christian Social Union (CSU), had taken a critical stance on monetary union.
13 In a newspaper interview in 1997, Schröder explained his position on European policy as follows:

> Kohl says Germans have to be bound to Europe or they will stir up old fears of the 'furor teutonicus'. I say that is not the case. I believe that Germans have become European not because they have to be, but because they want to be. That is the difference.

> (cited in Sloam 2003, 65)

14 After Lafontaine's resignation, his fiscal policy, inspired by neo-Keynesian principles, was abandoned. His successor as finance minister, Hans Eichel, unveiled an austerity package and promised budget consolidation. Also, the tax reform adopted in 2000 was largely based on supply-side considerations. Lafontaine's successor as SPD leader, Chancellor Schröder, had never shared Lafontaine's left-wing policy convictions. The failure of Lafontaine's endeavour for a European business cycle policy can be explained by domestic and internal party reasons. For more information on policy change and the subsequent disputes within the SPD, see Egle and Henkes (2004).
15 It has to be noted that Fischer was a senior Green Party official and presented his suggestions, not as a member of the government, but as a 'convinced European and German deputy' (Fischer 2000, 1).
16 See the increase in the competences on European policy of the *Länder* in the course of the approval of the Maastricht Treaty mentioned above.
17 In particular, the *Ministerpräsident* of Baden-Württemberg, Erwin Teufel, supported this position in the European Convention. Against the criticism, notably expressed by France, that Germany would try to transpose German federalism to the EU, that proposal regarding dual federalism in fact differs from the German 'joint-decision' model of federalism. Owing to the difficulties in reaching a decision, German federalism is no longer regarded by German elites as a model for Europe (Thielemann 2004).
18 In Germany as in most other EU member states, European Parliament election campaigns are predominantly focused on domestic issues, as was the case in 2004.
19 This notion is explicitly expressed in the SPD's new party programme as well: 'The European Union is first of all a project for peace' (SPD 2007, 14).
20 In fact, to make claims regarding the 'national interest' in a public political debate was almost a taboo until the re-unification of Germany in 1990.

3 The French Socialist Party and European integration

Faltering Europeanism

Philippe Marlière

> The reinforcement of European integration will be pursued but only on condition that it will not constitute an obstacle to the march towards socialism.
>
> (*Parti Socialiste* 1972, 183)[1]

> France is our homeland, Europe is our future.
>
> (Mitterrand 1988)

Introduction

This chapter focuses on the French *Parti Socialiste* (PS) and seeks to identify the origin and the nature of its preferences on European integration since its creation in 1905. The PS has been a self-proclaimed supporter of European integration throughout its history but – as this chapter will seek to demonstrate – a degree of nuance ought to be added to this professed view. In reality, the French Socialists have only conditionally embraced European integration, especially since the 1970s. The 'Europeanism' of the PS has been more functional than ideological. Despite committing itself officially to a 'federal Europe', the PS has always harboured strong reservations vis-à-vis the perceived neo-liberal and right-wing bias of the European project.

The first section of this chapter presents the main features of the French Socialist doctrine on Europe. It then examines how this doctrine has evolved over time to accommodate policy shifts in relation to European integration. First, it shows that the emphatic choice in favour of European integration after the Second World War was partly dictated by economic and diplomatic objectives. Such a stance should especially be understood as a commitment to reconstructing France under the auspices of the Marshall Plan in the wider context of the Cold War. Second, the persistence of a staunch pro-European agenda throughout the 1950s and 1960s was an attempt by the Socialists politically to differentiate themselves from the Gaullists and the Communists, both broadly Eurosceptics. Third, the first major departure from an unconditional support for European integration in the 1970s was the consequence of the adoption of a joint government programme by the PS and the *Parti Communiste Français* (PCF). Finally, since the early 1990s, the stance of the PS has evolved from a 'hyper Europeanism' under François Mitterrand to a much more critical position. In particular, since the mid-1990s, the EU's political orientation has been openly challenged by several groups within the PS. The party was split during the internal and national referendum campaigns on the Constitutional Treaty in 2004 and 2005. The politicisation of the debate in France and the hostility towards the Constitutional Treaty were such that the PS has had to tone down its traditional support in favour of European integration. The resounding '*non*' of the French people to the Constitutional Treaty in May 2005 forced the PS to adjust its narrative on Europe to the new political mood in France.

Doctrinal considerations

Republican ideas, as they progressively emerged and have been consolidated since the French Revolution, and a Marxist vulgate are the two major influences on French socialism (Ladrech and Marlière 1999, 67–8). For Jaurès, socialism was the complete application of the French republican motto: liberty, equality, fraternity. The French Socialists have always declared their attachment to internationalism and their solidarity with the people who, across the world, share the same values as them or are committed to the same socialist struggle. Therefore, as a French Socialist MEP put it, Europeanism was a popular cause among socialists as it offered one step in the direction of an international order based on peace and co-operation (interview with Harlem Désir, Socialist MEP, Paris, 26 January 2007). How were these republican values and internationalist ethos combined with Europe and European identity? Is there a clear socialist doctrine on Europe? Should the 'European identity' of the French Socialists be taken for granted? To answer those questions, one needs to revisit the discourse of the PS on European integration from the early years of French socialism.

The French Left and Europe

Is Europe a left-wing idea in France? It is tempting to say so in the light of Victor Hugo's seminal speech on the 'United States of Europe' on 21 August 1849 at the Peace Conference in Paris. Since then, Hugo's address has encapsulated the enduring attachment of the French Left to the idea of Europe and of European integration. From Hugo onwards, Europe has been synonymous with peace and with a stance against nationalism and war.[2] Following Hugo, the Left has supported the idea of peace, solidarity and co-operation across Europe. However, the European project has been a bone of contention between the three main traditions of the French Left: the republican Left has consistently been a staunch supporter of European integration; the Communists and the radical Left have opposed it or have been lukewarm with regard to it; and the Socialists have adopted a rather ambiguous stance on a subject matter that has, at times, seen them profoundly divided.

Internationalism and Europeanism

In the early twentieth century, the French Socialists, rallying around Jean Jaurès, were relentless peace activists. However, their credentials were more internationalist than Europeanist (Guyomarch, Machin and Ritchie 1998, 90–3). The European ideal did not feature prominently in the discourse of the *Section Française de l'Internationale Socialiste* (SFIO). Furthermore, political substance (socialist policies and the achievement of a socialist society) was given priority over political means (the creation of a supranational and European political framework). This meant that Socialists pursued their socialist objectives at the national rather than the European level (Frank 2005, 454). After the First World War, things changed radically. There was a first attempt at building a European movement as a way of preventing any further conflict on the Continent. However, this movement was neither a mass organisation, nor did it involve the European peoples. Léon Blum became one of the presidents of the French section of the Pan-European Movement in 1927 (Frank 2005, 456).

Blum contributed the first major doctrinal text on Europe. Arrested by the Vichy régime and while in detention, the leader of the Popular Front published *A L'Echelle Humaine* (Blum 1971). In this book, he outlined his views on socialism and on Europe. In the years after the Second World War and the reconstruction of the SFIO, those ideas were to exert significant influence on party preferences. Blum advocated the creation of an 'international body', with proper institutions in the form of a 'supreme state'. Nations would delegate part of their sovereignty to this 'super state', which would be empowered to make decisions that would have supremacy over those of its members. For the first time, a Socialist leader declared his support for supranationalism, agreeing publicly to the transfer of national competences to an independent set of institutions. In December 1943, the SFIO, again inspired by Blum, called for the establishment of the 'United Socialist States of Europe', as a first step towards a United States of the World. The French Socialists' assumptions were twofold. First, Nazism had been fuelled by nationalism, and the risk of revival of similar movements would remain in place as long as the nation was regarded as the supreme entity. Second, it was impossible to pursue reform in isolation, i.e. in the context of individual nation states, as such efforts would always face opposition from capitalist forces (Newman 1983, 18).

West European integration and the Cold War (1946–58)

After the Second World War, France saw in European integration the means to escape from a situation in which she remained (a) preoccupied with Germany, (b) subordinated to Britain – the 'natural ally' of the United States

– and (c) powerless vis-à-vis the USA. The idea was therefore to build a bloc, not only against the USSR, but also against the 'imperialist ambitions' of the USA. The Schuman Plan, which led to the establishment of the European Coal and Steel Community in 1951, was an attempt to achieve this objective: by entering into an international organisation on equal terms with Germany, France ended Germany's isolation and sought to reduce the likelihood of the revival of German nationalism. Later on, the SFIO was in office during the negotiations for the establishment of the EEC, but socialist values and policies did not appear to influence the European agenda of the Mollet government (Newman 1983, 12). The SFIO's commitment to European integration responded to two imperatives: first, the anchoring of France in the camp of Western liberal democracies against the 'Soviet threat'; second, this clear pro-Western stance enabled France to benefit from American aid that was essential to restore French economic power.

Europeanism, socialism and capitalism

After 1947, the Cold War brought about three major transformations in socialist thinking in France. First, Europe was reduced to 'Western' Europe. Second, any candidate aspiring to join a European organisation had to be a 'democratic' country. Finally, a debate between federalists and intergovernmentalists took place at the Hague peace congress of May 1948. The French Socialists (the Blumist right wing of the party led by Daniel Mayer, as well as Guy Mollet's Marxist left wing) supported Blum's federalist views. Another contentious issue was tackled by Blum in 1948: should the French Socialists be committed to establishing socialism in France prior to constructing 'Europe', or should they immediately pursue the latter alongside bourgeois governments? Blum's answer was that the political situation in 1948 was radically different from that of 1945, because of the Cold War and the rivalry between the two competing camps. Moreover, the United Nations had failed to establish a new order of peace and co-operation. Blum lamented the introduction of the right of veto in the San Francisco Charter – a right granted to all permanent members that, Blum argued, 'paralyses the UN's action'. The French Socialist leader concluded that the SFIO had to overcome the national egoisms at play in the UN by cultivating European federalism. To some extent, it was the UN's failure to brush aside nationalist instincts and interests that strengthened Blum's new federalist doctrine.[3] In April 1948, Blum presented his views on Europe at the Socialist International conference in Stresa. This intervention marked a turning point in the SFIO's doctrine with regard to Europe. Whereas the PCF rejected the Marshall Plan, Blum approved it on the grounds that it would help reconstruct the European economies and foster growth – a key condition for social reforms. Echoing his famous speech at the Tours conference in 1920, Blum insisted on the 'virtues of democracy against communist dictatorship' by insisting that poverty does not render the achievement of socialism any easier. Rather – he argued – prosperity is the mother of both socialism and peace. Thus, in the Blumist doctrine, European integration was construed as the pursuit of peace and democracy (or anti-communism), as well as a step towards the establishment of socialism at home (Office Universitaire de Recherche Socialiste, n.d.). Blum knew that the United States would seek to consolidate capitalism in Western Europe. However, he also believed that, under the Marshall Plan, Europe would offer a more favourable framework within which European states would be able to carry out social reforms. He also thought that it would be easier to 'socialise' domestic economies in a European context than if it was left to individual nation states. By 1947, the SFIO had revealed a deep-rooted commitment to European integration and had accepted (a) capitalist domination at home through support for the institutions of the Fourth Republic against working class unrest and (b) inclusion in a capitalist alliance abroad (Tartakowsky 1972).

Committed federalists

Guy Mollet's view on European integration did not differ from Blum's. The longest serving leader of the SFIO (from 1946 to 1969) did not diverge from the socialist doctrine as sketched out by Blum and his followers. In an important contribution to the debate published in 1965, Mollet distinguished between the 'federalist' and the 'intergovernmentalist' camps. He supported a federalist approach to European integration and argued that intergovernmentalism (mostly defended by Britain and the Scandinavian countries) was little more than a tactic whose aim was to slow down the process of integration (Office Universitaire de Recherche Socialiste, n.d.). Mollet also reiterated the need to fully integrate Germany into Europe and to work tirelessly to achieve economic and social integration, in order to create growth and wealth across Europe, and explicitly supported the federal model, the enhancement of the role and powers of the European Parliament (its approval ought to be required for treaty reform and the appointment of the Commission and it should have a greater role in budgetary decision-making), the direct election of its members and the merger of the executives of the ECSC, the Common Market and Euratom (Office Universitaire de Recherche Socialiste, n.d.). The direct election of MEPs in particular was essential, according to Mollet, as it would increase democracy at the European level. Such proposals appeared to be contentious and radical in the 1960s. On the economic objectives of European integration, Mollet distinguished between liberals and socialists. The objective of the former, he argued, was a free trade zone. The socialists, on the other hand, accepted free trade so long as it was accompanied by common socio-economic policies (e.g. harmonisation of employers' taxation).

The socialist Left and European integration

Political and electoral interests explain the choice in favour of Western European integration made by Léon Blum and Guy Mollet: between 1946 and

1958, their party was involved in a succession of coalition governments with centre-right parties. Anti-communism within the SFIO and in French society at large could not, at that time, be under-estimated. What is more surprising is the support of the socialist Left for the European project. In 1948, a Marxist tendency was present in the SFIO. The Socialists were able to present a united front on Europe because the party's left wing did not oppose European unification. This stance is exemplified by Pierre Rimbert and Marceau Pivert – two important figures of the Left at the time. Rimbert, a Marxist, was the party's main economic theorist. Like Blum, he thought that socialism could only triumph at the international level; that is, only once the framework of the nation state had been superseded:

> The division of the world into sovereign nations does not allow a single nation to remain behind. Universal competition between nations obliges each to advance ceaselessly. This necessitates the development of socialist forms of production, for only these are capable of increasing the economic power of each nation.
>
> (Rimbert 1948, 145)

Marceau Pivert, an eminent figure of the Left since the Popular Front, also argued that the creation of a United States of Europe was the major priority in order to prevent a third world war and to build socialism: 'International democratic socialism is leaving its infancy and entering its adolescence because it has finally found the material and economic framework, where its civilization can blossom, that is Europe' (Pivert 1948, 20). Both men loathed Stalinism and, although they often criticised the USA in very strong terms, their stance in favour of a federation of European countries led them to accept the Marshall Plan and West European integration.

The SFIO aimed to pursue a full employment policy at the European level. The party reckoned that socialists should co-operate with other political forces to build European institutions endowed with the power to promote a degree of economic integration. This did not mean the immediate construction of a Socialist United States of Europe, but the socialists thought that this would be possible as soon as the balance of power in Europe had become more favourable to socialist parties (Newman 1983, 24).

The Communist challenge

From the late 1940s onwards, the SFIO supported Western alignment, a *rapprochement* with West Germany and the modernisation of the economy through involvement in the international capitalist system. In all three respects, the PCF – the major party on the left of the political spectrum – opposed the Socialist position. Arguably the PCF's geopolitical standpoint indirectly influenced the SFIO's preferences on Europe. Given its close ties with the Soviet Union, the PCF's rejection of the Western alignment, which preceded the launch of the EEC, was totally predictable. Between 1941 and 1947, the PCF's objective was to use its influence to maintain East–West unity and to convince non-communist opinion that national independence depended on France alone, in close friendship with the Soviet Union (Newman 1983, 38). For the PCF, socialist talk of the establishment of a 'superstate' was 'escapism' from the real problems, and, if such an organisation were controlled by 'reactionary forces', it could lead to foreign control of French resources, the abolition of progressive domestic legislation and the destruction of French peasantry (Newman 1983, 38). After the start of the Cold War in 1947, the PCF argued that the struggle for national independence was actually proletarian internationalism in action, and solidarity with the Soviet Union was the practical application of such internationalism. Such an uncompromising stance gave the SFIO no room for manoeuvre.[4] A party in office, involved in coalition governments with centre-right parties and deeply anchored in the French political system, the SFIO could certainly not compromise on its position as a party of the establishment. What is more, the Communists' hard-line support for the USSR was an additional incentive for the SFIO to cultivate its political and ideological differences vis-à-vis the PCF, most notably its Atlanticism. In the name of democracy and freedom, the SFIO could only fall in line with the US-led liberal democracies of the West against the Soviet-led dictatorships of the East. This was notably the position adopted by all social democratic parties in the West (Marlière 1999, 5).

Socialist doctrine, the ECSC, the EDC and the EEC

For the SFIO, Robert Schuman's proposal for a European Coal and Steel Community in 1950 was not alien to socialist interests and ideas. Indeed, the project combined three socialist ideas, namely Franco–German *rapprochement*, the establishment of a supranational body as a first step towards a new international order, and European control over industries. However, by its general commitment to the principles of free competition at the European level, Schuman's document arguably also appeared to run counter to socialist beliefs. At its annual conference, the SFIO was broadly supportive of the project, although some reservations were also expressed. The Socialists wanted the ECSC to integrate as many nations as possible (notably Britain). They argued that the High Authority should have effective powers to impose its decisions; there should be a significant degree of worker representation; the ECSC should be responsible before a democratic international assembly; and, finally, the Ruhr industries should not return to private capitalism (Newman 1983, 26).

The Socialists were the largest group in the National Assembly among those who supported the treaty:

[The] acceptance of the Schuman Plan constituted a major step along the road of emasculation of any specifically socialist conception of West

European integration within the SFIO. However, the notion of Franco-German reconciliation within a supranational organisation was apparently so close to the aspirations of the socialists during the Resistance, that it was almost inevitable that the SFIO's welcome for the general characteristics of the plan would supersede the reservations they felt about its capitalist nature.

(Newman 1983, 29)

The Pleven Plan for a European Defence Community exacerbated the difficulties that the SFIO had encountered with the ECSC plan. On the one hand, the EDC appeared to constitute a major step towards the creation of a supranational Europe. On the other, it entailed the re-armament of Germany, which the Socialists totally opposed. The *anti-cédistes* argued that military integration threatened to undermine the socialist goal of European unity by reviving German militarism. It would therefore destabilise the young German democracy and would precipitate a nationalist backlash in other European countries. In reality, the *anti-cédistes* were challenging the policy of integration within the Atlantic Alliance. Mollet was determined to defeat them because he was preoccupied with strengthening the Western bloc against the USSR. In June 1954, at an extraordinary party conference, Guy Mollet managed to secure a decision in favour of ratification only by disregarding the normal voting procedures and by relying on the larger party federations of the North, which were unconditionally supporting his views (Newman 1983, 31). Despite the party's formal support for the EDC, fifty-three Socialist members of the National Assembly sided with the Gaullists and the Communists and voted against the ratification of the treaty in August 1954; only fifty voted in favour. This marked the death of the EDC and led to the expulsion from the SFIO's executive of the deputies who had voted against the EDC proposal in the National Assembly. Following this long and bitter dispute about the EDC, the party veered to the right: the *anti-cédistes* were all in the party's left wing, and the disciplinary measures against the recalcitrant deputies as well as the departure of party activists further strengthened Guy Mollet's centrist leadership (Newman 1983, 32).

The Mollet government was formed in 1956 and was resolutely 'Europeanist'. It promoted the establishment of a common market and an Atomic Energy community. Mollet handled most of the negotiations that led to the signing of the EEC and EURATOM treaties in 1957. The National Assembly voted in favour of the EURATOM treaty in July 1956 and ratified the Treaty of Rome in January 1957. Yet again, there was no significant opposition to this text from the Socialist ranks (Featherstone 1988, 117). The main opposition on the left came from the PCF. The Communists argued that West Germany would control economic policy in the EEC and therefore would dominate France once again. For that reason, the EEC was described in communist circles as 'fundamentally reactionary' (cited in Newman 1983, 50).

The Gaullist challenge (1958–71)

Despite maintaining their faith in an integrated and supranational Europe, the Socialists have had to reconsider the rather uncritical pro-EEC stance they had adopted from the late 1950s onwards. Until 1958, the SFIO participated in coalition governments alongside centre-right parties that were all pro-integrationist and supranationalist. The situation was to change with the return to power of Charles de Gaulle and the Gaullist party's subsequent political domination. Their robust defence of 'French interests' against the 'Brussels bureaucracy' was popular with voters. On the left, the SFIO had to compete with a strong and influential PCF. The Communists were equally critical of European integration and shared the nationalist stance of the Gaullists. Squeezed between these two forces, the SFIO was forced to acknowledge the neo-liberal foundations of the European construction and adopt a slightly more critical stance towards it.

'Atlanticist Europe' and 'European Europe'

Charles de Gaulle's return to power in 1958 provided a major challenge for the Left. De Gaulle sought to diminish the dominant role of the USA within NATO and to create an independent French nuclear capability. His decision to withdraw from NATO's military wing, eventually leading to the expulsion of American forces from France and the removal of the NATO headquarters from Paris, symbolised his determination to pursue an independent defence policy. Moreover, he pursued the policy of 'empty chair', which ended with the Luxembourg Compromise of January 1966. Instead of accepting the EEC as the European pillar of the Atlantic Alliance, he advocated a 'European Europe' that would determine its own interests and policies. De Gaulle argued that the interests of the nation states were both permanent and paramount. In the French case, these necessitated a search for *grandeur* (Newman 1983, 57). However, he favoured membership of the Atlantic Alliance and the EEC, so as to protect France from the Soviet threat and enhance the country's political and economic power, respectively. The French search for *grandeur* meant that it was absolutely legitimate to stand up to the United States and the European Commission when these appeared to threaten French interests. De Gaulle's stance in relation to the EEC and NATO was popular among the French public. Indeed, his views on foreign and European affairs helped the Gaullist party to secure the support of a significant segment of working-class voters (mostly traditional communist voters, but also some socialist sympathisers). Given de Gaulle's attitude towards the United States, the SFIO could no longer maintain its total solidarity with the Americans.[5] The Gaullist geopolitical approach can therefore be seen as a significant factor that led the Socialists (from the late 1950s onwards) to switch their support from a less 'Atlanticist Europe' to a more 'European Europe'. This also facilitated a *rapprochement* between the PS and the PCF. Both parties had an interest in uniting in both foreign and domestic affairs so as to respond to the Gaullist challenge.

From uncritical to critical support

From the late 1950s onward, the SFIO entered a phase of political and electoral decline. The party itself started to disintegrate. This meant that the Socialists' views on Europe became more volatile and diverse. However, in the last years of the Fourth Republic, the SFIO reiterated its traditional stance on Europe. It advocated a United States of Europe, supported NATO and remained hostile to the USSR. De Gaulle's opposition to Britain's membership of the EEC – which, in contrast, had been long supported by the SFIO – helped the Socialists to cultivate their 'internationalist credentials' (Featherstone 1988, 117). After 1958, the SFIO moved into opposition to Gaullism and began to move away from its uncritical acceptance of the EEC. Interestingly, Roger Quilliot, a member of the *Comité Directeur* (party executive), appeared to recognise the contradiction between the party's stated objective – socialism – and France's membership of NATO and the EEC, while highlighting the only route available to the party, namely reformism:

> We are members of NATO, Europe and the Common Market, our economic system overlaps with that of our partners and is essentially capitalist. How can our structures be radically modified in this context, without shaking the whole construction? . . . Could we claim to reconcile the irreconcilable? Everything indicates that we would, once again, be revolutionary in words and reformists in fact.
>
> (Quilliot 1963, 281)

Given de Gaulle's attitude vis-à-vis the United States, it became untenable for the Socialists to maintain total solidarity with the Americans.

For the *Centre d'Etudes, de Recherche et d'Education Socialistes* (CERES), a new Marxist faction within the SFIO (Hanley 1986), the fight against American political and economic hegemony had to be the priority – as it prevented the development of socialism in the West – and a French government of the Left could accept the EEC only if the latter did not interfere in French domestic policies. Furthermore, support for further integration would depend on the EEC taking concerted action in a manner capable of advancing socialism in France (Newman 1983, 74). The socialist Left argued that there must never be any contradiction between the programme of a government of the Left and the EEC. During the party conference held in 1967, the SFIO condemned the US as strongly as the Soviet Union and distinguished between (a) Socialist support for European integration and (b) the support provided by the proponents of capitalism (Newman 1983, 75).

On the other hand, François Mitterrand – a committed Europeanist, believed that European integration was a prerequisite for the advent of socialism in France and argued that it was not necessary to choose between furthering integration in a capitalist Europe and building socialism in France (Mitterrand 1969, 197). He argued that a 'European Europe' was possible only through socialism, and a government of the Left in France would have to further its own domestic programme, while impelling the members of the 'capitalist EEC' towards socialism. This line of reasoning reflected the influence of the socialist Left.

From the second half of the 1960s, the SFIO became increasingly critical of the USA and more assertive about the need to secure European independence. Charles de Gaulle supported the notion of independence from the USA, and so did the Communists. In this new context, the Socialists had to tone down their traditional Atlanticism. Yet, the SFIO's new stance was different from Gaullism, as it remained integrationist and supranationalist.

The Union of the Left and socialist Europe (1971–83)

Following the disintegration of the SFIO and the birth of the new PS in Epinay in 1971, the Socialists had to further review their preferences on European integration. Committed to a common programme of government and a 'union of the Left', the PS had no choice but to radicalise its stance on social and economic matters. In the light of a common programme that called for a break (*rupture*) with capitalism, the Socialists had to acknowledge that the EEC was not a left-wing project, but a capitalist venture that could prove an obstacle to the establishment of socialism in France and across Europe.

'Europe will either be socialist or will not be at all'

The birth of the PS marked a clear departure from the traditional socialist themes on Europe: in the long term, the PS still opted for federalism as a way of facilitating the construction of socialism at home. In the short term, it accepted free trade within the EEC, provided there was a degree of social policy harmonisation. From 1971 onwards, the Socialist narrative on Europe was notably revised. Mitterrand, under pressure from the CERES, decided to change the party's order of priorities: the construction of socialism in France became the priority. In fact however, he adopted a median position between (a) the SFIO's traditional line and (b) the CERES' view of the EEC as a 'liberal club'. Throughout the 1970s and until his victory in the presidential election of 1981, Mitterrand was concerned about the compatibility of his socialist programme at home with France's membership of the EEC (Bergounioux 2004, 7). In 1972, he famously wrote that Europe will either be socialist or it will not be at all (Duhamel 1998, 121), while, at the same time, calling for the pursuit of European integration. The CERES urged Mitterrand to clarify his position and to abandon this ambiguous stance. A specially convened national conference on Europe was organised in Bagnolet in 1973. The new PS aimed to produce a policy document on Europe. The CERES argued that the PS should only authorise the transfer of powers to a 'European Central Authority' after the Left had gained power in France. The decision would be taken after making an assessment of the political situation in Europe and of the intentions of other national governments (Hohl 2008, 92). Mitterrand dismissed the strict conditions set out by CERES and warned of the 'dangers of isolation' in Europe (Hohl 2008, 100).

Mitterrand's ambiguity prevailed in the end: on the one hand, European integration could go ahead without any delay or prerequisite, and, on the other, the majority of the party called for a 'Europe marching towards socialism' (Bergounioux 2004, 7). Two divergent interpretations of the text could be given: the supporters of integration thought that it endorsed their positions, whereas those holding a more critical view believed it offered conditional support to EEC membership. Mitterrand managed to rally 80 per cent of the delegates behind this ambivalent text.

At the same time, the relationship between the PS and other European social democratic parties was uneasy. Owing to their alliance at home with the PCF, the Socialists veered to the left and condemned, in theory, the 'excessive compromises' of social democracy. In practice, the PS needed the backing of its sister parties, most notably the German Social Democrats. The PS also turned to southern European socialist parties. They were operating in countries marked by influential communist parties (notably Italy and Spain) and with which they shared common values and policies – the emphasis on reforms to the structure of the economy, on the socialist ideology and also wider cultural similarities (Featherstone 1988, 121). In 1979, the PS refused to sign up to a common electoral platform with other social democratic parties ahead of the first direct elections for the European Parliament. The 'socialist project' of 1980 envisaged a 'break with capitalism' in France, despite the French commitment to the EEC. Indeed, the PS acceded to power in 1981 with a rather contradictory and ambiguous stance on Europe.

It was not surprising that the PCF toned down its fierce criticisms of European integration in the 1970s, when Socialists and Communists agreed to a joint government programme. However, after the defeat in the legislative elections of March 1978, and with the PS having secured dominance on the left, the PCF reverted to vehement criticism of the Socialists' European policies. Mitterrand did not give in and opted against reconsidering France's commitment to the EEC in case of an electoral victory of the Left. When the Left won the legislative elections in June 1981, the PCF signed a new common statement on the EEC and entered the government (but on a more junior basis than would have been the case if the Left had won the 1978 elections). Because of the changed balance of power between the PCF and the PS, the tone of the new statement was less critical than that of the joint government programme (Newman 1983, 90).

One can conclude that the fierce competition with the PCF in the context of the Cold War led the SFIO (and later the PS) to adopt an uncompromising Atlanticist and federalist stance with regard to European integration. The SFIO also aimed to occupy a more centrist position in the party system, compatible with participation in coalition governments (under the Fourth Republic) and political respectability in the domestic and foreign arenas. Conversely, in the context of the unity of the Left and with the PS in a dominant position on the left, the Socialist discourse on Europe shifted to the left and was more critical of European integration. This corresponded to the new Socialist strategy of conquest of power: the gathering of all left-wing forces behind a dominant PS, followed by the formation of a coalition government under a socialist president.

In 1980, the PS endorsed a 'Socialist project for France in the 1980s'. Drafted by Jean-Pierre Chevènement, the leader of the CERES, it made tough demands on enlargement in an effort to defend the 'national interest' (Featherstone 1988, 125). It also acknowledged the difficulty facing a government of the Left in France in reforming the EEC along socialist lines. However, the Socialists remained confident that this could be achieved through some kind of spillover effect:

> The realisation of a socialist project in France will be a shock within our European environment that will turn it into one that is less marked by liberalism and Atlanticism. Engaged in the construction of a socialist society, France will utilise the institutions to promote the convergence of the social struggles against unemployment and in favour of the reduction of working time, the control of multinational companies, the defence of liberties and the extension of democracy.
>
> (*Parti Socialiste* 1980, 352)

It is worth noting that, by the early 1980s, the PS was committed to a number of specific reforms in the EEC: the enhancement of the European Parliament, safeguards for French workers and industries affected by future enlargements, and the development of common policies against unemployment and for the reduction of working time and the control of multinational companies. Months before François Mitterrand's victory of 1981, the PS had laid out a set of measures for Europe, all specifically socialist in tone and content. This was much more than the SFIO ever did.

From a socialist to a social Europe

During the presidential election campaign, François Mitterrand had dismissed the 'Paris–Bonn axis' (of which Valéry Giscard d'Estaing, the incumbent president, was a strong advocate) and emphasised the need for the EEC to adopt a more 'social' role to gain the support of Europeans. Once in office, Mitterrand wished to increase the expenditure of the EEC, but was unwilling to accept any cuts to the Common Agricultural Policy (CAP), given French agricultural interests, nor was he willing to increase France's own budgetary contribution.[6]

After Mitterrand's victory in 1981, the Socialist government embarked on an extensive programme of economic reform involving nationalisations, a *dirigiste* industrial policy, planning, industrial relations legislation that favoured the trade unions, redistributive social programmes, and Keynesian economic stimulation, including public sector job creation and a large increase in subsidies granted to public enterprises. The minimum wage was increased by 15 per cent in real terms to stimulate demand and, as a consequence, economic recovery. However, this experience ran quickly into trouble. As the French government was pursuing the expansion of the French economy, its international and European trading partners were simultaneously seeking to slow down their national economies in an attempt to avoid inflation. The result was a surge in France's budget, trade deficit and inflation, as well as severe downward pressure on the franc. Mitterrand was faced with the choice of either maintaining his domestic economic policy, which would inevitably force the franc out the European Monetary System, or adapting his policy in order to keep the franc within the EMS. He chose – alone – the latter, after consulting a small group of advocates of both scenarios (Favier and Martin-Roland 1990, 438–53). At no point did he consult the trade unions or the party. The parliament followed those internal debates as a spectator (Halimi 1993, 434). By running a lower rate of inflation than its EU trading partners, the Socialist government hoped that French commodities could be sold at a lower price. Membership of the EMS and 'competitive disinflation' was a significant U-turn, for it marked the end of the social democratic experiment of the Mauroy government (1981–3). This crucial decision was perceived as Mitterrand's choice for Europe rather than socialism (Lemaire-Prosche 1990, 185). *The Economist* noted that Mitterrand's decision had 'enabled his government to adopt a reasonable policy' (cited in Halimi 1993, 436–7). The compliments of *The Economist* certainly meant that the radical reformism of 1981–2 was now dead and buried. Later on, Henri Emmanuelli, a senior left-wing party official, acknowledged the importance of the choice made by Mitterrand in March 1983: 'We did our Bad Godesberg. We did it on 23 March 1983 at 11 a.m. The day we decided to open up our borders and to stay in the EMS, we chose a market economy' (cited in Halimi 1993, 437).

These measures reduced French inflation from 9.6 per cent in 1983 to 2.7 per cent in 1986, but at the price of several years of growth below 2 per cent and an increase in unemployment from 8.3 per cent to 10.4 per cent (Levy 2000, 324). This major policy shift ended the policy of nationalisation and a subsequent reversal of French assistance to ailing public enterprises. This U-turn represented a shift from 'socialism in one country' to membership of EMS, the *franc fort* and a new set of policies clearly influenced by monetarism (Ross 1998b; Hall 1986).

From a doctrinal point of view, the narrative on Europe evolved considerably. After 1983, the French Socialists' objective was no longer the construction of a 'socialist Europe' (as in Mitterrand's famous slogan), but of a 'social Europe'. A 'social Europe' was definitely different from the free trade zone advocated by the neo-liberals. However, it was also very different from the goal of converting Europe to socialism stated both by the SFIO and the PS. From 1984 onwards, the 'call for Europe' came to replace the 'call for socialism'. It is not clear whether that conversion meant that the Socialists thought that European integration was a prerequisite for the construction of socialism in France, or whether they had given up all hope of achieving socialism in France, let alone in Europe. What is certain is that 'Mitterrand's choice for Europe' was not debated internally (interview with Laurent Fabius, Paris, 26 January 2007). The contradiction between a socialist discourse in France and another one accepting the capitalist nature of the EU in Brussels did not raise any objections within the party (Lemaire-Prosche 1990, 186). The PS replaced its slogans against a 'Europe of merchants' with a vague and more centrist discourse about a 'fairer and more efficient Europe' (Lemaire-Prosche 1990, 186).

A paradigm shift (1983–2007)?

After abandoning their effort to establish 'socialism in one country' against the backdrop of an increasingly neo-liberal Europe, the Socialists turned again to European integration. Strongly influenced by the leadership of François Mitterrand, they returned to their traditional stance of uncritical support for the EU. This new 'honeymoon period' with Europe hardly lasted ten years. In the aftermath of the Maastricht Treaty, a growing feeling of disillusionment could be detected among Socialists, culminating in the rejection, by more than 40 per cent of the activists and almost 60 per cent of socialist voters, of the Constitutional Treaty in 2005.

Hope and disillusionment

From 1983 onwards, Mitterrand turned his attention to Europe. European integration even became his pet topic: *relance* of European integration at the Fontainebleau[7] summit in 1984 and the appointent of Jacques Delors – a devoted Europeanist (Ross 1995) – as president of the Commission.

The adoption of the SEA in 1986 and the Treaty of Maastricht in 1992 highlighted the radical *aggiornamento* of the French Socialists in the space of a few years. In 1988, Mitterrand ran a solo presidential campaign where the themes of a 'United France' (i.e. both beyond socialism and Jacques Chirac's neo-liberalism) and European integration featured prominently. Yet again, at the Arche conference in 1991, the PS declared its strong attachment to European integration, albeit in a vague manner: 'Europe constitutes the relevant space to better master the future.' The choice of federalism was reiterated: 'The political union with a federalist objective will strengthen the identity of the current Community.' However, the commitment to Europe remained undefined and confused. What institutions should the EU have? What should the role of the nation state be? Which countries should join the EU? And, above all, which social policy should the EU pursue? All those underlying questions were not even debated at the conference.

The debate on the Maastricht Treaty was a turning point. Although the 'no camp' was still clearly in a minority in the early 1990s,[8] disenchantment with

European integration was growing among the Socialists. Even the most devoted pro-Europeans in the PS would then acknowledge that the main problem with the EU was that it had become fundamentally neo-liberal in nature (Frank 2005, 468). François Mitterrand himself toned down his marked preference for federalism before the referendum on the Maastricht Treaty. Challenged by *souverainistes*, both on the left (the PCF and Jean-Pierre Chevènement) and the right (Philippe Séguin and Charles Pasqua) of the political spectrum, the French president adopted an almost intergovernmentalist rhetoric in order to reassure the public shortly before the vote, arguing, for example, in favour of an increased role for the European Council and the principle of subsidiarity.

After an active campaign for the 'yes' vote, Mitterrand narrowly won (51 per cent against 49 per cent). This marginal victory indicated, in part, a crisis of confidence in France towards European integration as a whole. In particular, the vote registered, for the first time since the aborted Pleven Plan for the EDC in 1951, high levels of dissatisfaction among socialist activists and voters. The EU reforms de facto put an end to the party's 'socialist agenda' in Europe. The policy of the *franc fort* was maintained throughout the 1980s and 1990s and led to deflationary growth: inflation was avoided through a tight monetary policy, and the franc was informally anchored to the Deutschmark (Lordon 2001, 110–37).

By the mid 1990s, the relative optimism of the early stages of integration had gone and had been replaced by pessimism, if not anxiety. The success of the public sector strikes against the policies of the government of the Right in 1995 and the rise of the *altermondialiste* movements (such as Attac) and media (such as *Le Monde Diplomatique*) that were critical of neo-liberalism had an impact on many socialist activists. *Altermondialistes*, who argued that 'another world is possible' (George 2004), were very critical of *Eurolibéralisme*, that is a European Union that has created a deregulated market economy instead of an 'organised mixed economy' (Sapir 2006; Salesse 2004). François Mitterrand acknowledged this change of mood in France in an address to the European Parliament in 1995:

> I confess that I would have liked a more socially-orientated Maastricht Treaty than the one that we eventually got . . . We have now delimited the contours of social Europe, but it still lacks any substance at all.
> (Office Universitaire de Recherche Socialiste, n.d.)

This was indeed a remarkable admission, just a few weeks before his retirement from politics. From the mid-1990s onwards, European integration ceased to be a totemic reference in the socialist landscape. For the French Socialists, it was no longer taboo to question, challenge or even oppose certain EU policy choices (Moscovici 2004, 78–83). *Gauche Socialiste* (GS), the main one of the party's left-wing factions, criticised the 'naivety' of the PS on EMU. The GS argued that the party had been wrong to believe that economic integration would automatically pave the way to a 'new space of common norms and laws', which was needed in order to construct a 'social Europe' (Mélenchon 2007, 78–9). Some socialists argued that the crisis of the European project and the national crisis, as well as the crisis of social democracy, were all closely linked to each other and, therefore, had to be treated as a single problem (Peillon 2004, 85). After Maastricht, the French Socialists went beyond the old debate about 'more' or 'less Europe' (a debate in which all socialists agreed that there should ever be 'more Europe', that is more integration). The terms of the debate among Socialists had shifted: what kind of Europe do Socialists want? Is European integration going in the right direction? Is it compatible with the Socialists' objective of a 'social Europe'?

No French third way on Europe

In 1996, party activists debated the European question. The PS drafted a theoretical text on 'Globalisation, Europe and France' that was adopted at the party's Paris conference (*Parti Socialiste* 1996). The document placed emphasis on the economic, social, cultural and environmental impact of globalisation. It rejected 'liberal Europe', which, the French Socialists argued, had been gaining momentum. The PS criticised deregulation in the single market and the lack of common social policies. Instead, they argued that 'Maastricht must be overcome': the economic foundations have been laid, and now the time has come to establish a 'political' and 'social' Europe (*Parti Socialiste* 1996, 22). They also argued that a 'European government, submitted to a democratic control, should monitor the European Central Bank.' This European government should stimulate growth and job creation (*Parti Socialiste* 1996, 25). Finally, they acknowledged that the 'gamble of Maastricht' had not paid off. The Socialists had hoped that economic integration would pave the way for political integration. The document concluded that this had not been the case (*Parti Socialiste* 1996, 26).

Following the dissolution of the National Assembly by Jacques Chirac in 1997, the Left unexpectedly won the election. Taking into account the diffuse, but rapidly growing, disenchantment of left-wing voters with European integration, Lionel Jospin, the PS leader, stood on a platform advocating a softening of the austere fiscal policies associated with EMU.[9] He promised the creation of 700,000 new jobs, the reduction of the working week to 35 hours, an end to the privatisation of public services, and a 'dynamic Europe', i.e. one turned towards growth, employment and democracy (Ross 1998a, 22). In line with traditional socialist rhetoric and thinking on European integration, Jospin claimed to use the EU to support his attempt to democratise, regulate and manage the French economy. At the time, there was no specific reference to Mitterrand's 1983 U-turn. Jospin formed a coalition government – the *Gauche plurielle*[10] – which 'cohabitated' with President Jacques Chirac for five years. Hardly a week in post, Jospin had to attend an Intergovernmental

Conference in Amsterdam and was faced with the harsh reality of European integration. He was unable to change the terms of the convergence criteria and of the Stability and Growth Pact (SGP) – a promise that he had expressly made to the French public during the campaign. However, he secured the last-minute inclusion of a new chapter on employment in the Amsterdam Treaty. Jospin also defended (a) the idea of a European economic government that would provide democratic (and political) counterbalance to the 'technocratic' European Central Bank, as well as (b) more substantial European efforts in the area of social policy to offset the effects of the fiscal constraints linked to the convergence criteria and the SGP. None of these objectives was achieved in terms of concrete policy outcomes (Howarth 2002, 160–71). In order to meet the convergence criteria required for the adoption of the single currency, Jospin had to implement net reductions in public expenditure[11] while, at the same time, trying to please his more leftist constituents.[12]

In 2000 and 2001, a number of scenarios for the future of Europe were floated by several senior Socialists. Jacques Delors advocated the idea of a 'European vanguard', which would take the form of a federation of nation states. It would be linked to a 'larger Union' through a European Commission, in charge of both the 'larger Union' and of the 'vanguard'. The Commission would be responsible for the smooth operation of the two entities (Bergounioux 2004, 10–11). Laurent Fabius – a former prime minister – feared that, with enlargement, Europe would become 'bigger and more heterogeneous than it is today', and therefore 'all member states would not be able to go forward altogether. This would risk slowing down the march forward of Europe as a whole' (Fabius 2001, 48). However, the concept of 'vanguard' was short on specifics. Very little was said about how it would be established and operate, let alone who would be part of it. At the party conference in Grenoble (24–6 November 2000), the majority supported François Hollande's views (*motion* A), which emphasised the idea of a 'vanguard of a federal nature', the improved co-ordination of economic policy and the revision of the remit of the ECB, which should officially promote economic growth and job creation as well as price stability. Hollande and his allies also referred to a 'new Keynesianism on the European scale' (Hollande 2000, 19).

The *Gauche Socialiste* defended the direct election of a Constituent Assembly. The member states that voted in favour of it would subsequently form the 'European federation', the 'core of the Union'. The European Parliament would be bicameral. The second chamber would represent the member states and would elect a European government that would be accountable to the second chamber. The latter would control the ECB and have the power to dismiss its members. The *Gauche Socialiste* also called for (a) a 'social treaty', (b) a European directive to protect public services and (c) tax harmonisation (*Gauche Socialiste* 2000, 126). Henri Emmanuelli, also on the party's left (*motion* C), focused his criticisms on the democratic deficit of EU institutions 'inspired by neo-liberalism' (Emmanuelli, Vidalies and Bataille 2000, 153).

The tone and the content of the three sets of proposals were openly hostile to the way in which European integration had proceeded since the Maastricht Treaty. Far from facilitating a step closer towards more 'social' and 'political' integration (the major socialist objective), a growing number of Socialists seemed increasingly unhappy about what they perceived as the EU's neo-liberal drift.

During his time in Matignon, Lionel Jospin referred to the concept of 'federation of nation states', a term coined by Jacques Delors. This seemed to be less federalist than Joschka Fischer's bold speech calling for a 'Federation for Europe' in May 2000 (Fischer 2000). Jospin tried to make the 'new' social democratic argument in a series of speeches (Jospin 2002). On the one hand, it was an attempt to provide a more left-wing version of Tony Blair's Third Way (Marlière 2003, 161–76). On the other, it enabled Jospin to re-assert the traditional socialist claim of the EU as a vehicle through which genuine social democratic objectives can be pursued at the European level and facilitated at the domestic level (Clift 2003). Jospin advocated the promotion and the expansion of the 'European social model' (Jospin 2002, 36) and called for a 'genuine body of social legislation, establishing ambitious common standards', a 'European social treaty' to be agreed upon by EU member states (Jospin 2002, 17–18).

Tensions between the PS and other social democratic parties increased in spring 2001. The *Gauche Socialiste* went as far as to castigate the neo-liberal drift of New Labour, labelling it the 'inheritor of Thatcherism'. The PES was also accused of 'submission to the neo-liberal ideology' (Désir, Lienemann and Marlière 2001, 19). In March 2002, just a few months before the presidential election, Lionel Jospin committed France to raising the retirement age by five years and to the liberalisation of gas and electricity services at the meeting of the European Council in Barcelona. The decision went down badly with the French Left in general, as the Jospin government had not consulted with the ruling coalition's partners on the left of the PS or with the trade unions. Some saw it as another piece of evidence of (a) the anti-democratic and neo-liberal nature of the EU and (b) the acceptance by the Socialists of this state of affairs (Cassen 2002, 4). Nevertheless, it can be noted that such decisions had been reached in the final days of a tense *cohabitation* with the right-wing president Jacques Chirac. In the end, the Jospin government did not manage to find a French Third Way – i.e. a project for a 'social' and 'political' Europe that would differ from neo-liberalism and Tony Blair's market-orientated and Atlanticist Europe. By the end of Jospin's five-year term, the European policies of the Socialist government seemed on the whole in line with those of non-socialist governments in Europe.

The politicisation of European integration

The first round of the presidential election of 2002 was a disaster for the Socialists and for the Left in general, as Jospin was beaten by Jean-Marie Le Pen, the extreme right-wing candidate. For the first time since 1969, the Left was absent from the second and decisive round. As part of an introspective debate in the party about the '2002 debacle', most Socialists identified European integration as a major obstacle rather than the means to resolve France's socio-economic problems. From 2004 onwards, long and heated debates on the European Constitutional Treaty were to split the party.

During the operation of the European Convention, Arnaud Montebourg and Christian Paul – both in the left-wing faction *Nouveau Parti Socialiste*, asked, in the name of the 'socialist struggle for Europe', that any future enlargement be preceded by a referendum, because a Europe with twenty-seven member states would mean the 'end of resistances to neo-liberal globalisation and the triumph of Europe as a free market zone' (Montebourg and Paul 2002). Later on, the leaders of the *Nouveau Parti Socialiste* (NPS) were even harsher in their appraisal of the EU, depicting it as 'the Trojan horse of [economic] de-regulation' (Dray, Montebourg and Peillon 2002). In September 2002, *Nouveau Monde*, another left-wing faction within the PS, was launched. It declared its opposition to the essentially 'neo-liberal course' of European integration and to further enlargement that would enhance the neo-liberal nature of the EU. The party conference held in Dijon (16–18 May 2003) reflected the general mood of defiance and disillusionment vis-à-vis European integration. The majority's draft resolution (under François Hollande) argued that a 're-orientation' of European integration, both institutional and political, was a 'historic necessity'; otherwise, Europe would appear a 'feeble, constraining and technocratic' project.

It was therefore not surprising that the European Constitutional Treaty triggered passionate and politicised debates within the party in the autumn of 2004. François Hollande, the party leader, unexpectedly decided to hold an internal referendum to decide on the PS's stance on the Constitutional Treaty.[13] Supporters of the Constitutional Treaty acknowledged that it was a mistake to have a referendum in a party for which the 'European question' is an 'identity issue' (Moscovici 2007, 33). Some even thought that a referendum ran counter to the tradition of the PS, a party founded on compromises between organised factions. In a referendum, there is no such compromise: there can only be 'winners and losers' (interview with Pierre Moscovici, Paris, 25 January 2007). It was also a gamble, given that, in the PS, 'there had always been factions that were critical, if not frankly hostile to European construction' (Moscovici 2007, 34). In the end, the internal campaign was similar to an 'internal war' and left the party profoundly divided (Moscovici 2007, 35). However, it was also a true moment of party democracy, totally unique in Europe, which distinguished the PS from any other party of the PES. Over a four-month period, the PS debated the issue. Numerous rallies were organised across France, where activists discussed and analysed the most controversial articles of the Constitutional Treaty, which many had actually read. Party members voted in December 2004. The 'yes' camp, led by François Hollande, as well as the leaders of the biggest party federations (Nord, Pas-de-Calais, Paris, Bouches-du-Rhône), secured a relatively comfortable victory (58 per cent versus 42 per cent). However, the simple fact that an internal vote had been organised, and that an important minority of Socialists had rejected the Constitutional Treaty altogether, indicated the strength of the opposition to what many Socialists describe as 'neo-liberal Europe'. Proponents of the 'no' vote argued that the Socialists who had supported the Constitutional Treaty had missed the point: instead of campaigning for the treaty itself, they had defended the pursuit of European integration, a point to which the 'no' camp had not objected (Généreux 2005). In the PS, European integration had finally been *politicised*, in the sense that the Socialists no longer limited themselves to the examination of the pace of integration, but also pondered on the direction of this process, i.e. its nature. Europe had therefore become a debatable issue within the PS. All sections of the party could now express opinions about it according to ideological and policy preferences.

The *nonistes* in the PS felt vindicated after the national referendum of May 2005: 55 per cent of the French voters rejected the Constitutional Treaty, 59 per cent of whom were socialist voters. After the vote, a dispirited, but lucid, François Hollande acknowledged that

> the French vote is not about the rejection of Europe. 72% of voters have declared themselves in favour of the pursuit of European integration. The French 'no' is not predominantly a defiance vote vis-à-vis Europe, but largely a 'no' of social demand. For Europe has not kept its promises on the economic and social grounds. With the Single Market and the Euro, Europe was supposed to boost growth, create new jobs and fight unemployment. In truth, the EU has 20 million unemployed people. Here is, in my view, the profound meaning of the result of 29 May.
>
> (Hollande 2005, 4)

It is interesting to note that, throughout the six-month campaign, both camps kept referring positively to an elusive 'federalist' and 'social' Europe and called for the enhancement of the EU's supranational institutions. Critics who accused the supporters of the 'socialist no' of 'Euroscepticism', or even 'Europhobia', seem to have missed the point. It would be more accurate to describe 'Euroscepticism' in the PS as 'soft', policy-focused (rather than based on the national interest), as well as ideological (socialist) in nature. Socialists debated classic socialist topics (e.g. the regulation of markets in France and Europe, control of social and fiscal dumping, harmonisation of social rights, political control of the ECB) (Wagner 2008, 258). An in-depth study of the 2004 internal referendum on the Constitutional Treaty shows that

> there is no evidence of openly hard Euroscepticism in the PS: exit from the EU is not addressed at all, let alone endorsed. Moreover, around 66% of anti-ratification documents maintain that integration is necessary, with almost none arguing that it could be an optional process.
>
> (Wagner 2008, 266)

The Le Mans party conference of November 2005 aimed at restoring unity between *ouistes* and *nonistes*. Almost all factions rallied around a compromise motion (Marlière 2007, 21–2). In a conciliatory gesture, Benoît Hamon, a leader of the *noniste* NPS faction, was appointed party secretary responsible for European affairs. In the run-up to the 2007 presidential election, the Socialists declared that they

> will reject any European Constitutional Treaty similar to that which has been rejected on 29 May [2005]. We propose the drafting of a strictly institutional treaty . . . Once it has been renegotiated, such a treaty will be submitted to the people in a referendum.
>
> (*Parti Socialiste* 2006, 87)

Ségolène Royal, the party's presidential candidate, endorsed this proposal and included it in her *Pacte Présidentiel* (Royal 2007b). The signing of the Reform Treaty by the newly elected right-wing president, Nicolas Sarkozy, in Lisbon on 19 October 2007 tested the new unity of the PS on Europe to breaking point. The French president was one of the architects of the new treaty. He was also a fervent supporter of ratification of the new text by national parliaments rather than by referenda. Speaking to senior MEPs in Brussels, Sarkozy acknowledged that governments could not win popular votes on the new treaty. The French president argued that, 'France was just ahead of all the other countries in voting no. It would happen in all member states if they had a referendum. There is a cleavage between people and governments' (Waterfield 2007).

Such a candid admission, leaked to the Eurosceptic press in Britain, could only exacerbate the feeling of *malaise* within the PS. Earlier, the supporters of the new treaty in the PS had reneged on the party's promise to fight for a new referendum on the grounds that, during the presidential campaign, Nicolas Sarkozy had explicitly committed himself to ratification by parliament. Therefore, the *ouistes* thought that there was no point in opposing Sarkozy on the referendum issue, as he had just won the presidential election and was still a popular president. Opponents of ratification by referendum argued that, if they fought for a referendum, the PS would effectively offer the 'gift of division' to Nicolas Sarkozy (Peillon *et al.* 2007).

The *nonistes* considered that the changes to the Constitutional Treaty were only cosmetic. Notably, they argued that the Reform Treaty maintains the neo-liberal agenda of the previous text.[14] The *nonistes* received the indirect and involuntary backing of Valéry Giscard d'Estaing, the former president of the European Convention, who argued in public that, while the new treaty had re-ordered the 'toolkit', the tools had remained the same (Giscard d'Estaing 2007).

Following Sarkozy's crushing victory in May 2007, François Hollande gambled on the socialist apathy vis-à-vis the new treaty. On 6 November 2007, Hollande asked the *Bureau National* (the party's executive) to decide on the Reform Treaty. Though a clear majority (60 per cent) supported the new treaty,[15] this decision re-opened old wounds in the party. A few former *nonistes* supported the new treaty, and about as many former *ouistes* voted against it.[16] After the vote, François Hollande argued that the Socialists 'are turning the page. We are reaching the end of a long process on the European question in the PS. This issue is now behind us' (Soudais 2007).

In reality, this internal vote showed that the two camps, two years on, were still holding the same positions. Indeed, the arguments on both sides had not moved at all: the 'yes camp' acknowledged that, although the treaty was 'mediocre' (Guigou 2007) and 'fuzzy' (Bergounioux, Destot and Tasca 2007), it contained positive institutional changes (a stable president of the European Council; a significant enhancement of the role of the European Parliament; a more important role granted to national parliaments; the choice of the president of the Commission to take into account the political majority of the European Parliament; a stronger EU high representative for common foreign and security policy; a reference to a Charter of Fundamental Rights, even though Britain, Poland and, later on, the Czech Republic opted out). All these institutional improvements were deemed 'decisive' and were presented as improvements when compared with the Treaty of Nice. They argued that the Lisbon Treaty was needed to put Europe back on track and relaunch European integration (Moscovici and Poignant 2007). Furthermore, the supporters of the new treaty emphasised the need for the PS to stay in line with the rest of European social democracy, which by and large supports the new text. For the 'no camp', the new treaty was 'simplified' only in name. They considered that (a) the argument of 'institutional blockage' was largely exaggerated and hypocritical, and (b) the rules of majority voting decided at Nice in the Council of Ministers would remain in place until 2014 (or even until 2017, if a member state requested it), with or without the new treaty.

Having rejected the option of a new referendum, Nicolas Sarkozy used the parliamentary route, i.e. an ad hoc chamber, gathering parliamentarians from both the National Assembly and the Senate, who met at the Palace of Versailles on 4 February 2008. Parliamentarians first had to revise the French Constitution to adapt it to some provisions of the new treaty. This was a legal and decisive prerequisite for the ratification of the Treaty of Lisbon. Apart from a very small minority of Gaullist-minded rebels, Sarkozy could rely on the support of the vast majority of right-wing deputies and senators. In theory, this was not an easy vote to win, as a majority of 60 per cent of the votes cast was required for the amendment to the French Constitution. Out of a total of 907 parliamentarians, 893 turned out to vote, and 741 votes were cast (for or against the revision). The required majority of three-fifths was therefore 445; 560 voted in favour of the amendment to the French Constitution, and 181 against. The vote was comfortably won, thanks to the support or the abstention of Socialist parliamentarians. The official position of the PS was Byzantine, if not outright 'farcical' (Marlière 2008). The party leadership asked all Socialists to abstain on the grounds that the PS was in favour of a new referendum (Gil 2008). Left-wing critics within the PS argued that this was counter-productive and 'hypocritical' (Emmanuelli 2008). Crucially, by abstaining – or even, in some cases, voting with the Right – the PS helped Sarkozy amend the Constitution and avoid organising a new referendum. Although influential critics of the Constitutional Treaty (such as Laurent Fabius and Henri Emmanuelli) chose not to clash with the Hollande leadership again, other prominent left-wingers were angered by what they described as the party's 'unprincipled' stance (Jean-Luc Mélenchon, Marc Dolez, Gérard Filoche). Mélenchon denounced a 'shameful' vote and bitterly remarked that, if all Socialist parliamentarians had voted against instead of either abstaining or voting for the amendment (which is what 150 and 40 of them, respectively, did), the required majority would not have been formed. Abstention, he argued, had facilitated the amendment, because it had lowered the required threshold. If the PS had voted unanimously against the amendment, Nicolas Sarkozy would have been twelve votes short of the required majority (Mélenchon 2008a). On 6 and 7 February 2008, deputies and senators formally ratified the Treaty of Lisbon in their respective chambers. Here, a simple majority was required. The results were never in doubt, given the UMP (*Union pour un Mouvement Populaire*'s) absolute majority in both the National Assembly and the Senate.

The feud over Europe was briefly reignited in the spring of 2008, while the PS was busy drafting a new 'Declaration of Principles' (i.e. a kind of constitution that sets out the party's main values and objectives). It is worth noting that the reference to Europe did not even feature in the previous declarations of 1905, 1946 and 1969 (Ferenczi 2008, 2). It was only included in the last draft of the 1990 declaration despite the strong opposition of *Socialisme & République*, a left-wing faction led by Jean-Pierre Chevènement (Hohl 2008, 7). The text adopted in 1990 cautiously stated that the PS 'is committed to Europe in order to give nations that are part of it, the means to cope with the major challenges of the future' (Maret and Houlou 1990, 178). The new declaration adopted in June 2008 more boldly asserts that the PS 'is a European party. It acts in the European Union, which it has not only supported for a long time, but to whose founding it has also contributed' (*Parti Socialiste* 2008, 20). In this new declaration, the Socialists' commitment to Europe appears – on one reading – absolute and unconditional, whatever the policies or the political orientation of the EU. On the party's left, only Jean-Luc Mélenchon and Marc Dolez – two prominent advocates of the 'no' vote in 2005 – robustly criticised the inclusion of these statements in the new text prior to resigning from the PS in November 2008. Shortly after, they created the *Parti de Gauche* (PG – Left Party), a structure that is reminiscent of *Die Linke*, its German counterpart. A small splinter group of socialist activists joined the new party. On 29 November 2008, the PG was officially launched at a rally on the outskirts of Paris. Mélenchon – the leader of the PG – declared that the forthcoming European elections would be a 'political referendum on the Treaty of Lisbon', as many right-wing MPs, but also Socialist and Green MPs, had 'prevented French voters from directly voting on the Reform

Treaty'. According to Mélenchon, the European election would help answer a double question: do the 'French support a neo-liberal Europe', or do they 'demand instead a social, democratic and peaceful Europe, one that is not subjected to NATO?'. He also proposed the establishment of a *Front de gauche* (front of the Left), i.e. a loose confederation of leftist parties, including the *Nouveau Parti Anticapitaliste*, the PCF, the PG, Left Republicans, environmentalists and *altermondidalistes*. His ambition was to create a political alternative to the 'consensual management of economic and European affairs by the UMP and PS' (Mélenchon 2008a).

Within the PS, members elected the party leader following the Reims conference (16–18 November 2008). Martine Aubry narrowly defeated Ségolène Royal, after an acrimonious campaign. Accusations of electoral fraud came from the Royal camp. Elected thanks to the support of the party's left wing (whose prominent figures include Benoît Hamon, Henri Emmanuelli and Gérard Filoche), Aubry appointed a significant number of left-wing officials to the party executive. For the first time since 2005, partisans and opponents to the Constitutional Treaty jointly ran the party. In the run-up to the European elections of 2009, the party was united against the re-appointment of José Manuel Barroso as president of the European Commission because of his neo-liberal and Atlanticist views. At the meeting of the PES in Madrid (1 December 2008), Martine Aubry also argued that the PES should politicise the vote by presenting a candidate from its own ranks against the incumbent president of the Commission (*Parti Socialiste* 2009). This proposal was rejected by the British Labour Party, the Spanish PSOE and the Portuguese Socialists, who all publicly supported Barroso's re-election (see this volume's conclusion).

Conscious that the commitment of the PES to a 'social and democratic' Europe may not be radical enough, the PS drafted a 'French Manifesto' for its electorate, entitled *To Give Europe a New Direction*. In the context of the financial crisis, the document launched a fierce attack against 'neo-liberal ideology and laissez-faire policies which have dramatically failed' and targeted notably Nicolas Sarkozy in France and José Manuel Barroso in the EU, but did not mention the fact that the PES had to a large extent co-managed EU institutions (including the European Commission) with the EPP between 2004 and 2009 (Soudais 2009). The French manifesto advocated a 'European Pact for Social Progress', involving an increase in the EU budget, the harmonisation of business taxation (in order to combat fiscal and social dumping and stop outsourcing), greater co-ordination of economic policies and 'fairer trade with developing economies' (*Parti Socialiste* 2009).

The campaign of the PS ahead of the 2009 European elections was sluggish and unconvincing. On 7 June 2009, the party suffered big losses and obtained 16.48 per cent and fourteen seats (compared with 28.9 per cent and thirty-one seats in 2004). The UMP took 27.8 per cent of the votes and twenty-nine seats. The PS was narrowly ahead of *Europe Ecologie*, led by Daniel Cohn Bendit (16.28 per cent and fourteen seats). The *noniste* Left fared rather well:

Mélenchon's PG obtained 6 per cent of the votes and four seats, while Olivier Besancenot's NPA obtained 4.9 per cent, but no seats. These results seem to corroborate previous evidence that the absence of a consistent strategy with regard to European integration, and the public's perception that the PS is co-managing 'neo-liberal Europe' alongside its PES partners are increasingly vote-losers for the PS. Many working-class voters either abstained or voted for the Greens or radical left-wing parties (Marlière 2009, 17).

After the national referendum of 29 May 2005 and even more emphatically after the ratification by parliament of the Treaty of Lisbon in February 2008, it was clear that the Socialists' belief in Europe as a promoter of social justice and economic growth had been seriously questioned, if not undermined. In fact, after the signing of the Maastricht Treaty, an irresistible sentiment of disillusionment vis-à-vis European integration had started to grow among party activists. This is not to say that, since 1992, the Socialists had lost faith in their main objectives in Europe (the construction of a social and political Europe as a means to protect the French welfare state). It means that, for the first time since the 1970s, European integration – its method, its institutions and the policies that exemplify it – could be legitimately criticised or examined. For that reason, it can be argued that, since the mid-1990s, there has been a progressive change of paradigm vis-à-vis European integration.

Norms and interests: accounting for the paradigm shift

What accounts for the policy shifts of the PS with regard to European integration? The party has moved from being unequivocally supportive of the 'European project' between the late 1940s and the late 1950s, to being mildly critical of certain aspects of the EEC between the late 1950s and early 1970s, and very critical of it between the early 1970s and the mid-1980s. It then switched to vigorous support for the EU from the mid-1980s to the mid-1990s and, since then, it has been increasingly disillusioned by the EU as a whole. Several interpretations have been given of the social democrats' so-called 'turn to Europe'. However, the terms of the debate are problematic: they essentially concentrate on the turn to Europe by social democratic parties in northern Europe from the 1970s onwards. The more complex and erratic evolution of the preferences of the PS requires a different approach. Is the party's stance on Europe – as it has evolved since the 1970s – a simple adjustment of the doctrine or, conversely, a paradigm shift? The roles played by norms, ideas and beliefs deserve particular attention.

The PS and the 'turn to Europe' debate

By 'turn to Europe', one describes the progressive evolution of most social democratic parties from a certain 'weariness' with, if not outright hostility to, European integration to a strong pro-EU stance. From the end of the 1980s onwards, the notion that national economies can be more effectively regulated at the European level (Cafruny 1997, 109–28; Hirst and Thompson 1999,

191–225) had become a mainstream argument within the PES. In the case of the PS, it can explain and justify the 'choice for Europe' that François Mitterrand imposed in 1983. However, since the Maastricht Treaty in the early 1990s and more decisively after the referendum on the Constitutional Treaty in 2005, this argument lost much of its credibility. This point was acknowledged by Ségolène Royal, the Socialist candidate in the 2007 presidential election.[17] One common objection to the Constitutional Treaty by left-wing activists and voters was that the text was inspired by neo-liberal ideas and policies and, as a consequence, would facilitate the dismantling of the French welfare state.

The interpretation of the 'turn to Europe' as pragmatic adaptation to the environment is unconvincing. The institutions and policies of the EU have created a 'pressure to overcome internal factors until now precluding support for EC integration' (Ladrech 1993, 208). The notion that the increasing permanence of the EU makes political strategies that attempt to overturn or reverse integration less viable, thereby making engagement with the EU more attractive to social democratic parties (Ladrech 2000), does not suit the French situation, as it tends to present a rather apolitical explanation of the social democratic parties' engagement with the EU. The French case shows conversely that the 'turn to Europe' in 1983 and the subsequent relative detachment from European integration have taken place in the context of *politicised* debates.

Third, ideological moderation suggests that traditional social democratic values, which formed the basis of social democratic policies, are now in decline. Thus, the new engagement with the EU is seen as further evidence that social democratic parties have rejected many of their traditional values. 'New social democracy' (best epitomised by the Blairite Third Way) underwent major ideological and organisational transformation during the 1980s and 1990s. The social democrats' attitude towards the EU is a major aspect of this ideological and political shift from the left to the centre of the political spectrum (Kitschelt 1994; Moschonas 2002; Glyn 2001). This thesis presupposes that a 'Blairite' social democracy is firmly in command across Europe and that it is here to stay in the long run. This does not apply to the French case, where 'economic Blairism' (i.e. the acceptance of neo-liberal globalisation in general) has been challenged and rejected – at least rhetorically – by a large majority of French Socialists (Marlière 2003, 161–76).

Finally, the obfuscation thesis (Bailey 2004) could suit the French case rather well. However, it also suggests that socialist governments and party leaders are cynics who have voluntarily committed their party and France to European integration in order to play down the neo-liberal nature of their policies at home. Furthermore, this looks like a deliberate ploy to lie to people or conceal the truth. There is no clear evidence that such a ploy exists at the level of social democracy at large and in the PS in particular. Therefore, none of the aforementioned interpretations accounts fully for the very perception of integration by the Socialists and the transformations of the Socialist doctrine and narrative about Europe.

Norms and paradigm change

Why have the French Socialists become increasingly critical of, if not hostile to, European integration since the early 1990s? Why did they progressively depart from their traditional supranationalist and uncritical stance with regard to the EU institutions? An explanation for such ideational change reads as follows: 'norms influence [the process of change] when the reforms that embody them are perceived to be broadly congruent with the interests of the powerful decision takers and when they resolve real political problems' (Dimitrakopoulos 2005, 676).

In the case of the PS, the largely uncritical support of the PS for European integration started to falter when the PS realised that the French public no longer believed that a Europe dominated by neo-liberal ideas and policies offered the right framework to protect the French welfare state. The two referenda of 1992 and 2005 marked, in this respect, watershed moments. Since Maastricht, the PS has publicly accepted that the EU as a whole had to achieve more in the domain of redistribution and social protection in order to curb the present wave of Euroscepticism in France and other member states. The new socialist discourse more readily acknowledges the 'social deficit' at the heart of European integration.

In that sense, one can argue that the party's new normative stance on Europe has conferred legitimacy on some policy changes. This being said, it remains to be seen whether the new Socialist approach can help achieve the elusive 'social Europe'. In the run-up to the financial and economic crisis that commenced in 2008, the PS seemed to be politically isolated within the PES.[18]

Paradigm shifts entail dramatic changes (Hall 1993, 284). For instance, when monetarism replaced Keynesianism as the template guiding policy in Britain since 1979, a radical policy shift took place. Furthermore, these changes were accompanied by changes in the discourse employed by policy- and opinion-makers. In the French case, this stage has not yet been reached. Facts and events have – arguably – proved the PS mostly wrong on European integration. Consequently, the normative appraisal of the EU has changed from uncritical to relatively critical. Evidence of 'policy paradigm' change exists. The 1996 document on 'Europe, globalisation and France' contained quite robust attacks on 'neo-liberal Europe' and also reservations about an enlarged EU with no proper political foundations. Nevertheless, the party's stance remains resolutely pro-European, that is in favour of the pursuit of integration. This said, the support for the EU is increasingly conditional. It largely depends on the need at least to abandon some of the EU's neo-liberal features. Following the 'no' vote in May 2005, this more critical stance has had political effects: the decision by the party's majority to endorse the Treaty of Lisbon has yet again provoked reactions of unease or even outright hostility within the party.

Conclusion

The French Socialists have perceived European integration as a means to transform society and to construct socialism. However, if the majority of European governments are hostile to socialist ideas and policies, Europe becomes an obstacle to the very construction of socialism in France – hence the ambivalence of the PS with regard to European integration. On the one hand, integration has appealed to Socialists because it has represented a concrete development of their professed internationalism. On the other, integration has challenged the long-term objectives of French socialism, i.e. the radical transformation of French and European capitalisms.

Since the end of the Second World War, the party's Europeanism has been, on the whole, of a supranational and federalist nature. This pro-integration stance has been accompanied by a rather radical and ambitious vision for Europe. From Blum to Mitterrand, it was argued that the European frame-work was no obstacle to the implementation of socialist policies at home. Furthermore, the French Socialists have claimed that Europe as a whole could be converted to socialism.

Political competition from the Left (PCF) and the Right (Gaullism) forced the SFIO to adapt its discourse and stance on Europe. Faced with the communist challenge in the early days of the Cold War era, the SFIO chose the Atlanticist and capitalist camp against the 'Soviet threat'. This accentuated the Socialist commitment to a federalist Europe and the acceptance of the Treaty of Rome. Later on, having to respond to the Gaullist challenge, the SFIO once more readjusted its position on European integration: it adopted a more independent and critical stance vis-à-vis the United States as a way to compete with De Gaulle's policy of *grandeur* and national independence. This led to a *rapprochement* with its communist rival and the adoption of a more critical position with regard to the EEC.

After a very long period in opposition, the PS had, yet again, to revise its approach to European integration. Once in power, the Socialists had to deal with the consequences of their redistributive reforms and Keynesian economic stimulation, which proved too inflationary. Mitterrand was faced with the choice of either maintaining his domestic economic policy, which would have forced the franc out of the EMS, or espousing monetarism in line with the policies pursued by France's European partners. Mitterrand 'chose Europe' and bid farewell to the old Socialist objective of a 'socialist Europe'. It can be argued that, throughout the 1980s, an idiosyncratic 'Euro-pean ideology' progressively replaced the traditional 'Socialist ideology'. This meant resolute – and some would allege – blind faith in the so-called 'positive' and 'inevitable' effects of European integration. The new 'European ideology' was very influential in large segments of the PS and was couched in the deep belief that the EU possessed extraordinary virtues and offered infinite possibilities. For Socialist pro-Europeans, every social, economic or cultural issue had to have European solutions; all things European were deemed 'good'. For that reason, Socialists refrained from criticising the institutions or the policies of the EU. Consequently, little attention was paid to the content of European policies (Landais, Monville, Yaghlekdjian 2008, 11). What is more, some Socialists assumed that all the countries that had joined the Union shared the same fervour for the 'European project' (Jennar 2007, 23).

The goal of a 'social Europe' has also proved elusive: the treaties of Maastricht and Amsterdam, which only contain very mild market-correcting policies, have disappointed the French Socialists. Disenchantment among a growing number of Socialists replaced the blind faith in the 'European project' of the 1950s, 1960s and 1970s. Unhappy about the neo-liberal drift of the EU, the Socialists politicised the European question. The debate on the Constitutional Treaty shed light on the existing tensions and contradictions within the party. An important minority rejected the text on the grounds that it 'constitutionalised' neo-liberalism. It argued that such a treaty would have further restricted the room for manoeuvre of any future Socialist government. The internal vote and the national referendum that followed undermined the Socialists' belief that traditional social democratic policies (including the regulation of neo-liberal globalisation) can be successfully pursued at the European level.

This case study shows that ideas play a role in shaping new political behaviours and policies when political parties feel that such policy changes are a political and electoral necessity. As for the PS, it became increasingly clear from the mid-1990s that the post-Maastricht order would not live up to its expectations. The PS has subsequently radicalised its critique of European integration. This critical stance has even hardened after the rejection of the Constitutional Treaty by French voters. Since then, the discourse on Europe has tended to be more critical, and the support for further enlargement has been more conditional.

The French Socialists have now come to terms with the fact that there is no obvious correlation between the pursuit of European integration and the achievement of their socialist ideals. Their faltering Europeanism does not mean that they have become staunch nationalists or Eurosceptics. Rather, it means that, for them, European integration has become politicised. They regard it as an area of political struggle where the Left and the Right compete in an effort to impose their views and policies.

Appendix: list of interviewees

Harlem Désir, Socialist MEP, Paris, 26 January 2007.
Laurent Fabius, Socialist member of the *Assemblée Nationale*, former prime minister, Paris, 26 January 2007.
Pierre Moscovici, Socialist member of the *Assemblée Nationale*, former minister of European affairs, Paris, 25 January 2007.

Notes

1 All translations are the author's own.

2 The day will come when there will be no other battlefields than markets opening up to trade and minds to ideas. A day will come when bullets and bombs will be replaced by the ballot, the universal suffrage of the people, by the venerable *arbitrage* of a great sovereign Senate that will be for Europe, what the Parliament is to England, what the Diet is to Germany, or what the legislative Assembly is to France.

(Hugo n.d. [1849])

3 Léon Blum was not alone in his defence of 'European federalism'. André Philip, a party official on the right wing of the SFIO, emerged at the time as the dominant influence on the issue.

4 When the Schuman Plan was announced, the Cold War was at its peak. The communist propaganda reached a new peak. For instance, François Billoux, one of the three ministers expelled from the government in 1947, claimed:

Thus, Robert Schuman, former minister of Pétain, is achieving the Pétain-Hitler plan for the de-industrialisation of France. It would lead our country to become the outlet for German war industry while French workers were reduced to unemployment or starvation salaries, and French peasants could sell their agricultural products only at a loss, or export at knock-down prices.

(cited in Newman 1983, 43)

5 This was particularly true in the late 1960s, i.e. the last years of the Vietnam war, which was deeply unpopular with the Left in France and across Europe.

6 Enlargement to Spain and Portugal could make France a net contributor and threaten its agriculture.

7 Mitterrand was also instrumental in resolving the problem of the British contribution to the budget in Fontainebleau.

8 When the *Mouvement des Citoyens* (MDC – a republican and Eurosceptic party led by Jean-Pierre Chevènement, a former senior Socialist minister) faction quit the party in 1993, the Socialist parliamentary party lost only three deputies.

9 The dissolution of the National Assembly was a direct consequence of public opposition to the reforms carried out by the Juppé government between 1995 and 1997. Those austerity measures were aimed at meeting the criteria set by the SGP and ensuring France's participation in the final stage of EMU. This resulted in five weeks of social unrest and strikes among public workers across France in November and December 1995 (Leneveu and Vakaloulis 1998).

10 The *Gauche plurielle* consisted of members of the Socialist, Communist, Green and Radical parties, as well as the small MDC.

11 These measures entailed cuts in defence expenditure, the introduction of means-testing of family allowances and, most notably, a record number of privatisations (Fondation Copernic 2001).

12 These measures included the 35-hour working week, combined with state subsidies, the *Couverture Maladie Universelle* (aiming to make health care available to low-income groups) and the *Programme Emploi Jeunes*, i.e. a system of state subsidies aiming to ensure that young unemployed people gain work experience in public and not-for-profit organisations.

13 Hollande was accused by many in the PS of using the vote as a device to rally the party behind him and isolate Lionel Jospin and Laurent Fabius, his two major rivals in the race for the party nomination ahead of the next presidential election.

14 They point out that the fight against inflation remains the main target for the European Central Bank, a choice that is 'detrimental to production, growth and

better salaries'. They also argue that it is impossible to raise and harmonise social regulation and systems of social protection and that, although the principle of 'unfettered market competition' has been removed from part II of the treaty, it appears in an appendix.

15 Thirty-six members supported it, twenty voted against, two abstained, and one member did not take part in the ballot.

16 It is worth noting that Serge Janquin, the leader of the party's second most important regional federation (Pas-de-Calais) switched to the 'no camp'. In May 2005, more than 60 per cent of the electorate of this region had rejected the Constitutional Treaty.

17 'My objective is to reconcile the French people who have voted yes and no in the referendum on the European Constitutional Treaty. I know that all of them would like a more pro-active and a more protective Europe against the negative effects of globalisation' (Royal 2007a).

18 According to Pierre Moscovici, a Socialist former minister of European affairs, only the Greek PASOK and the Belgian PS fully share the French reservations vis-à-vis the EU's 'neo-liberal drift' (interview, Paris, 25 January 2007).

4 The Labour Party and European integration

An awkward relationship

Hussein Kassim

Introduction[1]

The Labour Party has had a famously difficult relationship with Europe, or at least with the Europe of the Europeans.[2] Singling out Labour's discomfiture for special attention, Donald Sassoon (1996, 339) observes in his magisterial history of the West European Left that: 'No party of the Left has exhibited such profound uncertainty on the question of Europe' (see also Featherstone 1988, 41). This judgement is only partly fair. Labour opposed the supranational model of integration that emerged from 1950, but it played an important part in the development of Europe's post-war architecture – a contribution that is often forgotten. As with its counterparts on the Continent, European integration proved, however, to be an intensely problematic issue for the party. The issue of membership was deeply divisive across the labour movement and at all levels (Broad 2001; Featherstone 1988; Newman 1983; Robins 1979; Young 1998). Like its sister parties, Labour eventually abandoned its hostility, though not all its reservations, but, in contrast to them, it never had its Bad Godesberg moment (see Egle, this volume). Its European journey has been complex, tortuous and often contradictory, and, even as Labour has become Britain's main pro-European party, it remains circumspect about integration.

The purpose of this chapter is to examine Labour's preferences on Europe and how they were shaped. In taking such an approach, the analysis presented below departs from the two main tendencies in the existing literature. In the first, scholars survey Labour's attitudes to Europe over the post-war period and attempt to account for its vicissitudes over six decades in terms of a single factor. Thus, Labour's 'reluctance' – the usual focus of inquiries of this kind – has been explained variously in terms of the changing nature of the international system (Mullen 2007), developments in the European Union (Delaney 2002), British exceptionalism (Gamble 2003), nationalism (Nairn 1972), and party management against the background of a struggle between traditionalists and revisionists (Robins 1979). The second focuses principally on the 1980s, the period of transition to a pro-membership position. Scholars taking this approach inevitably (and correctly) highlight the role played by Neil Kinnock (leader 1983–92) (Holden 2002), but contend that parties of the Left came to support European integration, because it offered possibilities for achieving either objectives, such as market regulation, at the EU level that were no longer attainable at the national level (the 'instrumental thesis'; see introduction), compensation for 'failure and retrenchment at home', even in the absence of social democratic outputs at EU level (the 'obfuscation thesis'; see Bailey 2005), or participation rights in structuring a regulatory environment that shapes their destiny and from which it would be costly to be excluded (the 'dependence thesis'; see Haahr 1993). Both literatures have important limitations. While the first attempts to explain Labour preferences over a sixty-year period in terms of a single variable, the second approach is focused on a relatively short time period and dramatically oversimplifies the pressures at work in the 1980s.

Against this background, approaching Labour and Europe through the concepts of preference and preference formation offers a number of analytical advantages. First, while attentive to the complex trajectory of Labour's position on Europe, it enables the more enduring dispositions that lie behind changes in policy and strategy to be explored. Second, the preferences and preference formation approach problematises the origins of the party's disposition towards Europe. It corrects an important imbalance in the literature, which – to paraphrase Wildavsky (1987, 3), cited by Dimitrakopoulos (see Chapter 1) – has been more concerned with what actors want than the processes by which they come to decide what they want. Third, preference formation proposes a less mechanistic conceptualisation of how preferences are formulated than many in the existing literature. This allows for the possibility that preferences do not correlate simply with, and so cannot be read off, more fundamental economic or ideological commitments. Indeed, it implies the involvement of a broader range of influences than the machinery involved in formal decision-making or the balance of power between opposing factions. It is also historically sensitive, permitting appreciation of (in fact, it problematises) how preference formation changes over time.

Three arguments are made in this chapter. The first is that it is important to qualify the conventional wisdom concerning Labour's European policy expressed in many of the claims about the party's troubled relationship. Labour's difficulties with Europe have related specifically to integration according to the Monnet model, where supranational bodies take the lead, and national governments are constrained. Labour has been far less troubled by UK involvement in more orthodox forms of international co-operation. Indeed, Ernest Bevin, foreign secretary between 1945 and 1951, was one of the principal architects of the family of regional and international bodies that was created in the immediate post-war period (Young 1998, 26–70; Bullock 1983). Thus, generalisations about Labour and Europe need to distinguish between the party's difficulties with the first model and its achievements in relation to the second.

The second is that the complexities of Labour's European policy since 1945 conceal several important continuities. Though individual members and groupings have been enthusiastically pro-European and even federalist,[3]

Labour as a party has never been an idealist supporter of integration nor has it ever seen 'Europe' other than as an arena in which Britain might pursue its interests. It has favoured a minimalist conception of integration, been keen to preserve British sovereignty and typically regarded Britain's relationship with Europe as secondary to its wider international interests. At the same time, it has been pragmatic, prepared to move in a supranational direction where it is persuaded that Britain's interests can be furthered by so doing. A further element of continuity, though not strictly speaking a preference, is Labour's didactic approach to Britain's European partners. The party has consistently made clear its belief that Britain has a leading role to play in Europe.

The third argument is that, although no single factor or set of factors can account for the preferences that Labour has expressed throughout the post-war period, several of the variables identified by Dimitrakopoulos in the introduction to this volume have been important. For a supposedly non-doctrinaire party, ideas have been surprisingly influential. As well as a general preference for maintaining Britain's freedom of action, Labour's approach to European integration has been shaped by the claims of democratic socialism (in the 1950s and 1960s), by the calls of the Left in the 1970s and early 1980s for radical state interventionism, and, from the 1990s, by New Labour's pro-market, pro-business agenda. Interests have also been important. Labour's conception of Britain as a major world power, with geopolitical concerns and economic interests that reach far beyond the European continent, has been influential throughout. Institutions, meanwhile, have had a major impact. Party organisation in particular has been a key factor. Preferences have generally been set by the party leader, but the autonomy of the incumbent and the powers of the office have varied considerably over the period under discussion. The transition from an organisation without a single centre of authority, and in which the trade unions had at times a deciding voice, to one that is dominated by the leader and where unions, though still present, are more marginal had far-reaching implications in this regard.

The discussion that follows is organised into three main sections. The first provides a brief historical overview of Labour's European policy from 1945. Its aim is to contextualise the analysis of preferences and preference formation that follows. The second section describes and examines Labour's preferences towards 'Europe'. It identifies five preferences that have remained relatively constant across the post-war period, despite the often dramatic changes in the party's European policy. The third part examines the variables that have shaped the Labour Party's European preferences.

Labour and 'Europe': a historical overview

Labour's post-war European policy, which defies easy summary, is perhaps best viewed in terms of six periods: active support for intergovernmental co-operation and rejection of supranational integration (1945–62); conditional acceptance of British membership (1962–79); support for withdrawal (1979–83);

growing commitment to the Community (1984–94); and qualified pro-Europeanism (1994–2009).

Labour and 'European unity'

In the 1920s, Labour was avowedly internationalist. However, the party opposed regional co-operation, despite its commitment to world government and its support for the League of Nations.[4] The experience of the 1930s brought a change of outlook. In defining Labour's aims for the peace on the eve of war, for example, Clement Attlee (party leader from 1935 until 1955), contended that:

> in the common interest there must be recognition of an international authority superior to the individual States and endowed not only with rights over them, but with power to make them effective, operating not only in the political, but the economic sphere . . . Europe must federate or perish.
> (Labour Party 1939, 13, quoted in Featherstone 1988, 43)[5]

In the immediate post-war period, Europe appeared not to be a major priority for the Labour Party. Elected in 1945, its main foreign policy goal was to preserve Britain's global status, which it sought to pursue through the Empire, the Commonwealth and relations with the Allied Powers. However, the party soon discovered that it could not stand aloof from developments on the Continent. Labour in general, and Bevin in particular, became a major protagonist of European unity (see Bullock 1983; Newman 1983, 121–55; Young 1984, 77–95; 1993).[6] However, in opposition to calls to federate espoused by the federalist movement that had grown up during the war and to the supranational schemes that came later, Labour wanted to strengthen Europe through the permanent involvement of the US in its defence and intergovernmental co-operation among European states. Thus, although Bevin welcomed Marshall's June 1947 proposal of a European Recovery Programme (Broad 2001, 11–14), he opposed the creation of independent institutions to administer the aid and insisted that the 'continuing organisation' for the planning and implementation of the programme (the Organisation for European Economic Co-operation was established in April 1948) should be intergovernmental. US pressure for a customs union as part of the recovery programme was similarly resisted.

Once it became apparent that a working relationship with the Soviet Union was no longer possible, and that Europe's recovery and security would depend on Washington, Labour sought to promote intergovernmental co-operation 'in firm alliance with the US . . . and . . . simultaneously tried to impede the process of supranational integration' (Newman 1983, 122). It was more successful in the first than the second. Bevin's proposal in October 1948 for a North Atlantic security pact that would involve the US permanently in Western Europe defence was instrumental in the creation of NATO. The government extended the Dunkirk Treaty – a treaty of mutual defence and cultural co-operation that it had signed with France in 1947, formally directed at Germany, though with one eye on Moscow – to Belgium, Luxembourg and the Netherlands, to form the Brussels Treaty Organisation in March 1948.[7] It also sought to discourage Labour members and representatives of other socialist parties from attending The Hague Congress of May 1948 (Broad 2001, 14–17), and rejected as premature the West European Assembly called for by Churchill. Though the government participated in the negotiations that led to the formation of the Council of Europe, it was concerned to steer participants away from political union and towards a structure in which governments would retain final decision-making authority (Young 1984, 108–17).[8] Although the government signed up to the Convention on Human Rights, it did so only on the condition that the UK would have an opt-out from certain provisions.[9]

When the Schuman Plan was announced, Labour found unacceptable the condition on which France insisted in advance of negotiations: namely, that parties should accept the principle that coal and steel would be removed from national control and submitted to a supranational authority.[10] After an exchange that lasted four weeks, the government announced its decision not to participate. It expressed similar reservations about the supranational dimensions of the Pleven Plan, which it interpreted as 'not simply a plan for achieving the rearmament of Germany, but . . . a military counterpart of the Schuman Plan and . . . another step in the "making of Europe"' (Camps 1964, 13).[11] It also made clear its commitment to Atlanticism, declaring that NATO should be the custodian of Western Europe's defence.[12]

Labour's position remained unchanged after its return to opposition in 1951. The party lent its support to a series of government initiatives, including the Eden Plan for reorganising the Council of Europe, association with the ECSC, and the recasting of the Brussels Treaty Organisation as the West European Union.[13] Having hoped that the failure of the European Defence Community would signal the end of the supranational dream of the Europeans, it was as sceptical as the Conservative Party concerning the outcome of the 1955 Messina Conference and, in the summer of 1956, backed the government's counter-proposal for a free trade area that would include Britain, the Six and members of the OEEC. When these negotiations collapsed in November 1958, Labour supported the Conservatives' proposal of a free trade association, which led, in 1959, to the creation of the European Free Trade Association.

A decade of bipartisan consensus came to an end in 1961, however, when the Conservative government led by Harold Macmillan announced its decision to apply for membership of the European Communities.[14] Labour's response was not outright opposition, which some in the party had wanted. Instead, it insisted that accession would be acceptable if five conditions were satisfied: strong and binding safeguards for trade and other interests in the Commonwealth; a pledge to Britain's EFTA partners; the right to plan the British economy; guarantees for the protection of British agriculture; and freedom to pursue an independent foreign policy (Newman 1983, 174; Broad 2001, 41).

Its position hardened when Hugh Gaitskell (1955–63) declared at the 1962 party conference that membership of a 'federation of Europe' would mark, not only 'the end of a thousand years of history', but of Britain 'as an independent nation state' (Labour Party Annual Conference Report 1962, 159, cited by Broad 2001, 52). Labour thereby assumed the mantle of the party for national independence and British greatness (Broad 2001, 47–53; Newman 1983, 191–5).[15]

Conditional acceptance

Labour's insistence on the five conditions marked the beginning of an era of calculated ambiguity, which the party maintained after de Gaulle's 1963 veto and continued to uphold until the late 1970s. It allowed the party, without taking a position on the *principle* of the UK accession (Broad 2001, 54–71), to criticise the Conservatives, to contain divisions within its own ranks, and, later, to remain in the Communities at the same time as renegotiating the terms of British entry.[16] Its manifestos of the mid-1960s reflected this ambivalence. In 1964, it promised that: 'Though we shall seek to achieve closer links with our European neighbours, the Labour Party is convinced that the first responsibility for a British Government is to the Commonwealth', while, in 1966, it once again emphasized Gaitskell's five conditions. Shortly thereafter, however, having reviewed the party's options and having travelled to Brussels for a 'probing visit' by George Brown and himself to EEC capitals (Broad 2001), Harold Wilson (party leader from 1963 until 1976) announced in 1967 that the government would be submitting an application for membership. Once again, de Gaulle delivered the *coup de grâce* when, on 22 November 1967, he vetoed British entry for a second time. Wilson made clear, in the face of considerable internal opposition, that the UK's application remained on the table (Robins 1979, 71; Featherstone 1988, 58).

When Georges Pompidou, de Gaulle's successor, lifted the veto at The Hague summit,[17] Labour continued to argue that membership would only be acceptable if the terms were right and, thereby, to differentiate itself from the alleged readiness of the Tories to enter the Community at any cost. Although Labour lost the June election, the incoming Conservative government, led by Edward Heath, inherited Labour's negotiating briefs and proceeded with the ministerial talks with EEC member states that had been planned under Labour. Despite the fact that the Heath government took up where the Labour government had left off, Wilson criticised the conditions of accession and opposed 'entry on Tory terms'. In a climate of heightened ideological differences between government and opposition, and a deepening schism between the party's left and right wings, Labour split on a government motion approving the principle of entry on 28 October 1971, with sixty-nine MPs, christened the 'October traitors', defying party conference and the whips by voting with the government.

In the face of multiplying calls from Labour backbenchers and other parts of the Labour movement for the British people to be consulted on the issue, the Shadow Cabinet gradually shifted in favour of a referendum.[18] Wilson calculated that, by accepting the idea, he could outflank the Tories and defuse tensions within his increasingly divided party.[19] Although the public's interest in the issue waned after accession in 1973, Labour affirmed its policy of renegotiation and consultation in its February 1974 manifesto:

> it is the policy of the Labour party that, in view of the unique importance of the decisions, the people should have the right to decide the issue through a General Election or a Consultative Referendum. If these two tests are passed, a successful renegotiation and the expressed approval of the majority of the British people, then we shall be ready to play our full part in developing a new and wider Europe.
>
> (quoted by Byrd 1975, 476)

Two months after a narrow election victory, the minority Labour government set out its terms to its European partners and agreed that renegotiations would be followed by a binding referendum. Following a second general election in October 1974, Labour, now with a slender majority of four, pressed ahead with renegotiation. Although the process proceeded relatively quickly, and was concluded at the Dublin summit in March 1975, the party was split from top to bottom on whether the terms were acceptable. The government won the vote in the Commons the following month, but only with the support of Conservative and Liberal MPs.

The campaign for the referendum that followed – an unprecedented event in British politics – was run on non-party lines.[20] From the Labour Party, Jenkins and Williams were leading figures in the 'Yes' campaign, and Benn for the 'No' campaign. Wilson and James Callaghan (then foreign secretary) took a low-key approach throughout, though Wilson came to believe that the referendum had to be won.[21] The vote took place on 6 June 1975. Two-thirds (67 per cent) of voters expressed their support for continued British membership on a turn-out of 64 per cent. Although it might reasonably have been expected that the result would resolve the issue, Labour opponents of the decision, who were mainly on the left wing of the Party, refused, to paraphrase Broad (2001, 120), to 'take "yes" for an answer'.[22] When the government introduced deflationary measures, the Left claimed that the Community was the source of the deficit and that it was preventing the use of policy instruments that could otherwise be used to remedy the UK's circumstances.

More broadly, both the government and the party struck an increasingly defensive stance. Following a special day-long meeting on 29 July 1977, where discussion was dedicated to the issue (Owen 1992, 329–32), the Cabinet adopted what one interviewee described as 'a coherent anti-federalist position' (private correspondence, 23 November 2009). This position, which was supported by some leading left-wing critics, including Michael Foot, informed a letter that James Callaghan addressed to the NEC on the eve of the party conference in early October 1977 and provided the basis for the government's decision to sign up to an agreement on the European Monetary System, not to participate in the Exchange Rate Mechanism in late 1978 (Owen 1992, 376–77). Sentiment within the party remained yet more hostile. When proposals for the EMS were put forward in 1977, the NEC reminded the government that the 1976 programme had rejected 'any form of economic or monetary union which compelled us to accept unemployment for the sake of maintaining a fixed parity' (Newman 1983, 242). The 1978 party conference, meanwhile, saw the adoption of a resolution that called for amendment of the 1972 European Communities Act; CAP reform; the rewriting of the Treaty of Rome; a rejection of moves towards economic and monetary union or strengthening of the Common Assembly; protection of indigenous fuels for the British people; and the transformation of the EEC into a larger, flexible and more open institution (Newman 1983, 242).

Labour's manifesto for the 1979 election, which was drafted on 6 April 1979 and finalised at an eight-hour joint meeting of the Cabinet and the NEC, reflected the anti-federalist position that the Cabinet had developed two years before. A commitment to repeal section 2 (1) of the 1972 European Communities Act, according to which Community legislation takes direct effect in the member states, was rejected, but the manifesto included the promise that a future Labour government would make ministers more accountable to the House of Commons before they signed up to decisions in the Council of Ministers (Owen 1992, 410). Only manifesto pledges to remedy the most egregious problems related to Britain's membership of the Community and the concern of the left wing's leading figures to maintain party unity defused the issue in the run-up to the elections.

Towards withdrawal

Following the 1979 election defeat, the precarious compromise over 'Europe' soon broke down. While Michael Foot, the new party leader (1979–83), and Peter Shore committed themselves to upholding the manifesto position, other anti-marketeers announced that they intended to vote for withdrawal at the party conference. At the same time, leading pro-marketeers, including David Owen, Bill Rodgers and Shirley Williams, declared their support for continued membership. The 1980 conference passed a motion calling for withdrawal and decided the following year that there would be no further referendum.[23] Following a special party conference in January 1981, the 'gang of four' (Owen, Rodgers, Williams and Roy Jenkins, an early pro-European, who served as Commission president between 1977 and 1981) left the Labour Party to form the Social Democratic Party (SDP). One unintended consequence was that anti-marketeers were in a majority in the Shadow Cabinet. It was little surprise that Labour's 1983 manifesto – the party's most radical of the post-war period[24] – committed the party to withdrawal from the Community in the following terms:

Geography and history determine that Britain is part of Europe, and Labour wants to see Europe safe and prosperous. But the European Economic Community, which does not even include the whole of Western Europe, was never devised to suit us, and our experience as a member of it has made it more difficult for us to deal with our economic and industrial problems. It has sometimes weakened our ability to achieve the objectives of Labour's international policy.

The next Labour government, committed to radical, socialist policies for reviving the British economy, is bound to find continued membership a most serious obstacle to the fulfilment of those policies. In particular the rules of the Treaty of Rome are bound to conflict with our strategy for economic growth and full employment, our proposals on industrial policy and for increasing trade, and our need to restore exchange controls and to regulate direct overseas investment. Moreover, by preventing us from buying food from the best sources of world supply, they would run counter to our plans to control prices and inflation.

For all these reasons, British withdrawal from the Community is the right policy for Britain – to be completed well within the lifetime of the parliament. That is our commitment.

(Labour Party 1983, available at www.politicsresources. net/area/uk/man.htm)

A pro-European party

The 1983 election, at which the party received its lowest share of the vote since 1918, proved to be a turning point for Labour's European policy and the party more generally. Its dismal performance provoked an intense debate about its future (see Whiteley 1983). A new leadership team, Neil Kinnock (1983–92) and Roy Hattersley (deputy leader, 1983–92), embarked upon a process of modernisation. As well as organisational changes aimed at improving the effectiveness of the Labour's campaigning and preventing an activist fringe from determining the party's positions on key issues, the reform included a review of party policy. A shift towards a pro-European policy was both a part and an expression of this transformation. Although Kinnock later recalled that it had been easier to change the party's policy on Europe than on other issues, such as nationalisation, trade union ballots and especially defence (Kinnock 1994; Westlake 2001, chapter 16; Broad 2001, 158; Hughes and Wintour 1990), the process took no fewer than three parliamentary terms nevertheless.

An instinctive internationalist, though not a lifelong pro-European, Kinnock had made clear his commitment to continued membership of the Community in his leadership manifesto.[25] In sharp contrast to his predecessors, he began to engage with Labour members of the European Parliament and to develop closer relations with sister parties of the Centre-Left bilaterally[26] and multilaterally through the 'Confed'[27] For the first time, Labour signed up to most elements of the common manifesto. On policy, Kinnock was initially cautious,[28] but its 1984 European manifesto demonstrated how far and how quickly the party had moved, declaring that Britain's immediate future lay in Europe and identifying the benefits that the Community afforded to the Labour movement (see Broad 2001, 159). At the same time, the manifesto noted that Britain retained the right of withdrawal. It also declared the party's opposition to expanding the European Parliament's legislative powers, demanded the return of certain powers to Westminster, and called for a fundamental reform of the Common Agricultural Policy.[29] The poll results – Labour's share of the votes was 36.5 per cent – were interpreted as an encouraging sign that the new strategy was working. Thereafter, the party continued its shift towards pro-Europeanism. The debate over the SEA marked a major milestone in this process. Hattersley commented, for example, that it represented 'the last throes of the old unthinking anti-Market position' (Hattersley, quoted in Broad 2001, 167).[30] The leadership argued that Labour could benefit from Community action, but would need to engage positively with Europe in order to shape it.

The 1987 manifesto committed the party to 'work constructively with our EEC partners to promote economic expansion and combat unemployment', though the message was balanced by a declaration that Labour would 'stand up for British interests within the European Community' and that 'like other member countries, [we] reject EEC interference with our policy for national recovery and renewal' (Daniels 1998, 76).[31] Though it dealt with 'Europe' in a single paragraph, the focus was mostly on how the Community could be used to Labour's advantage. The election results were not as good as the leadership had hoped, but the upturn in its fortunes, the recapture of ground from the SDP and the praise that the professionalism of the campaign had attracted (Shaw 1996, 181) reinforced support for the direction in which Kinnock was taking the party.[32] Shortly thereafter, at the leader's initiative, the party began a Policy Review. Seven groups were created, each of which included representatives from the Shadow Cabinet and the NEC. The group 'Britain and the world' was jointly convened by Gerald Kaufman MP and Tony Clarke (Deputy Secretary General of the Union of Communications Workers), but the European Union was a common thread running through the review.[33] Although the Policy Review endorsed the single European market, it called for co-ordination among the member states on environmental protection, workers' rights, social security and reflationary economic policy. While supporting co-operation in foreign policy, it opposed the possible development of the Community into a superpower. It supported the retention of the national veto and called for enhanced scrutiny by Westminster in dealing with EC legislation. The report was approved by the 1989 Party Conference.

Labour's embrace of 'Europe' was one of a series of new policies intended to move the party towards the centre of the political spectrum. The party also saw that it might be possible to establish rights at the Community level that had been abolished in Britain (Daniels 1998, 88). On 20 September 1988, Margaret Thatcher had delivered her famous 'Bruges speech', in which she opposed the development of a social dimension at the EU level only a few days after Jacques Delors had spoken of the need to protect workers' rights, as well as a statute for European companies and a right to life-long education (Radice 1992, 170), in his historic address to the TUC Conference. With the Conservative Party becoming increasingly Eurosceptic and growing tensions between senior members of the government, Labour was able to fight the 1989 European elections as the pro-Europe party. The result represented the first victory that Labour had enjoyed over the Conservatives in fifteen years.[34] Despite John Major's initial attempt to reclaim Europe for the Conservatives, Labour remained the pro-European party as divisions over the issue in the Conservative Party hardened and Euroscepticism became increasingly influential.

By 1992, Labour had completed its conversion to 'Europe'. After Kinnock had resigned following Labour's fourth successive general election defeat, the leadership battle pitted John Smith and Bryan Gould. Smith was a lifelong pro-European who had been one of the sixty-nine Labour MPs to defy the party whip in 1972 and one of the main architects of the Labour Party's new economic policy, in which British membership of the European Exchange Rate Mechanism (ERM) played a central part (Stuart 2005, 179–94).[35] Gould, by contrast, was an old-fashioned Keynesian and opponent of the ERM and Maastricht. Smith's victory confirmed that Labour was now a pro-European party. Although a lifelong supporter of British membership, Smith was a practical European rather than a federal visionary, who believed that domestic action alone was no longer sufficient to achieve the Party's key economic and social goals (Beckett 2007). During Smith's brief but eventful leadership, which included both the ratification of the Maastricht Treaty (Stuart 2005, 276–87) and 'Black Wednesday', when speculation forced the pound out of the ERM, the party consolidated and strengthened its European credentials.[36]

The episode, which undermined credibility in the Conservative Party's economic management for a generation, was not without cost to Labour, however. The government's decision to enter the ERM with an overvalued pound and high interest rates had worsened the recession (October 1990 to September 1992), but, because Labour had supported the principle of entry, its ability to criticise the government's decision was limited, and, when the pound fell out of the ERM, the party found it difficult to respond to the argument that the whole experience had demonstrated the folly of fixed exchange rates (Stuart 2005, 255–60). Labour's response was continued support for the ERM, but insisting that it be accompanied by co-ordinated economic and industrial policy, and for the single currency, on the grounds that it could counter the kind of currency speculation that had caused the ERM crisis.[37]

Qualified pro-Europeanism

The party's pro-Europeanism continued after its rebranding as New Labour.[38] Indeed, 'Europe' played an important part in New Labour thinking. Tony Blair (1994–2007), who became leader following the death of John Smith,[39] had, like Kinnock, not been an instinctive pro-European, but saw action through the European Union as a key part of New Labour's modernising project, linked to its Third Way agenda of economic reform and the pursuit of competitiveness and prosperity in a globalised world (Mandelson and Liddle 1996). Blair pledged to end Britain's difficult relationship with the Union, declaring to the 1996 Labour Party conference that: 'Under my leadership, I will never allow this country to be isolated or left behind in Europe', (Rawnsley 2000, 73). Promising to put Britain at the centre of Europe, he emphasized the need to: 'end the isolation of the last twenty years and be a leading partner in Europe' (Blair 1997). New Labour's support in principle for the UK's participation in economic and monetary union lent credibility to the party's broader economic policy and contrasted the predictability that membership would bring with the uncertainty that the British economy had experienced under the Tories. Again, like Kinnock, Blair invested in establishing good relations with Labour's sister parties, as well as with Labour MEPs (Messmer 2003), and, in office, with other heads of government.[40] Contacts were established with other EU member states, and attempts were made to mobilise support for the Third Way. A later initiative (in 1998) saw an attempt to bring about a 'step change' in Britain's relations with its partners by seeking to forge enduring relationship at all levels of government (Smith and Tsatsas 2002). The PM also promoted initiatives with partners, including Aznar, Berlusconi and Chirac, in areas of shared concern.[41]

In practice, New Labour's pro-Europeanism was somewhat guarded. Its hesitancy became evident soon after the election victory of May 1997. The new government was immediately thrust into the 1996–7 IGC and, though it won plaudits for its constructive approach, which contrasted sharply with its predecessor's negative approach, its substantive positions were often not so dissimilar. The same was true of its involvement in the 2000 IGC, the Convention on the Future of Europe and the 2002–3 and 2007 IGCs, where it showed itself determined to preserve British sovereignty in certain policy areas. In terms of policy, although it signed up immediately to the Social Chapter in 1997, this marked the extent of its commitment to European social policy. New Labour was decidedly less enthusiastic in general about EU efforts to create new social rights or to introduce measures to regulate the labour market. It has also been famously ambivalent on the euro.[42] In government, it remained silent on the issue until – to the dismay of its EU partners – it announced first that Britain would not be signing up and then, in autumn 1997, in an echo of the early 1960s, that it would have to be assured that five tests had been satisfied before it could contemplate entry.[43]

Soon after the five tests were announced, the government effectively stopped discussing the euro. Labour frontbenchers generally avoided any mention of 'Europe', while Blair's interventions on the subject were a rarity and usually delivered abroad, as for example his speech in Warsaw (2000) and address to the European Parliament (2005). There was little change in the party's willingness to attempt to change public opinion or to counter Eurosceptic claims, even after Blair had conceded calls for a referendum on the Constitutional Treaty. New Labour's insistence on red lines, ambivalence towards EU social policy and the single currency, and its failure to engage in domestic debate about Europe suggest that, in power, it has proved less pro-European than the party of the late 1980s and early 1990s or than in opposition in the mid 1990s (Paterson, Henson and Shipley 1995).[44]

Nor was there any sign that Labour would take a more positive approach to the domestic debate when Gordon Brown (2007–) succeeded Blair as party leader and prime minister.[45] Brown has certainly been no less timid concerning the Treaty of Lisbon and was conspicuously absent from the signing ceremony on 13 December 2007. His low-key approach to Europe has been in keeping with his reported disdain for continental Europe, which he regards as backward and stagnant, and his impatience with how the EU conducts its business (Peston 2005; O'Donnell and Whitman 2007). Despite his concern for competitiveness and meeting the challenges of globalisation, Brown scarcely mentioned the EU in his early speeches, such as his keynote address of November 2007 (Brown 2007). When he has broached the topic, as in a speech on 14 January 2008, he has said little about Britain's relationship with, or role in, the EU, and presented a somewhat negative image of the Union as a 'trade bloc Europe' (O'Donnell and Whitman 2007, 255; see also Brown 2005).[46] By contrast, and somewhat uncharacteristically for the party in this era, Labour's manifesto for the 2009 European elections presented the reasons for Britain's engagement with the Union at length and in detail.[47] As well as outlining the benefits for business, it pointed to the Union's record on consumer protection, underlined the need to work collectively with Britain's EU partners to address common problems such as climate change, security, trafficking and the credit crisis, and emphasised the advantage of co-operation on issues such as international development.

Labour Party preferences

Approaching Labour European policy from the perspective of preferences and preference formation makes possible the identification of continuities and discontinuities in the party's disposition towards Europe over time.

Aims and scope

Although, as the preceding discussion shows, its attitudes have fluctuated considerably since 1945, some of the party's preferences concerning the aims and, therefore, the scope of integration have proved remarkably stable. Beneath the policy shifts, close examination reveals five constants. The first relates more to the spirit in which preferences have been held rather than to their content. Though at all times since 1945 there have been enthusiasts for integration and even federalists within the party, Labour has never been idealistic about integration. Until the mid-1960s, it opposed the supranational conception of European unity, but, even when it contemplated and finally proposed British entry in 1966–7, it did so less because it was inspired by the idea of membership than because other possibilities were no longer available.[48] Its unease has been evident from 1973. In opposition after entry, it refused to join the Confed and, in government from 1974 to 1979, it found itself at odds with its partners over a wide range of policies. It was not surprising that the party gravitated towards a policy of withdrawal between 1979 and 1983. Even since the early 1980s, when it became a pro-European party, Labour has seen Europe in instrumental or pragmatic terms, viewing the Communities and later the Union as an arena for advancing the interests of the United Kingdom. Its leaders have rarely made reference to the general or intrinsic benefits of integration, still less suggested that there should be any cause to celebrate British membership of the Union. New Labour's silence on the issue during more than a decade in government has already been remarked upon (see also Kassim 2008). Its failure to mark publicly the major anniversaries of Britain's accession in 1998 and 2003 was especially conspicuous.

A second constant, related to the first, is that Labour has regarded Brussels as a venue through which the party can pursue its goals, rather than an actor with interests of its own that are above those of the member states. Like the UK Conservative Party, Labour has been attached to the preservation of national sovereignty; hence, its support for intergovernmental co-operation as an alternative to supranational integration. Since accession, it has favoured a conception of the Union where the UK is not overly constrained. Accordingly, Labour has generally been reluctant to broaden the Communities' competencies. When it has been unable to prevent its partners from agreeing common measures, it has managed either to negotiate opt-outs for the UK with regard to, for example, asylum, visas and immigration, tax policy and social security, or, over successive rounds of treaty reform, the entire justice and home affairs domain, or to ensure that particular instruments or measures would have limited impact in the UK. Thus, Blair secured a written guarantee in the Treaty of Lisbon that the Charter of Fundamental Rights cannot be used by the European Court of Justice to alter British labour law. However, there are some exceptions, which are discussed below. It has also resisted the adoption of policies at EU level that it considers harmful to British interests. These have ranged from Wilson and Callaghan's opposition to proposals concerning the CAP, budget and fisheries, to New Labour's opposition to regulation of the financial markets.

Third, Labour has never taken a Europeanist view of Europe similar to that espoused, for example, by the *Parti Socialiste* in France under François Mitterrand. Instead, it has always seen the UK's relationship with 'Europe' more fundamentally, in the wider context of the country's broader international interests. The conception of these interests has, of course, changed over time. The initial foreign policy priority for the Attlee government was to strengthen Britain's relations with the Empire and the Commonwealth, and to continue its privileged alliance with the Allied powers. 'Europe' began to feature only as the Cold War developed. In opposition, in the early 1960s and, similarly, a decade later, Labour condemned Conservative governments for neglecting the Commonwealth in their determination to join the common market. Since the 1990s, by contrast, Labour leaders have underscored the importance of Atlanticism in security and defence, and pointed to Britain's financial and trading interests in all corners of the globe. Blair's support for US intervention in Iraq, which was opposed by Paris and Bonn, was regarded by many as emblematic in revealing that New Labour's fundamental loyalty was to Washington.[49]

Since it first countenanced British entry in the mid-1960s, Labour has generally favoured a minimalist conception of integration, based on the common or single market – a fourth preference. This preference is somewhat paradoxical for two reasons. First, when the Labour government decided to apply for membership, it was motivated more by geopolitical concerns related to the desire to maintain British *grandeur* than by economic concerns to boost British industry. Indeed, the 1970 White Paper prepared by the Wilson government concluded that, insofar as there was an economic argument for entry, it was extremely finely balanced. Second, when it returned to government in 1974 following accession, Labour showed little sympathy for, or indeed understanding of, market-making and what it implied. As noted above, during the Wilson–Callaghan era, it was frequently opposed to proposals for common policies in the economic domain that were supported by other member states. Only with the SEA did the party accept integration as an economic project (though see below), although New Labour has, of course, been extremely comfortable with the market-making element of the European project.

There have, however, been two main, if limited, exceptions to Labour's preference for a minimalist conception of Europe. The first is the party's advocacy, during the late 1980s and early 1990s, of a social dimension to complement the single market. Under Kinnock, the party pressed for recognition and protection of worker rights at the Community level. In the 1992 election campaign, the party called for high employment standards and committed itself to signing up to the Social Chapter, thereby reversing one of the opt-outs that the Major government had secured at Maastricht. Smith not only saw the Social Chapter as 'essential in transforming a market for business into a Community for people' (*Hansard*, 20 October 1992, cited by Dimitrakopoulos 2009, 14–15), but also viewed the British opt-out as 'an absurdity' tantamount to denying British citizens 'the social rights, the social opportunities and the social advantages which the whole Community wants for its citizens' (*Hansard*, 23 July 1993, cited by Dimitrakopoulos 2009, 14–15). As well as underlining the party's commitment to social justice, its decision regarding the Social Chapter was intended to signal that its election would inaugurate an era of positive engagement with 'Europe'. Although New Labour carried out its promise when it won power in 1997, it showed little enthusiasm thereafter for a social Europe, much to the disappointment of its supporters in the trade union movement. Its insistence on the preservation of the individual opt-out in the working time directive in order to minimise its impact in Britain and its reservations about measures concerning temporary and part-time workers are illustrative and indicative of its views on labour market regulation.[50]

A second exception is foreign policy. For much of its history, Labour has been strongly opposed to political integration. However, in the early 1990s, it championed the development of a European military capability that could be mobilised independently of NATO. The 1998 St Malo agreement, signed by Britain and France, was an important landmark in the development of a common European policy in security and defence, since successive British governments had previously blocked any move that might threaten NATO's position as the guardian of European security. Blair took from Europe's failure to intervene in Kosovo the lesson that the Union should have 'the capacity for autonomous action, backed up by credible military forces' and that co-operation should take place within the EU framework. More typical has been Labour's ambivalence with respect to economic and monetary union.

A fifth and final constant has been Labour's assumption that Britain should lead in Europe. This attitude was evident under the Attlee administration, when Britain played a key part in the creation of several regional and international organisations, while at the same time blocking federalist initiatives and denouncing supranational schemes. It was apparent in opposition in the 1950s, as shown by Labour's support for various government proposals to outflank or emasculate the EEC. The same view was present in the late 1960s. George Brown's exclamation to the German chancellor, 'Willy, you must get us in, so that we can take the lead' (cited in Broad 2001, 63), is an excellent example. It has also been a New Labour theme. The party's 1997 manifesto promised that a Labour government

> will stand up for Britain's interests in Europe after the shambles of the last six years, but, more than that, we will lead a campaign for reform in Europe. Europe isn't working in the way this country and Europe need. But to lead means to be involved, to be constructive, to be capable of getting our own way.

Even more forcefully, Blair opined that, for Britain to remain at the edge of Europe, rather than take up a leading role at the centre of Europe, would be 'to deny our historical role in the world' (Rawnsley 2000, 73).

Institutions

Unsurprisingly, given its emphasis on sovereignty and its instrumentalist conception of integration, Labour has generally preferred power to be exercised by the organs of the Union that represent the governments of the member states – the Council and the European Council. It has not been a supporter of the European Parliament and has shown great reluctance to allow that body's powers to be extended. It has been relatively quiet on the subject of the European Commission. Interventions of the sort made by Tony Blair, where, in the debate on the future of Europe, he discussed the need for the Commission to act as an independent arbiter and regulator, have been rare indeed among Labour leaders. At the same, Labour has been prepared to accept, and indeed has sometimes advocated, the extension of qualified majority voting in the Council. Thus, for example, it agreed to expansions through the Treaties of Amsterdam, Nice and Lisbon.

More surprisingly, given its general preference for fewer rather than more competencies to be exercised at the EU level and for treaty reform, for which there has never been any great appetite within the party, it agreed at the meeting of the European Council in Laeken in 2001 to the calling of a convention to draw up a draft constitutional treaty, rather than insisting on the traditional method of treaty reform, which privileges national governments (Dimitrakopoulos 2008a). This may, however, prove to be a one-off that can be explained as a reaction to the circumstances surrounding the 2000 IGC, where the machinations of the French presidency at the Nice European Council led to considerable ill-feeling. Blair was one of the heads of state and government quoted as commenting that: 'we cannot do business like this in the future' (*The Independent*, 12 December 2000, 1).

Preference formation

The formulation of the Labour Party's preferences in regard to European integration cannot be explained in terms of a single factor or along a single dimension. Preference formation within a political party is a complex process, where multiple variables are at work and where their relative weight is not constant. The sets of variables described by Dimitrakopoulos in the introduction to this volume offer a useful framework for explaining how and why Labour adopted the preferences outlined above.

Ideas

Despite Labour's reputation as a non-doctrinaire party, ideas and ideology have had an important influence in shaping the party's preferences towards Europe.[51] The relationship has not been straightforward. In the 1940s and 1950s, it was the ideological commitments of the mainstream of the party that were incompatible with British participation in the Communities. Although, since the 1960s, the Left of the party has generally been more Eurosceptic than the Right, sceptics and supporters could be found on both wings of the party.[52] Moreover, the views of many individual members changed over time. Even during the 1970s and early 1980s, when the party became increasingly polarised and the Left vociferously anti-European, Europe remained a cross-cutting issue. Ideas were no less important in the party's transition to pro-Europeanism, nor have they been less significant during the New Labour era.

Democratic socialism was especially important in the first two decades after the war, but its influence was more enduring. The commitment to reformist socialism was rooted in the achievements of the Attlee government. As well as nationalisation of key industries, the administration introduced economic planning, created the National Health Service and established comprehensive social security provision. As it was widely believed within the movement that continental European socialist parties were so weak,[53] and the accomplishments of the Attlee government so monumental, many party members considered Labour to be the only left European party capable of implementing a socialist programme. The sentiment that the British Labour Party was special, a pioneer in some way in advance of its sister parties, persisted until at least the 1980s.

Moreover, the policies and freedom of action that democratic socialism required were, as Bevin was one of the earliest to point out, incompatible with the obligations imposed by membership of a supranational organisation (see Newman 1983, 134). Siminlarly, when socialist parties met in London in 1950 to discuss the Schuman Plan, Hugh Dalton and Dennis Healey elaborated further on this theme:

> No socialist party with the prospect for forming a government could accept a system by which important fields of national policy were surrendered to a supranational European representative authority, since such an authority would have a permanent anti-socialist majority and would arouse the hostility of European workers.[54]
>
> (cited in Featherstone 1988, 49)

These ideas faded in the early 1960s – indeed, Sassoon attributes Wilson's 1967 bid to join the Community to the failure of the 'modernised version of the domestic road to socialism' (1996, 342) – but reappeared in a different guise towards the end of that decade as part of the programme of the party's left wing, which was beginning to grow in influence. Reacting to what it regarded as the policy failures of the Labour administrations of the 1960s, the party's left wing demanded 'a more vigorous socialist platform on which to fight against Conservative policies' (Featherstone 1988, 58).[55] Not only was the radical economic programme it proposed inconsistent with Britain's membership of the Community, but it considered the legislation enacted by the Heath government to amount to nothing less than outright class warfare and interpreted Heath's negotiation of Britain's entry as part of the same programme.[56] 'Europe' became a salient issue for the left wing of the party and, for the first time, was treated as a question of domestic policy. Not only did anti-marketeers explicitly link the government's attempt to curb the power of the unions with entry into the Community, arguing – however implausibly – that membership would assist the Conservatives in implementing their anti-union agenda, but, in a climate of intensified partisan difference, they argued that it was the duty of Labour members and supporters to oppose all actions of the Heath government in the defence of the working class (Frankel 1975, 243).[57]

Nor was the party's left wing placated when Labour returned to power in 1974. It blamed the Community for the government's deflationary policy and for preventing the government from using policy instruments that could otherwise be used to remedy the UK's position, and attacked Community policies. An economic programme, which had been developed in 1973, was launched as the Alternative Economic Strategy in 1976. It included measures to redistribute income and opportunities to the working class, import controls to protect manufacturing industries, and a state-directed industrial policy, the implementation of which would be incompatible with Community rules (see Seyd 1987). Although the party leadership was able to prevent these radical proposals from being included in the 1979 manifesto, the growing influence of the party's left wing and the election of Michael Foot as party leader to succeed Callaghan led to a significant shift after that date. By 1981, the party had committed itself to an alternative economic strategy, a non-nuclear defence policy, abolition of private education and private medicine, and withdrawal from the EEC. These policies were included in the 1983 manifesto.

Democratic socialism, and the belief that a programme of the Left could be achieved only by a Britain that was fully sovereign, began to recede in the 1980s, when the constraints imposed by economic interdependence came to be more widely understood within the party.[58] The idea of a choice between the restraints imposed by Brussels and the freedom of the deep blue sea came to be seen as false. This lesson was reinforced by the failure in France of the 'Mitterrand experiment' in the early 1980s (MacShane 1988). The Left's attachment to socialism in one country, as well as the 'widespread conviction, at grassroots level, that we are the only real socialists in Europe' (Morrell 1987, quoted in Broad 2001, 169) came increasingly into question. In addition, a debate among the trade unions that had begun in 1983 seemed by 1986–7 to have been resolved in favour of the Community. The conclusion that Britain could not unilaterally implement a socialist programme marked an important step towards a preparedness to accept Community membership and to realise that certain economic and social objectives could only be achieved through collective action at the level of the EC.

With a new outlook predicated on interdependence, the party was ready to embrace Europe – or at least it recognised, as in the 1960s, that there were no other options. Socialism-in-one-country gave way to a model of regulated capitalism. The new aim was, in John Smith's words: 'the creation of a high-productivity, high-skill and high-wage economy in Britain and in the Community, instead of seeking to compete on the basis of low costs and low skills' (*Hansard*, 23 June 1993, cited in Dimitrakopoulos 2009, 14–15). For Labour under Kinnock and Smith in particular, the opportunities presented by the Community to influence the shape of economic Europe and to develop a social dimension at the EC level, when trade union and workers' rights had been rolled back in the UK, were important to explore. The trade union movement reached a similar assessment (Rosamond 1993). Under New Labour, the assumption of interdependence has persisted. However, married with the party's pro-business outlook, the emphasis has switched from restraining capitalism to liberalisation, light touch regulation and a neo-liberal conception of social policy. Thus, New Labour has sought to promote economic reform through the Lisbon Agenda, championed impact assessment and better regulation, and opposed labour market regulation and the broadening and strengthening of worker rights.

Interests

Interests have also played a major part in shaping the Labour Party's European preferences. Britain's island status has been important.[59] In contrast to its continental counterparts, for whom geography made the 'German problem' a necessary preoccupation, the Attlee government was not moved by fears for its immediate security to favour European co-operation. Britain had emerged from the war not only stronger economically than its European counterparts, but victorious and unoccupied (Camps 1964, 3–4). While the nation state in continental Europe had been called into question by the war, and the crises and instability that had preceded it, this was not true in Britain (Newman 1983, 123).[60] There was also a broader sentiment, widely shared in the party, that Britain was different in character from other European countries.[61] In short, there was little reason for Britain to look to the Continent to solve its problems.

More generally, though the content may have changed over time, the party's attitude towards Europe at each stage has been strongly influenced by its conception of Britain's place in the world. For most of the post-war period, the party has cast Britain's interests in international, rather than regional, terms. Attlee pledged in 1943 that Britain would 'continue to carry [its] full weight in the post-war world with the US and the USSR' (quoted by Broad 2001, 5) and carried this commitment into government. Indeed, as Newman has observed: 'Almost every policy statement, public and private, produced by the post-war Labour Government was predicated on the supposition of Britain's enduring grandeur' (1983, 123). Stafford Cripps's explanation to the House of Commons in May 1950 of why the government had decided not to participate in the Schuman Plan provides an illustration of a perception that prevailed for at least two decades after 1945: 'In our view, participation in a political federation, limited to Western Europe, is not compatible with either our Commonwealth ties, our obligations as a member of the wider Atlantic community, or as a world power' (quoted in Robins 1979, 21; see also Windrich 1952, 200–3).

Wilson's decision to apply for entry to the Communities marked a departure from the conception of Britain as a world power. For that particular 'Labour government, the progression towards Europe was a story of collapsing alternatives' (Lieber 1970, 261; see also Camps 1966, 194; and Robins 1979, 58). It was borne out of a realisation that the Commonwealth could not serve as a vehicle for projecting Britain's power in the world, awareness of the country's subordinate status within the 'special relationship', and lack of interest on the part of the Community in a *rapprochement* between the EEC and EFTA. In short, it was motivated by the realisation that Britain was no longer a great power and the fear that its importance would further diminish if it remained outside the Community. Labour's conception of Britain's position in the world became still narrower in the 1970s and 1980s, as the party became increasingly isolationist. To that extent, its policy of withdrawal from the Community reflected a 'Little Englander' outlook. However, the view of Britain as a global power began to re-emerge under Kinnock, was reinforced by Smith and has been considerably strengthened under New Labour. Since the 1980s, Labour has supported European integration at least in part because it has concluded that Britain's influence is greater within the Union than it could be without.

Labour's commitment to Atlanticism – a second conception of Britain's wider international outlook – has also been an important influence in how the party defined its European preferences. For much of the post-war period, and certainly between 1945 and 1964 and after 1994, the party has also been strongly Atlanticist.[62] For the Attlee government, the relationship with the US was important from the outset, only to become even more so as the Cold War developed. For New Labour, Washington has been at least as important as Brussels (Stephens 2005, 19–21). The personal relationship between Blair and President George W. Bush and Brown's admiration for the American model have been important influences.

For at least three decades after 1945, its conception of Britain's relationship with the Commonwealth – a third geopolitical interest – also shaped Labour's preferences in regard to integration. The party presented itself as the party of the Commonwealth (and initially the Empire) first, with Europe some way in the distance. There was an affinity between Britain and the Commonwealth that could not be matched by its relations with the countries of Western Europe. This romantic view was given eloquent expression by Hugh Dalton:

> It is no good denying that we are very much closer, in all respects except distance, to Australia and New Zealand than we are to Western Europe. Australia and New Zealand are populated by our kinsmen. They live under Labour governments, they are democracies, they speak our language, they have high standards of life and have the same political ideals as we have.
> (cited in Newman 1983, 130)[63]

The Commonwealth was also important to Britain's place in the world. Labour had no intention of forming other associations that would harm Britain's position as the 'nerve centre of the Commonwealth and the banker of the Sterling Area', as Hugh Dalton and Dennis Healey put it (quoted in Featherstone 1988, 49).

Labour criticised the Conservative Party for abandoning the Commonwealth when the Macmillan government announced its decision to apply for entry to the Communities and levelled the same charge at Heath ten years later. It also invoked the Commonwealth when it took the decision to renegotiate the terms of Britain's membership. However, the Commonwealth appeared to have fallen away when Wilson launched Labour's bid for membership in 1967: realising perhaps that it could no longer serve as a vehicle for projecting Britain's power in the world nor act as a force for peace contributed to his decision to apply for British entry. Not only was Britain's relationship with the Commonwealth changing – while Britain's trade with Europe had doubled since 1958, trade with the Commonwealth had remained static (Newman 1983, 205) – but it was becoming increasingly apparent that the Commonwealth was an unlikely platform for the country's aspiration to remain a world power (Sassoon 1996, 342). The relationship with the Commonwealth was revived as an issue by Labour when Heath negotiated entry in 1972, but not with the same conviction as it had done a decade previously. Although there were some echoes as concessions for certain Commonwealth products were sought during the renegotiations, the Commonwealth all but disappeared as a theme after the mid-1970s.

Surprisingly, economic interests have, for the most part, been less influential than ideology or geopolitical interests as factors influencing Labour preferences on Europe (see, e.g., Broad 2001, 62). The Attlee government, which ruled out participating in the Schuman Plan on economic grounds, is a possible exception. Addressing the House of Commons on 26 June 1950, Sir Stafford Cripps, who had succeeded Dalton as Chancellor of the Exchequer, emphasised that Britain produced half of Western Europe's total coal output and more steel than any other country, and therefore that: 'we have a greater economic interest in these proposals than any other country and we must, therefore, be very concerned with them' (quoted in Featherstone 1988, 48). More generally, Labour politicians have not tended to make the case for membership of the Communities on economic grounds. As a member of the Communities, however, a particular conception of Britain's economic interest has informed the party's preferences on specific issues. This was true of Labour's early positions on energy, the CAP, fisheries and the Community budget (George 1998, 71–136), and of New Labour's advocacy of economic reform, ambivalence on the euro and resistance to financial regulation that might undermine the City.

Interest in terms of vote maximisation has played its part, though in different ways at different times. The only generalisation that can perhaps can be sustained is that, despite evidence of widespread Euroscepticism among the British population, the electorate has appeared not to reward parties according to whether they are pro- or anti-European – though no avowedly anti-European party has won a general election since 1973 – but to punish parties when they take an extreme position, as in the case of Labour in 1983 (and perhaps the Conservatives in 2001).

Institutions

The third series of variables outlined by Dimitrakopoulos in the introduction to this volume relates to institutions. Three have been especially important in shaping Labour's preferences. The first is the electoral system. The first-past-the-post system generally encourages parties to take up moderate positions on key issues, in contrast to the ideologically pure manifestos that parties under proportional representation can put forward. At the same time, the government–opposition dynamic in a two-party system creates a strong imperative for Labour and the Conservatives to differentiate and exaggerate the differences between them. In the 1960s, Labour responded to the Conservatives' decision to seek membership by adopting a conditional approach to the question of British entry, focusing on the terms and questioning the implications for the Commonwealth. It continued, in the 1970s, to criticise the conditions on which the Heath government had taken Britain into the Communities, even though these had been largely determined by the preceding Wilson government. Moreover, Labour struck this sceptical stance, arguing that it could do better and even submitting its own application in 1967, without strong support for membership within the party. Since the 1980s, the parties have effectively switched positions on Europe, and New Labour seems to have benefited, at least in general elections, from its pro-European position.

The second and, arguably, the most important institutional variable has been party organisation. Gamble's notion that there has been a succession of Labour parties since 1906 is a useful way to approach the history of its organization (2003, 196–202). Who makes decisions and how, and the way that structures have changed, have had a profound impact on Labour's European preferences. Processes of decision-making offer an especially sharp illustration of Schattschneider's insight that 'organization is itself a mobilization of bias' (1960, 30). In broad terms, the party's organisation has undergone a two-fold transformation: from a segmented party, where leadership was contingent on the compliance of trade union bosses, to an activist-centred organisation, and then to a leadership party.[64] Although, at each stage, the leader initiated policy, the amount of discretion enjoyed by the incumbent, the constraints imposed by party structures, as well as trade unions, which have been ever present, and the availability of personal structures of support have varied considerably over time.

The party's original structure was markedly disaggregated, with three separate and largely distinct centres of authority that reflected its federal and extra-parliamentary beginnings (Seyd 1987, 3–5; Byrd 1975; see also Russell 2005). While the National Executive Committee (NEC), the party's 'administrative authority', and the annual party conference were responsible for deciding party policy, the Parliamentary Labour Party (PLP) implemented policy as decided at conference, but always rejected the idea that it was dictated to by conference (Seyd 1987, 4). The division between parliamentary and extra-parliamentary structures posed obvious challenges to the party leadership, as a conference vote that went against its wishes was likely to undermine its authority. Much depended, therefore, on the composition of the NEC and party conference.

Trade unions and other affiliated organisations, as well as local parties, were guaranteed representation in both bodies. Indeed, the trade unions controlled 90 per cent of votes at conference, most seats on the NEC and often constituency-level general committees. Each national affiliated organisation and constituency party was entitled to submit one motion per year for conference. These motions were reduced to a manageable number of composite resolutions prior to the conference. Any motion supported by a two-thirds majority at the conference became part of the party's policy programme. The conference also voted on statements from the NEC, which effectively determined its policy direction, and on proposed changes to party rules (Russell 2005, 11–12). Though the PLP elected the party leaders, Labour MPs had no right to vote at Party Conferences.

Until the 1960s, neither the structure of the party nor the power of the unions posed problems for the leadership. An implicit understanding allowed the unions to set the terms of industrial policy, but allowed the parliamentary leadership freedom in other areas (Harrison 1960; Minkin 1980; 1991; Russell 2005, 13). Thus, the PLP brought forward initiatives that were endorsed by the NEC and supported by the Conference.[65] Until the 1960s, trade union leaders generally came from the same wing as the party leadership, and party leaders could usually secure the decisions they were seeking. However, this began to change in the late 1960s, when a new generation of left-leaning union leaders emerged,[66] and the left wing's influence in the NEC and party conference, as well as in the PLP and among the grass roots, began to grow. The party leadership found itself advocating different policies from those adopted by these other party bodies.[67] In order to maintain party unity, and aware that the issue had 'the potential to destroy the government from within' (Young 1993, 119), Wilson attempted to please all sides. However, he was under permanent pressure from the NEC and Party Conference. Though sometimes he succumbed, he regularly found himself committing the party to positions that ran counter to decisions adopted by these bodies (see Broad 2001, 88–103, 120–38).

The party's left wing not only demanded changes in policy; it also called for organisational reform to promote greater democracy within the party. It argued that: 'the Party conference should determine the Party's policies and should elect the Party leadership; the NEC should determine the election manifesto; and the local Party General Committee should have the regular right to reject its incumbent Labour MP' (Seyd 1987, 34).

Its success in securing its objectives in the late 1970s and early 1980s was a major factor in explaining the radicalisation of the party's policies, including withdrawal from the Community.[68] After the 1983 defeat, however, first Kinnock, then Smith and later Blair sought to reverse the organisational changes that the party's left wing had introduced, to prevent party policy from being decided by activists, and to strengthen the party leadership. Under Kinnock, 'one man, one vote' (OMOV) was introduced for the selection of European parliamentary candidates and the election of NEC members, while the bloc vote was reduced to 70 per cent and the share of the local electoral college to 40 per cent. Smith abolished the block vote at party conferences, replacing it in 1993 with OMOV. Under New Labour, the policy-making powers of the NEC and conference have been weakened, NEC elections have been reformed, and the National Policy Forum has been created to discuss and decide party policy.[69] An important effect of the modernising reforms was to increase the decisional autonomy of the party leader.

Variations in the processes of decision-making within the party have had a profound effect on Labour's preference formation in respect to European integration. Although the dependence on the party conference and the NEC was not a problem for Attlee or Gaitskell, Wilson, as noted above, frequently found himself at odds with both bodies. Callaghan faced the same problem. After the Cabinet had approved direct elections to the European Parliament, including a proposal that MEPs would be elected by proportional representation – to please the Liberal Party, who were keeping a minority Labour government in power, but supported by the foreign secretary (Owen 1992, 325–6; Young 1993, 132) – and the government had reported the decision to its European partners, the NEC took a contrary view and, in September 1976, party conference rejected the decision. Although Callaghan was able to secure a reversal the following year (though he had to drop proportional representation), the episode illustrated the constraints to which the party leader was subject.[70]

The experience of Smith and, especially, Blair and Brown as party leaders has been very different from that of their predecessors.[71] Decision-making in the party has been streamlined and power centralised as the result of a succession of modernising reforms implemented since the 1980s. The leader is considerably less constrained and has greater freedom to shape policy. The independent and competing power centres that used to exist within the party have been abolished or sidelined. Post modernisation, leaders have only rarely confronted opposition and hostility from the NEC or its committees, the Trades Union Conference or party conference, which were all too familiar to Wilson and Callaghan. In addition, leaders have had their own support staff, which has increased their autonomy. Kinnock was the transitional figure in relation to both. With the old structures in place, Kinnock had to tread carefully in his first parliamentary term. For example, the 1984 party conference defeat on OMOV underlined his early vulnerability. However, Kinnock continued to work hard behind the scenes to secure the support of backbenchers and trade union leaders. His position was gradually strengthened by electoral success, the marginalisation of Militant and the reorganisation of party HQ (Minkin 1991, 602).[72] The Joint Policy Committees, meanwhile, enabled him to build a personal staff. By contrast, for Blair, Gamble notes that:

> the parliamentary leadership achieved a level of dominance over both the parliamentary party and the party in the country which several previous leaders had sought, but none had achieved to the same degree. That

familiar battle in the history of the Labour Party, the degree of autonomy exercised by the parliamentary leadership and its independence from the party organisation, appeared to have reached a climax under Blair.

(Gamble 2003, 194)

Blair solicited advice on Europe, not only from the party machine or the civil service, but from personal advisers, such as Roger Liddle and Derek Scott, pollsters, media figures and experts from business.

The third concerns the structure of the executive. Labour's experience demonstrates that the Cabinet system imposes important constraints on British prime ministers. Not only are they under pressure to ensure that all sections of the party are represented, but the departmental responsibilities and Cabinet status of ministers give them an important authority, while the administrative resources of Number 10 are relatively weak. As a consequence, Cabinet government is considerably less presidential, at least in the sense that power is strongly concentrated in the hands of the PM, than is often argued. Wilson's Cabinet, for example, which had to include pro- and anti-marketeers, was rarely united, and the PM had constantly to find ways to reconcile or minimise differences. The decision to call a referendum, for example, was a remarkable admission of the limits of prime ministerial power.

Blair, often thought to be the presidential PM *par excellence* (Heffernan and Webb 2007, 63–87), also found himself constrained by his Cabinet colleagues, and in particular the chancellor. For example, it was the chancellor and his advisers that decided on the five tests for the adoption of the euro – from all accounts, without the PM's participation (see Rawnsley 2000, 72–88).[73] This move, which entrusted the Treasury with the power to determine whether the tests had been satisfied – 'How Gordon fixed Tony', as Rawnsley put it (*The Observer*, 11 May 2003) – essentially gave Brown ownership of the issue, enabling him to prevent other frontbenchers, including the foreign secretary (Cook 2004, 168–71), from inveighing against the subject.[74] This was by no means Brown's only intervention on EU matters. As chancellor, he was also behind many of Britain's 'red lines' at the 2003–4 IGC (Menon 2004) and sent his second secretary at the Treasury to accompany Blair in negotiations on the EU budget review (*European Voice*, 17 July 2008, 10).[75] Moreover, Brown was not the only minister whose ability to take the lead in particular policy areas challenges the view that the PM is the overlord on European issues. In successive treaty negotiations, the government's position was effectively decided by ministers. This was the case, for example, during the Convention of the Future of Europe, when the then Home Secretary, David Blunkett, was one of a number of ministers who took an active lead in defining the UK's position.

Conclusion

Approaching the Labour Party's European policy from the perspective of preferences and preference formation sheds important new light on a topic that has generated a voluminous literature. It reveals that, beneath often dramatic shifts in position, there has been strong continuity in the party's underlying dispositions towards Europe. Although Labour has occupied multiple positions on the pro- and anti-integration spectrum, it has proceeded from an international or global conception of British interests, preferred to preserve sovereignty where possible, and has regarded 'Europe' as an arena through which to pursue British interests, rather than as an inherently noble cause.

The focus on preference formation, moreover, highlights the range of factors that have shaped Labour's views of Europe and how these have changed over time. Rather than forcing a reading of the development of Labour's preferences in a particular direction, or assuming that they can be inferred from any of the party's more fundamental ideological commitments, this perspective makes it possible to arrive at a multivariate account of the underlying processes. Ideology, geopolitical interests and party organisation have been the most important influences on the formation of Labour's preferences, but their relative impact has varied across time. This finding questions attempts to explain the post-war development of Labour policy in terms of a single factor and suggests that the processes that led to the turn towards pro-Europeanism in the 1980s need to be set in historical perspective.

Appendix: list of interviewees

Charles Clarke MP, former Labour minister, London, 28 March 2007.

Lord Kinnock, former Leader of the Labour Party, London, 26 April 2007.

Roger Liddle, special adviser on European affairs to Prime Minister Tony Blair, London, 3 April 2007.

Lord McNally, former political adviser to Foreign Secretary James Callaghan, head of Prime Minister Callaghan's political office, member of the Social Democratic Party, and leader of the Liberal Democrats in the House of Lords, London, 24 April 2007.

Lord Owen, former Labour foreign secretary and founder of the Social Democratic Party, London, 19 April 2007.

Lord Radice, former Labour frontbencher, London, 30 April 2007.

Sir Stephen Wall, former head of the European Secretariat in the Cabinet office in London and EU adviser to Prime Minister Tony Blair, London, 21 November 2005.

Notes

1   I should like to express my gratitude to the five former Labour frontbenchers, the former member of Tony Blair's staff at 10 Downing Street, the former international secretary, the Labour Party official, the former special adviser at the Foreign and Commonwealth office, the two senior civil servants and the trade union official who kindly granted interviews in 2007. Their insights were invaluable. Thanks are also due to Dionyssis G. Dimitrakopoulos for helpful comments on earlier versions of this chapter, the participants at the workshops hosted in the School of Politics and Sociology, Birkbeck, University of London in 2006 and 2007, where earlier versions of this paper were presented, and especially to Anand Menon for very useful feedback on previous drafts. Last but not least, Sara Connolly offered

encouragement and showed her usual forbearance as the paper underwent yet another round of revision. The usual disclaimer applies.

2 Authors do not always differentiate between European integration, understood as specifically supranational integration, and other forms of regional co-operation. 'The Europeans' was a term used in earlier debates within the Labour Party to refer to the former Continental advocates of supranational integration.

3 In the late 1940s, Keep Left, Federalists and the Committee of Study and Action for a United Socialist States of Europe were the main pro-European groupings. Keep Left and Federalists later merged to form the All Party Committee and the Labour Europe Group. In the 1960s, pro-Europeans pressed their case through the cross-party Common Market Campaign, the Campaign for Democratic Socialism, which published the *Common Market Broadsheet*, and the Labour Common Market Committee. Roy Jenkins and Bill Rodgers were active in the latter, which worked closely with the Federal Union. Labour pro-Europeans were also active in the European Movement. The main opposing group within the Labour Party was the Britain and the Common Market group, which later became the Common Market Safeguards Campaign.

4 For example, it had rejected Briand's proposal for a united Europe on the grounds that: 'an exclusive and independent European Union of the kind proposed might emphasize or create tendencies to inter-continental rivalries and hostilities' (cited in Featherstone 1988, 43; see also Boyce 1980).

5 As with the similar pronouncements made by Winston Churchill (Young 1998, 5–25), it is not clear whether Attlee believed that Britain should be part of these federalising efforts.

6 Bevin's hope was that European unity would enable the Red Army to be kept at bay 'until such time as the economic buoyancy of Britain and the Commonwealth could restore the country to equality with the United States and the Soviet Union' (Broad 2001, 9).

7 Bevin's actions in 1948 drew the admiration of pro-integrationists hopeful of British leadership, such as Paul-Henri Spaak (see Young 1984).

8 Bevin commented on the possibility of European Union as follows: 'I don't like it. I don't like it. When you open that Pandora's Box you'll find it full of Trojan horses' (Lord Strang, *Home and Abroad*, quoted by Young 1984, 206).

9 Namely, Articles 25 and 46. Justifying this position in an address to the Commons, Bevin declared: 'we are not prepared, without further thought, to hand over . . . appeal rights to another body' (Broad 2001, 26).

10 As Bevin was in hospital, Attlee on holiday, and Sir Stafford Cripps sick, France's ultimatum was directed to Herbert Morrison, as acting PM. Morrison's reaction ('It's no good. We cannot do it. The Durham miners won't wear it'), as Broad notes (2001, 20), 'has passed into folklore'.

11 As Newman suggests (1983, 159), Labour saw EDC as a way of securing French agreement, which was a precondition of German rearmament, and the restoration of sovereignty. Ultimately, however, these objectives were met via another route. Following the rejection of EDC by the French parliament and at the initiative of Anthony Eden, a Conservative government negotiated the Paris agreements that led to the creation of the WEU.

12 However, it also made clear that, provided certain conditions were met (Newman 1983, 196, fn. 9), it would not stand in the way of other countries.

13 The WEU was stripped of the supranational aspects of the EDC.

14 See Newman (1983, 163–201) and Robins (1979, 11–43) for accounts of internal party discussions. The terms were set largely by a memorandum prepared by David Ennals, following a request of the NEC's Home Committee to the Financial and Economic Policy Sub-Committee. The central issue, it appeared, was not whether

Britain should or should not accede, but on what terms. The paper highlighted six key areas for negotiation. These included the impact of accession on economic growth; the protection of key agricultural products; the impact on British industry; the right of other EFTA states to join at the same time and on similar terms as the UK; the importance of not harming the economic interests of the Commonwealth; and the wider consequences of membership for the Commonwealth and the UK's independent world role.

15 Gaitskell later claimed to have been embarrassed by his extreme rhetoric, which he insisted did not reflect his true views (Broad 2001, 51–3).

16 Its immediate response to de Gaulle's veto was to try to debunk a 'new Conservative myth . . . [that the] Government were within an ace of achieving a satisfactory agreement only to find the prize snatched from their grasp by an intransigent Frenchman [and invoking] vital national and Commonwealth interests' (quoted in Camps 1966, 128).

17 Although he insisted at the same time that financing arrangements for the CAP would need to be agreed by the Six before enlargement negotiations could begin.

18 The idea was first proposed by Douglas Jay in 1968 and taken up by Tony Benn and the NEC.

19 However, the decision provoked the resignation of four of its members: Roy Jenkins, Shirley Williams, Bill Rodgers and David Owen.

20 See Butler and Kitzinger (1976).

21 Wilson had invited Helmut Schmidt to talk to the Cabinet and to address a special conference of the Labour Party in November 1974 and, as one interviewee indicated to the current author was, from that moment, convinced that he must win the referendum. See Young (1998, 282–3) and Zeigler (1993, 43, 430, 432, 439).

22 Following the announcement of the results, Wilson voiced the hope that '[t]he political argument in Britain is over' (Byrd 1975), while Benn declared: 'I have just been in receipt of a very clear message from the British people' (*The Times*, 7 June 1975).

23 Owen responded to Shore's remark that Community membership amounted to 'a rape of the British people and of their rights and constitution', by pointing to the hypocrisy of those who had insisted on 'a constitutional outrage first to let the British people decide in 1975', but now would 'not even give them a chance to determine their own destiny'.

24 Gerald Kaufman called it famously 'the longest suicide note in history'.

25 'I made it clear that that party policy would have to change . . . It was very clear that the integration of economies by then meant that unilateral action was not going to be enough . . . It was coming home to me, as it was coming home to Trade Unionists, that unless we were calling from the inside, we weren't calling' (Kinnock, quoted in Pappamikail 1998, 207).

26 Regular seminars were held with socialists from France and Germany in 1985–6, and Kinnock began to cultivate relations with leading figures on the Left across the Continent.

27 Although Labour was entitled to join the Confederation of the Socialist Parties of the European Community ('Confed') on accession in 1973, the party refused to fight on a joint manifesto in 1979 (Pappamikail 1998, 207). In addition, the Labour delegation to the European Parliament quickly gained a reputation for being 'more Gaullist than the Gaullists' (quoted in Featherstone 1988, 60), demonstrating very quickly how mistaken had been the remark attributed to James Callaghan: 'I don't think we are going to be any more troublesome than the French' (*The Economist*, 28 June 1975, cited in Featherstone 1988, 41).

28 In an article in the *New Socialist* in 1984, Kinnock called for a 'new Messina conference', to decide whether to 'reject, revise or rewrite' the Rome Treaty, and

far-reaching institutional reform, which, as one commentator suggested, was a wishlist so broad it 'suggests it was a smokescreen behind which he could manoeuvre' (Broad 2001, 158).

29 It read:

> Labour's aim is to work constructively with our EEC partners to promote economic expansion and combat unemployment. However, we will stand up for British interests within the European Community and will seek to put an end to the abuses and scandals of the CAP. We shall, like other member countries, reject EEC interference with our policy for national recovery and renewal.

30 Both Shore and Foot, for example, spoke out against QMV and the co-operation procedure. Even the leadership had expressed fears that the SEA might represent 'the triumph of Euro-Thatcherism' (Judge, quoted in Broad 2001, 166).

31 There was also the familiar denunciation of the CAP.

32 Kinnock (1994, 543) reports that he had always thought in terms of 'two innings'.

33 Their work was supplemented by the Economic Sub-Committee of the Shadow Cabinet, set up in early 1988 and in which the Cambridge economist, John Eatwell, played a leading role. The Shadow Communications Agency under Philip Gould also had an input.

34 The 1989 European elections were significant, not least because Labour withdrew its opposition to the formation of a Party of European Socialists and joined the Socialist Group in the European Parliament (Pappamikail 1998, 209). In recognition of his personal role in this rapprochement, the Confed approached Kinnock in 1992 after his resignation as Labour leader with a view to his becoming its president (Westlake 2001, 637).

35 As Margaret Beckett recalled, commenting on Smith's contribution to the policy review process two decades later, 'just five years earlier [these views] had been very far from accepted doctrine within the Labour Party' (2007).

36 The fact that Smith had been a long-standing pro-European made him less vulnerable to the charges of opportunism that had been laid against Kinnock.

37 One interviewee mused that, had the Deutschmark been revalued, as Labour's outgoing leader, Neil Kinnock, had urged in a letter published by the *Financial Times* on 17 or 18 July 1992, the pressure on the main EMS economies might have been eased, and Black Wednesday and its consequences avoided (private correspondence, 18 November 2009).

38 See Shaw (2007) for a discussion of New Labour in office.

39 Margaret Beckett, as party deputy, had been acting leader of the party.

40 As well as cultivating relationships through personal visits, the party sought to put an infrastructure in place to make and manage relationships. Blair entrusted a member of the policy unit with responsibility for keeping in contact with prime ministers' offices in other EU states, and Peter Mandelson, minister without portfolio, for contact with parties of the Centre-Left.

41 Proposals were launched on European defence with France, in 1998 (the St Malo Declaration); on economic reform with Spain, in 2000, which fed into the Lisbon summit; on immigration with Italy and Spain, in 2002; and on several issues with various partners at different stages of the Convention on the Future of Europe (Menon 2004).

42 Peston (2005, 191) suggests that Balls and Brown were concerned by Blair's decision in March 1996 to match the Conservatives' pledge to hold a referendum on adoption of the euro, and considered for several months how they might best pre-empt problematic outcomes.

43 These concern: the extent to which business cycles and economic structures are compatible, so that the UK and others could exist comfortably with interest rates

on a permanent basis; whether there is sufficient flexibility to deal with any problems that emerge; whether joining EMU would create better conditions for companies making long-term decisions to invest in Britain; the impact of EMU entry on the competitive position of the UK's financial services industry; and whether EMU will promote higher growth, stability and lasting increase in jobs (HM Treasury n.d.).

44 As a senior EU official remarked, 'Blair was a first-class leader in Europe. But he failed to make the case for Europe in Britain or to use his influence with the US effectively' (http://news.bbc.co.uk/1/hi/uk_politics/6760937.stm). Sir Stephen Wall, former head of the European Secretariat of the Cabinet Office and adviser to the prime minister on Europe, has contended that Blair's timidity in regard to the press was at least partly responsible. In an interview published some months after his resignation, Sir Stephen recalled that he had 'thought then, when I read that Tony Blair was going off to Australia to secure the support of Rupert Murdoch, that this is going to put the kibosh on European policy', adding that:

> Maintaining the support of the Murdoch press is obviously very critical to Labour's interest – or that is how it seemed. I do regret that with the most massive majority in post-war history we couldn't have done more to turn it round.
>
> (*Daily Telegraph*, 25 September 2004, online at www.openeurope.
> org.uk/media-centre/article.aspx?newsid= 51,
> accessed on 29 December 2009)

45 The reorganisation of the staff at Number 10, which involved the amalgamation of foreign and EU affairs, suggested that Europe would not have the importance that it had under his predecessor.

46 My vision of Europe moving forward is global Europe – not just an internal single market that looks inwards but a driving force of the new fast-changing global market place. An open, outward looking, flexible global Europe competing on and prosperous because of its skills, its innovation and its creative talents. In this way the enlarged Europe moves forward from its original objective of preserving the peace to its future achievement – widening and deepening opportunity and prosperity not just for some but for all. That is why I am confident that – momentous as the challenges we are currently facing are – we can, by making the right long term decisions, meet and master them.

47 Labour took 15.7 per cent of the votes cast in 2009, its worst ever showing in a national election, and nearly seven percentage points down on 2004, which was its previous lowest share since 1918.

48 The Labour Party had been elected on a programme of economic modernisation, but the technological revolution had failed to materialise, the National Plan had been quietly forgotten, and the pound was embattled (see Padgett and Paterson 1991, 150–2; Howell 1976, 251).

49 It is important, however, to put the disagreement between the three larger member states into context and to recall that US intervention divided, not only the three larger member states, but the EU-15 – and, after 1 May 2004, the EU-25 – and that it was France and Germany, not the UK, that were in the minority (Smith 2005, 715). Under these circumstances, it could not credibly be claimed that the UK had betrayed Europe. Still, EU divisions and London's support for Washington did appear to undermine Blair's oft-repeated claim that Britain did not need to choose between Europe and America, but could be a bridge between the two.

50 As one interviewee observed in private correspondence with the current author,

> It was a long journey (particularly for the Left of the Party) to see Social Europe as the best protector of workers' rights rather than as a capitalist conspiracy

against them. The tragedy is that, having made that journey, the Party under Blair and Brown retained the fixation with Atlanticism and the Anglo-Saxon model rather than embracing Europe more whole-heartedly.

(17 November 2009)

51 Labour had organised relatively late in Britain and was not formed as a revolutionary socialist or Marxist party. The party had a distinctly labourist ethos. Internationalism and fraternity were not well developed within the party.

52 On the left, for example, Tony Benn supported the 1967 membership bid (see Robins 1979, 57). On the right, Douglas Jay, Denis Healey, Peter Shore and Austin Mitchell were Eurosceptics.

53 Bevin told the House of Commons on 15 September that the proposed constitution for European Union 'will not stand the test of examination for a moment' and suggested that the economic weakness of Europe was now 'an obstacle rather than a spur' (Featherstone 1988, 46). At the negotiations, the Labour Group, led by Dalton, opposed plans where the assembly would play a central role and insisted on an executive composed of foreign ministers acting by unanimity.

54 Dalton explained the party's opposition to membership at the 1953 party conference as follows:

> We are not prepared to hand over to a supranational authority that might well be dominated by reactionary elements' decisions on matters which we judge vital to our national life; such matters as the scope of socialisation, the means of maintaining full employment or the distribution of wealth through the policy of fair shares.

(Cited in Featherstone 1988, 50)

55 See Wickham-Jones (1996) for a discussion of Labour's economic policy from 1970 until the early 1980s.

56 Concerns about the standard of living had been raised in the 1960s in relation to the impact on the 'ordinary people of Britain' of Labour's deflationary policies and about the consequences of Britain's entry to the EEC for the price of food. The White Paper, *In place of strife*, published in 1969, had further exacerbated intra-party tensions with its proposals for tighter regulation of industrial relations. The same sensitivities about an assault on the working class were re-ignited by the Heath government's 'Selsdon man' agenda, which was interpreted as an attempt to end the post-war consensus, and the same government's Industrial Relations and Housing Finance Acts provoked particular hostility.

57 One delegate at the special Party Congress in 1971 gave voice to this heightened sense of partisanship as follows: 'if the Tories are in favour of it . . . if Ted Heath is in favour of it, I am against it' (quoted in Newman 1983, 222). See also the remarks made by Neil Kinnock at the special Labour Party Congress, 1971, quoted in Robins (1979: 82).

58 See Hill (2001) for a discussion of the development of the Labour Party's economic strategy between 1979 and 1997.

59 Attlee commented in 1937 that:

> The age-long immunity from attack of this country has created a habit of mind in the people that is deeply seated . . . This insularity has always made it difficult for British Socialists to understand completely their Continental comrades. Continental Socialists are often puzzled by the attitudes of British Labour representatives.

(Quoted in Broad 2001, 2)

Two years later, in words that, as Broad (2001, 3) notes, proved remarkably prescient, G. D. H. Cole remarked on the same ambiguity:

We socialists are, broadly speaking, the only internationalists: we alone have a clear vision of a system transcending national frontiers . . . [Yet at the same time] . . . It is quite on the cards that Great Britain, with the British Dominions, instead of entering into a supra-national state system based on Western Europe, will become an economical and political satellite of the United States, and that Europe will make its plans without the participation of the British Empire.

60 Dalton wrote to Bevin in 1950, in the wake of the Schuman Plan, that: 'No doubt . . . the experiences of war, including the experience of being occupied by the enemy has broken the back of nationalist pride in many of these countries and this helps to popularise the federalist myth' (quoted in Newman 1983, 123).

61 As Bevin commented in 1949, 'We must remain, as we have always been in the past, different in character from other European nations and fundamentally incapable of wholehearted integration with them' (cited in Bullock 1983, 734).

62 Wilson was not a strong Atlanticist, and Smith was only mildly so. The party under Foot was isolationist, whereas, under Kinnock, the party's commitment to unilateral disarmament made his relationship with the US government difficult.

63 In similar vein, Dalton told the 1953 party conference that, 'we as Socialists and members of the Commonwealth hold ourselves responsible for making our contribution towards bridging the gap between the living standards of the developed and of the under-developed countries.'

64 See Russell (2005) for further details.

65 For this reason, McKenzie (1963, 635) concluded his study of power in the Conservative and Labour Parties with the observation that:

Whatever the role granted in theory to the extra-parliamentary wings of the parties, in practice final authority rests in both parties with the parliamentary party and its leadership. In this fundamental respect the distribution of power within the two major parties is the same.

66 For example, Hugh Scanlon of the AUEW.

67 At the 1969 conference, for example, a TGWU resolution, accepted by the NEC, had laid down strict terms for British entry, while, a year later, conference had passed a resolution supporting membership on acceptable terms, but the unions had led a groundswell of opposition.

68 In addition, the 1980 party conference decided to include the extra-parliamentary party in the election of the party leader, and a special party conference in January 1981 agreed that the PLP should have a minority of votes in the new electoral college.

69 The National Policy Forum works to a three-year cycle, drawing on internal and external policy sources. It meets every six months, without journalists present. The process is dominated by frontbenchers.

70 Interview conducted by the author with a former Labour frontbencher, 20 April 2007.

71 As was Foot's, though for quite different reasons.

72 Kinnock's achievement was to transform a 'party that was divided, electorally defeated, disorganised and dominated by the Left into a united social democratic party that could provide a significant electoral threat to the Conservative Party' (Smith 1994, 560).

73 For a discussion, see Rawnsley (2000, 72–88).

74 Brown made a number of media interventions on 'Europe' (see, e.g., *The Guardian*, 29 May 2003, the *Daily Telegraph*, 19 September 2003, the *Wall Street Journal*, 24 October 2005) while he was chancellor. Although Blair could, in theory, have moved him to another ministerial position or even sacked him, such

a move would perhaps have been impossible in practice, given Brown's seniority within the party and his status as a joint architect of New Labour. With Blair and Brown taking opposite sides, other Cabinet members rarely ventured views on 'Europe' (interview with former senior official).

75 As to the source of red lines at the 2003–4 IGC, see Menon 2004.

5 The Panhellenic Socialist Movement and European integration

The primacy of the leader

Dionyssis G. Dimitrakopoulos and
Argyris G. Passas

Introduction[1]

This chapter focuses on the Panhellenic Socialist Movement (PASOK) and seeks to trace the origin and the content of its preferences on European integration since its establishment in 1974. It challenges the established view that – couched as it is in PASOK's rhetoric in the immediate post-1974 era – construes PASOK as an initially instinctively anti-European political party that subsequently performed a policy U-turn, a true political transformation by turning from a vocal anti-EEC stance to a pro-European (even federalist) attitude (Tsardanidis 1998, 295, 299, 300; Kazakos 1994, 5; Verney 1987, 259–60, 263; Featherstone 1988, 178; Couloumbis 1993, 126; Featherstone 1994, 158–9). It also takes issue with more nuanced accounts that refer to a 'subtle metamorphosis' of PASOK's stance since 1977, resulting from the exigencies of PASOK's political competition strategy – as well as shifts in public opinion and a 'pragmatic adjustment' to the requirements of governing Greece (Verney 1994, 347–9; Loulis 1984, 379; Coufoudakis 1987, 238–40). The chapter advances four claims.

First, PASOK did not perform a U-turn, because it did not have a clearly elaborated and explicitly articulated policy on European integration from which to depart. This is demonstrated, not by the absence of a rhetorically robust thesis, as the 'ΕΟΚ και ΝΑΤΟ το ίδιο συνδικάτο'[2] slogan and opposition to accession to the European Communities were unequivocal, but by the absence of a clear definition of the kind of Europe that it stood *for* in the second half of the 1970s.[3] In the absence of a response to this question, it is impossible to refer to a 'U-turn'. Second, electoral, economic and geo-strategic interests, ideas (populism, initially; modernisation along social democratic lines in the second half of the 1990s) and, more importantly, institutions (specifically, the autonomy of the leader vis-à-vis the party organisation and membership) played a major role in the gradual definition of PASOK's views on European integration. The interplay of these factors and their outcome are time sensitive. Although it is exemplified by specific events (such as the decision to support the ratification of the Maastricht Treaty and the determined pursuit of accession to the third stage of economic and monetary union (EMU)), it ought to be construed as a *process*. Third, the gradual elaboration and determined pursuit of advanced preferences regarding the future of Europe – couched in the social democratic tradition as well as practical considerations – were the hallmark of the Simitis era (1996–2004); it is only during this time that PASOK (then the ruling party) had a clear objective regarding the future of Europe, as well as a clear strategy regarding the country's involvement therein. Finally, although this marked the high point in the history of the party's policy on European integration, their adoption and pursuit have been ephemeral since they do not appear to enjoy the support of powerful 'carriers' or a majority within the party; in that sense, the Simitis era can be likened to a Europeanist 'intermezzo'. Indeed, as will be demonstrated in this chapter, under George A. Papandreou, PASOK appears to have abandoned the left-wing federalist Europeanism doggedly pursued under the leadership of Costas Simitis.

The discussion of the content and the origins of PASOK's rhetoric and practice regarding European integration since 1974 can be divided into four phases: 1974–84; 1985–95; 1996–2004 and 2004–to date.

Rhetoric and tactics as substitutes for policy

The origins of radical rhetoric

Since its establishment in September 1974, PASOK has had to reconcile competing and often contradictory demands. This is so despite its initially narrow electoral basis[4] and Andreas Papandreou's decision to break with *Enossi Kentrou* (EK), the dominant but factious party of the Centre-Left of the pre-1967 period. During this period, and especially the crucial years that preceded its accession to power, the remarkable diversity of PASOK's leadership, cadres and voters was a key source of the multiple messages that emanated from it, with regard to both European integration and other issues. Indeed, three groups can be identified at the point of PASOK's establishment, namely the 'leftists', the 'technocrats' and, finally, the 'conformists' (i.e. centrists) who stemmed from EK – the Declaration of 3 September 1974, the party's founding document, reflects an attempt to reconcile their demands (Spourdalakis 1998, 21–2).[5]

The first group brought together mainly young activists who had participated in the anti-junta struggle at home and abroad and relied on a Marxist understanding of contemporary Greek politics and society, coupled with nationalist overtones, as well as influences stemming from dependence theory. Their rhetoric enabled PASOK gradually to attract voters from older generations (especially those who had been defeated in the civil war of the late 1940s) who had hitherto supported other parties of the Left, especially the Communist Party. The second group was composed mainly of well-educated supporters of the Centre-Left, many of whom had become politically active (on the basis of a modernisation agenda) during the turbulent years that preceded the advent of the dictatorial regime in 1967. The final group brought together mainly MPs and aspiring politicians, many of whom had close personal ties with Andreas Papandreou and his father, the last leader of EK, and brought with them an unparalleled understanding of grass-roots politics. Many of the leftists and the 'conformists' were steeped in populism. Nationalism was an additional hallmark of their worldview and rhetoric. Nationalism, anti-Americanism and wider anti-Western attitudes largely stemmed from the country's recent history. They were founded not only on the American support for the military junta but also on a sense of humiliation after the Turkish invasion of Cyprus in the summer of 1974. As a result, PASOK's formative statements reflected the prevalent feeling of anti-Americanism that dominated Greek politics in the aftermath of the fall of the dictatorial regime. This often provided fertile ground for the leftists, who attacked the EEC as a sidekick of the USA that was dominated by large member states. They construed the EEC as part of the West, whose interests conflicted with those of the nation.

Much of PASOK's early rhetoric on European integration and other issues reflected this understanding. This contributed to PASOK being seen as little more than a protest movement. However, much of that rhetoric also mirrored real political and socio-economic issues that the country faced. Though Andreas Papandreou's charisma enabled him to become the focal point for the aforementioned diverse groups,[6] in reality it was his decision to base PASOK's establishment on three common and fundamental issues that brought these groups together. These issues concerned (a) Greece's place in the world, (b) the make-up and the actual operation of the country's democratic institutions and (c) significant social inequalities.

PASOK's early slogans, such as 'Η Ελλάδα ανήκει στους Έλληνες',[7] and the demands for social justice (captured in the constant references to PASOK as the party of the 'non-privileged Greeks') reflected both profound economic and social inequalities, which had dogged the country at least since the end of the civil war in the late 1940s, and a prevalent sense of the need to emancipate the country from ties that had often served its allies but not its own interests (Coufoudakis 1987, 232). At the same time, the nationalist rhetoric enabled PASOK to distance itself from both of its main political rivals. Nea Dimokratia (ND), established in 1974 and led by Konstantinos Karamanlis, was the dominant party of the Centre-Right, whose unequivocal pro-Western orientation was exemplified by its leader's statement that 'ανήκομεν εις τη Δύση'.[8] PASOK also sought to distance itself from (without challenging) the Communist Party, while wooing its electorate.[9] Although it rejected the Soviet model, much of its rhetoric reflected both the concerns and the terminology of Communist Party voters. The nationalist overtones of PASOK's anti-Western rhetoric reflected the nascent political movement's need to carve out its own space (and message) in the rapidly changing Greek political landscape of the mid-to late-1970s, but it also mirrored a powerful demand for the confident reassertion of the nation's independence.

At the same time, significant social inequalities reflected both the country's under-developed economy and the results of more than two decades of bitter internal political strife that followed the end of the civil war. The latter created and perpetuated a profound feeling of exclusion or even oppression[10] inflicted on those who were (or were thought to be) on the 'wrong side' of the political centre ground, while the former had led, not only to large and successive waves of emigration (predominantly to the West) during the 1950s and 1960s, but also to the perpetuation of major economic problems, including the dominant role of family enterprises of a primitive character (especially in agriculture and tourism), an overgrown service sector, an ineffective civil service that was based on (and the victim of) patronage, and an uncompetitive industrial sector that relied on protection from foreign imports and was mainly geared towards internal demand (Tsoukalas 1969, chapter 9). These economic structures largely reflected a quasi-institutionalised emphasis of public policies on short-term gains, irrespective of medium- and long-term consequences, as well as the short-term logic and speculative character of Greek capitalists, who were more interested in maximising income from public subsidies than in modernising their business practices (Tsakalotos 2001, 142).

Finally, the domestic political landscape of the mid-1970s was also marked by the compelling popular demand for the real democratisation of the Greek polity. This was the logical consequence of decades of bitter internal political strife in which the royal family, segments of the armed and security forces, and powerful families often conspired with their foreign allies and acted against the wishes of the people. Thus, the inclusion of the objective of veritable popular sovereignty and substantive democratisation in PASOK's founding declaration of September 1974 came as no surprise.

Against this background, it is hard to see why a newly established political party should have sought to develop a set of fully fledged proposals or objectives regarding the future of the then stagnating EC, which, at that point in time, had little to offer in terms of direct assistance to an under-developed economy. Nevertheless, Prime Minister Karamanlis's historic decision to seek Greece's quick accession to the EC provided a major impetus for a fierce political debate on the issue of membership; it is in that context that PASOK's robust rhetorical statements became the substitute for a coherent policy. This debate was marked by PASOK's sustained rejection (until the general election of 1977) of the notion of membership. This marked a radical change from the consensus between the two main parties of the Centre-Left and the Right, which (unlike the Left) supported the Association agreement (including the prospect of membership) in the early 1960s (Pateras 1984, chapter 1; Verney 1987, 256). Two important caveats ought to be added here.

First, although Karamanlis's decision to relaunch[11] Greece's accession bid was explicitly based on *political* considerations (especially the need to strengthen democracy, secure the nation's territorial integrity against its aggressive eastern neighbour and reduce the country's dependence on the USA), PASOK's criticism was founded on primarily *economic* grounds, though political considerations were present too.[12] This pronounced emphasis on the economic aspects of membership (and European integration as a whole) has remained a central feature of PASOK's stance ever since.[13] Second, the debate regarding accession to the EC became a key political battleground for PASOK. The public debate attracted attention, and Andreas Papandreou used it skilfully as a platform for the presentation of simplistic, at times ill-defined and often contradictory views, whose main strength lay in their capacity to echo (and often amplify) fears, and a wider defensive attitude, as well as legitimate concerns regarding the country's economy.

These contradictions are extremely revealing. Papandreou made masterful use of leftist political rhetoric essentially in an effort to turn PASOK from a protest movement and an elite party[14] to a broad political alliance (of often competing interests and views) and, subsequently, a mass party whose vocation was to govern the country. This is unsurprising, as the issue of membership of the EC combined two major strands of his thinking, namely the Harvard-educated and former Berkeley economics professor's preoccupation with issues of economic development and the political leader's interest in broader geopolitical issues such as the Cold War and the North–South divide. Three factors account for PASOK's initial formal rejection of the principle of membership.

First, given that the Left had opposed the Association agreement[15] and the principle of membership after 1974, a party such as PASOK that aspired to become the main anti-right actor in Greek politics could not afford to be seen to support one of the core choices of the conservative ND. Rather, the issue of membership of the EC was an excellent opportunity for the nascent party to shape and reflect the (often assumed) wishes of the electorate that it aspired to represent. Second, given PASOK's analysis of the country's economic problems and its position in the world, support for membership (which carries both opportunities and duties) could have blurred the simple message that its leader wanted it to carry. Indeed, PASOK's formal analysis drew not only on Marxism but also on dependence theory (especially the work of André Gunder Frank and Samir Amin) and saw the country as part not only of Europe but also of the Balkans and the Mediterranean, i.e. the periphery whose interests differed from those of the imperialist centre. As a result, the exigencies of its economic development and political emancipation could not be reconciled with membership of a Western organisation that was (a) composed of prosperous capitalist states and (b) lacking the means to engage in market intervention, which was one of PASOK's explicitly chosen means to promote economic development. PASOK expressed the fear that, as the EC was the junior partner of the USA, it 'would trade full membership of the EC for concessions on Cyprus and the Aegean which would satisfy the Americans' (Verney 1987, 259). Third, in addition to these considerations, one key institutional factor helped shape PASOK's initial declarations on the principle of membership, namely the predominant role of its leader in intra-party politics. Although PASOK's establishment had been followed by an unprecedented political dialogue at the grass-roots level, most of the party's pronouncements on major issues reflected its leader's tactical and strategic choices. This was the result of his hegemonic position within the party that, nevertheless, could not conceal the often uneasy co-existence of activists and members of the leadership whose views differed remarkably. Indeed, at least until 1977, the party had not debated the issue of membership of the EC (interviews with former PASOK Cabinet ministers). Rather, Andreas Papandreou's pronouncements were treated as the party's policy (Verney 1994, 298).

The party could not aspire to capture power without expressing the wishes of a large (and diverse) part of the electorate. Papandreou's public pronouncements on the principle of membership reflected this need even from an early stage. For example, on the occasion of the visit of the then French president, Valéry Giscard d'Estaing, in 1975, *Exormisi*, the party's newspaper, denounced Karamanlis's pursuit of membership as a 'sell-out' and a threat to national sovereignty, but Papandreou stated that, although PASOK was an opposition party, it supported Karamanlis's policy on France and the EC (Spourdalakis 1998, 41 fn. 33). In addition, during the early 1960s, Papandreou had publicly supported[16] the Association agreement, largely on the basis of the fact that it could facilitate the country's economic modernisation. Such contradictory statements reflected Papandreou's efforts to build a *volkspartei* capable of reflecting the wishes of large segments of public opinion.[17]

Preparing for government

The general election of 1977 marked a turning point in PASOK's handling of the issue of membership of the EC. PASOK became the main opposition party by nearly doubling its share of the vote (to 25 per cent, which corresponded to almost one-third of the seats in parliament). Papandreou's astute (and audacious) political calculation of 1974 was beginning to pay dividends. By choosing to create a new political party in 1974 instead of leading EK, he broke not with EK's traditional electorate but with that party's ageing leadership. His objective was to attract EK's rather heterogeneous electorate without being associated with that party's leadership. Indeed, EK was the main source of PASOK's new voters in the 1977 election. Despite Papandreou's disappointment, other senior PASOK officials interpreted this result as an indication that the electorate was beginning to see it as a party of governmental vocation (interview with former PASOK Cabinet minister). The newly established party had already made significant progress towards becoming part of the mainstream of Greek politics, but it still fell short of having the support of the majority of voters. Rhetorical devices would not enable it to overcome this barrier. Rather, the party had to have a programme and be seen to be mature enough to govern the country.

While Karamanlis was actively pursuing the objective of membership, Papandreou's task was equally Herculean. He had to (a) steer the party towards a realistic programme and (b) attract even more centrist voters. These combined needs provided a major impetus for the gradual disengagement from both the previous extreme statements rejecting the prospect of membership of the EC and the notion that, as PASOK was in opposition, its leader could say in public whatever he wanted. Indeed, Papandreou was, at the time, taking the prospect of membership much more seriously (and realistically) than his earlier public statements would suggest (interview). There are two major indications of this fact. First, when he appointed a committee (chaired by economics professor Apostolos Lazaris) to draft (in 1977) PASOK's programme on the basis of which he was planning to fight the 1981 general election, he appointed Grigoris Varfis (a former senior civil servant in the Ministry of National Economy who was not a party member) to ensure that PASOK's commitments would be compatible with obligations deriving from membership of the EC (interview). Varfis, an economist, had unsurpassed inside knowledge of these negotiations, because he had been a senior member of the Greek negotiating team, from which he resigned in January 1977 as a result of his disagreement with Prime Minister Karamanlis's efforts to achieve membership without paying particular attention to its terms.[18] Second, although he was aware of the public's preference for a clear (i.e. 'yes' or 'no') answer to the question of membership, Papandreou began gradually to move away from explicit references to withdrawal from the EC. Instead, he made increasing references to 'a special agreement'[19] and, closer to the 1981 general election, the renegotiation of the terms of membership and a referendum. Indeed, the party's 1981 electoral manifesto did not refer to withdrawal but to the renegotiation of the terms of membership (interview with former PASOK Cabinet minister).

The claims regarding renegotiation reflected an effort to portray PASOK as a party that was capable of promoting the national interest (unlike the Right, which was allegedly pursuing a 'sell-out'). The promise of a referendum mirrored PASOK's claim to protect 'popular sovereignty' while also drawing on the Labour government's experience and the British referendum of June 1975. The references to a 'special agreement' are more revealing in the sense that they support one of the key claims made in this chapter: PASOK did not have a clear view of the kind of Europe that it preferred in the late 1970s; rather, it was much more aware of (and vocal about) what it opposed. As a result, it was drawing selectively both on its own fuzzy ideology and events that were taking place primarily in the Greek, but also (though to a lesser extent) the broader international environment. In that respect, Norway's arrangement with the EC was used to lend credence to PASOK's claim regarding the 'special agreement' that it appeared to prefer over membership. Two compelling questions remained unanswered.

First, what would be the precise content of this special arrangement? Again, PASOK's rhetoric was much more explicit about what it sought to avoid – namely restrictions on macro-economic policy and surrendering controls over the movement of capital and goods – than what it sought to promote. Second, how far (if at all) could a country such as Greece rely on the example of

Norway, i.e. a prosperous country whose geopolitical position differed markedly from that of Greece? More importantly, if the EC was – as PASOK's analysis claimed – dominated by the large member states, how would a small *non*-member (with the characteristics of Greece) influence decision-making therein? If the claim regarding the Norwegian example was meant to show that there was an alternative to full membership, the claim regarding the referendum was part of a subtle but important strategic change whose aim was to shift the emphasis of PASOK's attacks from the EC to the government's handling of the negotiations (Verney 1994, 352).

The impact of the domestic political environment was becoming increasingly clear. While this process of change was taking place at the level of the national political landscape, disagreements within the party – exacerbated by the prospect of membership of the EC and the decisive election of 1981 – were beginning to surface. One important incident was indicative of the party's uneasy internal balance of power. Costas Simitis – a social democrat, academic and active member of the anti-junta resistance movement – resigned on 13 June 1979 on the occasion of the party's decision to withdraw a poster that, echoing Euro-communist views, indicated a more nuanced view on European integration: 'Όχι στην Ευρώπη των μονοπωλίων – Ναι στην Ευρώπη των λαών', it read[20] (Simitis 2005, 25). Although Papandreou's decision was partly motivated by his wish to limit the party political prospects of one of the party's most knowledgeable and respected senior cadres, it was also proof of the uneasy co-existence of leftists, centrists and social democrats. This incident also demonstrated the clear limits of Papandreou's strategy of papering over the party's internal ideological (and broader political) divisions. That this incident took place in June 1979 is not a coincidence. The accession agreement had been signed in Athens just a month earlier, and the parliament was about to debate its ratification. Although this meant that Papandreou had an excellent opportunity to prepare and present the party's own vision for the future of Europe and the country's role therein, he made a decision that was illustrative of his own tactical nous as well as his party's inability to provide a credible answer to a major political and economic issue: after making a brief statement, he chose to lead his party's MPs out of the chamber just as the debate was about to begin. The decision was made by the party's Executive Bureau in an emergency session literally minutes before the beginning of the parliamentary session. As a result, only two senior MPs (the centrists Alevras and Haralambopoulos) were aware of his decision prior to the commencement of the debate in parliament (Verney 1994, 354). The terminology that Papandreou used in his brief statement was indicative of his decision to maximise the political damage inflicted on the government (which, in turn, was expected to portray accession as a major success of its foreign policy) and steal the thunder from the Communist Party whose MPs had also decided to avoid the debate. He denounced the decision of the government (and the European Commission) to withhold the 'minutes' of the negotiations, for only they would enable parliament to know what concessions the government had made. He argued that this was an indication of the government's 'subservience' to foreign powers and claimed that membership would dilute popular sovereignty as a result of the supremacy of EC law. This was, he claimed, a major reason why PASOK rejected the principle of membership. Instead, PASOK refused to legitimise the process that the government had chosen and promised to first inform the people 'comprehensively and objectively' and then hold a referendum (Hellenic Parliament debate, 25 June 1979, 5499–500).

The major tactical strength of this decision lay in the idea that the government had turned membership into a *fait accompli*, despite PASOK's protests regarding its implications for national sovereignty. Coupled with the Greeks' endemic sense of the 'underdog', which politicians often cultivated, and the call for a referendum (which required the assent of the president of the Republic, a post that Karamanlis was expected to occupy at a later stage), Papandreou's decision was designed to provide an escape route for PASOK by amplifying the notion that membership was now a fact, indeed one with which a future PASOK-led government would have to deal. In other words, the issue of membership had been resolved, de facto, by Karamanlis (interview with former PASOK Cabinet minister). Papandreou's conviction about this is demonstrated by his subsequent public references to the costs of withdrawal and the notion that they would perhaps be greater than the cost of membership (Varfis n.d., 1).

In addition to these tactical considerations, Papandreou's decision also reflected the 'ideological agnosticism' that had permeated PASOK since its establishment. PASOK did not have a clearly defined ideological position on the EC; in fact, it is hard to pinpoint precisely PASOK's general ideological position (interview with former PASOK Cabinet minister). The rapid growth in PASOK's electoral support exacerbated the problem of its internal coherence. The internal divisions became more evident when the Committee for Analysis and Programming begun to develop PASOK's programme. As a leading member of the committee acknowledged, the end result was a combination of conservative, socialist, centrist and other viewpoints (interview with former PASOK Cabinet minister). The closer PASOK moved to becoming a catch-all party, in an effort to win the general election, the less adequate its frame of reference was. Greece joined the EC in January 1981, and nine months later PASOK won a landslide victory in the general election. Confronted with the reality of membership and the exigencies of governing the country, PASOK was compelled to move clearly and unequivocally from populist rhetoric to concrete action.

From rhetoric to praxis

PASOK's first four years in power were marked by the use of declarations as a substitute for action[21] on core foreign policy issues (Coufoudakis 1987, 248). In terms of EC policy, PASOK had to find a way out of its electoral pledges. The issue of membership was resolved in a typically incremental manner.

On the one hand, Papandreou quickly (and quietly) abandoned the pledge to organise a referendum. On the other hand, the government sought to renegotiate the terms of the country's membership, thus beginning to deal in a much more pragmatic way with serious (and undoubtedly real) economic problems.

Another part of Papandreou's problem had to do with the political personnel that he had at his disposal. Indeed, he was the only member of the first PASOK Cabinet who had ministerial experience, and even that dated back from the mid-1960s. Moreover, his government had to face a rather hostile civil service, which he intended to reform. A former technocrat himself, he appreciated the importance of expertise and experience in the management of government business. This is why he appointed Grigoris Varfis as European affairs minister, in charge of dealing with the entire EC portfolio, apart from European Political Co-operation (EPC) business, which remained the responsibility of Foreign Secretary Ioannis Haralambopoulos (a centrist). Varfis's main task was not only to manage relations with the EC but, crucially, to prepare a memorandum for the future of Greece's relationship with the EC. Varfis was extremely well placed to do it, not only because he had first-hand experience from the negotiations for Greece's accession, but also because he had considerable experience as a senior official with the Ministry of Co-ordination (then Ministry of National Economy, now Finance) and was well aware of the weaknesses of the Greek economy. In addition, Papandreou appointed Costas Simitis (who, at the time, was not an MP) to the crucial post of minister of agriculture.[22] Varfis drafted the memorandum with the assistance of a small team of civil servants, but without the direct input of party officials. The memorandum, presented to the EC in March 1982, is a remarkable text for three reasons.

First, far from echoing the populism of PASOK's rhetoric of the mid-to-late 1970s, it provided a dispassionate and balanced account of Greek demands that reflected the major problems that the Greek economy was likely to face in the context of the EC, as well as the unevenness of the accession agreement. After a concise and frank presentation of the structural weaknesses of the Greek economy, the memorandum referred clearly, not only to the responsibility of the Greek government to ensure the modernisation of the economy, but also to the harmonious development and the convergence of the economies of the member states as key objectives of the Treaty of Rome. The Greek government claimed that its efforts to resolve the country's economic problems (which had been exacerbated by the international crisis of the late 1970s) was not only part of the national interest but was in line with the EC's repeated calls for Community action for the reduction of the discrepancies between regions and states, though this action had been hampered by the absence of appropriate mechanisms, the inefficiencies of existing mechanisms and the absence of adequate funding (Hellenic Government 1982, 7–8). Highlighting the extremely modest redistributive capacity of the EC budget, the Greek government argued that EC membership was very likely to exacerbate the country's economic problems. Crucially, it pointed out that the Community's preferential treatment of the products of other Mediterranean member states had not been extended to Greek produce. In addition, although the Common Agricultural Policy covered on average 95 per cent of the agricultural products of the nine member states, it covered only 75 per cent of Greek produce and did so in a less intensive manner. Arguing that the fight against regional inequalities should be a top priority for the EC, the Greek government proposed the intro-duction of a new set of arrangements – including exemptions for reasonable periods of time – and the provision of funding to Greece under EC financial mechaisms. Highlighting the importance of its own five-year economic growth plan that the PASOK government was to implement, the Greek government also asked for EC support for domestic regional and sectoral policies – especially small and medium-sized companies and tourism; the flexible implementation of competition rules in a manner that would take into account the objectives of economic growth and the improvement of the population's living standards; and the revision of EC rules for the provision of funding in a manner that would take into account the peculiarities of the Greek economy, including the small size and low productivity of farms and the high inflation rate. Though the concluding section referred to the Greek government's belief that these measures were minimal requirements for the establishment of a regime that would not go against vital national interests, the document did not refer to the prospect of withdrawal from the EC. When Papandreou presented the draft memorandum to senior party officials, one of them asked for an explicit reference to a threat of withdrawal to be included in the text. Never-theless, Papandreou assured the authors of the memorandum that this would not be necessary and that he had already liaised with Karamanlis[23] about it (interview). This was, effectively, the end of PASOK's references to with-drawal from the EC. Indeed, when a foreign journalist asked Papandreou whether the rejection of the Greek memorandum would lead to the country's withdrawal from the EC, Papandreou stated that he had won an election, rather than organise a revolution (Varfis n.d., 1).

Second, unlike most of the public statements of PASOK officials and MPs who criticised the EC, the memorandum also made positive (though certainly limited) proposals for EC-wide changes, including the enhancement and the improved co-ordination of structural funds, a theme that the EC would subsequently deal with in the 1986 and the 1990–1 IGCs.

Finally, although the memorandum was consistent with PASOK's pre-electoral emphasis on the economic aspects of membership, the absence of any reference to political integration was striking. A left-wing government of a small member state that was facing clear security threats could, perhaps, be expected to at least raise the issue of solidarity. The absence of such references is indicative of a deeply embedded (though gradually weakening) sense of political distrust vis-à-vis Western Europe. This was exemplified by the Greek presidency's[24] decision to veto (under EPC procedures) a statement condemning the destruction by the Soviet Union's air force of a Korean civilian airliner in 1983. This led some MEPs to condemn Greek foreign policy as 'a blow to the whole idea of political co-operation', claiming that Greek foreign policy was 'more aligned with Moscow's than with those of (its) European friends' (cited in *Financial Times*, 16 September 1983, 2). Moreover, when the European Parliament voted on the 1984 Draft Treaty on European Union, PASOK MEPs chose to abstain.

The economic demands contained in the memorandum had two direct implications. First, the Commission agreed that, although the Greek government's five-year economic plan ought to be consistent with EC commitments,

a)   special provision would be made for financial assistance on infrastructure projects, employment and social policy measures, agriculture, transport and the environment, to the tune of more than £450m;
b)   more substantial aid amounting to nearly £1.6bn would be available under the Integrated Mediterranean Programmes, with Greece being the second largest beneficiary from this £3.97bn package, which would also cover parts of Italy and France;[25]
c)   £740m would be allocated to Greek agriculture between 1985 and 1991, £72m to forestry, £84m to fishing and £630m to 'general economic development'; and, in addition
d)   efforts would be made to improve Greece's 'take up' of EEC funds despite (or, rather, because of) the deficiencies of the Athenian bureaucracy (*Financial Times*, 6 May 1983, 2).

Second, this outcome allowed Papandreou to claim that his strategy had been vindicated and that his government had honoured the pledge to renegotiate (and improve) the terms of Greek membership of the EC. In hindsight, one can therefore claim that, instead of preparing the country's withdrawal, Papandreou's anti-EC rhetoric was meant to prepare the EC for the renegotiation of the terms of Greek membership, while serving the crucial tactical task of turning PASOK into the main vehicle for the expression of the anti-right political forces in post-junta Greece.

From rhetoric to reality

Between populism and modernisation

PASOK remained in power during the second half of the 1980s. In the absence of any serious debate within the party, government action became the means by which PASOK identified and pursued its preferences on European integration. It is in that context that spectacular contradictions between various aspects of its action became evident. Government action highlighted the serious (if not irreconcilable) tensions between not only the government's European and domestic policies but also (if not more importantly) various aspects of PASOK's domestic policies. The most important novel characteristic of PASOK's action was the de facto recognition on the part of the government that membership of the EC offered the country constraints as well as opportunities.[26] This subtle but significant change was facilitated by the experience acquired after four years of membership (during which PASOK was in government), but also by the gradual emergence of a group of senior officials who took centre stage in the government. Costas Simitis, who became the minister of national economy after PASOK's electoral victory in 1985, and Theodoros Pangalos, who occupied the post of deputy foreign minister[27] in charge of European affairs, are two individuals who stand out. Both were social democrats and convinced pro-Europeans and had acquired considerable experience in European affairs since 1981.[28]

As regards the government's action at the European level, three major developments forced it to adopt a more active stance in the mid-1980s, namely, the prospect of the accession of Spain and Portugal, the likely relaunch of the single market project and the first revision of the Treaty of Rome. The Greek government linked these three issues in an effort to promote the enhancement of the EC's redistributive capacity, from which Greece stood to gain. Arguably, this reflected more the country's needs than the party's social democratic views. As the accession of Spain and Portugal was certain to increase competition for Greek agricultural products, the Greek government repeatedly threatened to veto the Iberian enlargement if Greek economic interests were not taken into account. At the same time, it tried (unsuccessfully) to block the decision to convene the IGC that eventually led to the SEA of 1986.[29] Tactical considerations account for Papandreou's stance. First, speaking in the European Parliament two years earlier, he had made an explicit plea in favour of the reform of the EC's institutional framework; indeed, he called for a 'new Messina conference' that would enable the EC to deal with new problems without distancing itself from the spirit of the Treaty of Rome. Second, Theodoros Pangalos argued that, although the reform of the EC was a necessity, it could be achieved without an IGC (Kazakos 1987, 436–7).

Though the party had not been involved in the formulation of the proposals submitted by the Greek government to the IGC, their content echoed the defensive attitude vis-à-vis the EC that had taken root within the party and the government. The process that led to the Dooge report (which was meant to prepare the IGC) demonstrated the disparity[30] between the Greek views and those of other governments (Kazakos 1987, 436). A major characteristic of the Greek proposals was the vociferous support for intergovernmental institutions and a cautious (or even hostile) attitude vis-à-vis supranational institutions. For example, Greece opposed both the involvement of the European Parliament in the appointment of the Commission and the proposal to give it veto power over future enlargements and association agreements (Ioakimidis 1996, 15–16).

Despite its initial objections, the Greek government agreed to the SEA and presented it to the Greek Parliament as an agreement that favoured Greek interests (Hellenic Parliament debate, 14 January 1987, 2616). The terminology used by some majority MPs in parliament reflected the defensive attitude of the party vis-à-vis the integration process. For example, the inclusion of provisions regarding foreign and security policy in the SEA was presented very timidly, the emphasis being on consensus as a key procedural requirement that ensured that decisions could not go against Greek interests. Moreover, majority MPs were quick to point out the fact that the Luxembourg compromise had been preserved (Hellenic Parliament debate, 14 January 1987, 2615). Nevertheless, the speech made by the then deputy foreign minister in charge of European affairs indicated that a robustly pro-European and decidedly social democratic discourse was now a central feature of PASOK's stance on Europe. Two aspects of his speech stand out. First, Pangalos did not confine his speech to the merits of the SEA. Rather, he passionately presented a social democratic platform for a united Europe that would entail a 'unified political entity' able and willing to determine the future of European peoples independently of the other major powers, promoting peace and prosperity (Hellenic Parliament debate, 14 January 1987, 2623–7). He also highlighted the importance of economic and social cohesion as a key (constitutional) objective of the EC and the future predominance of the political over the economic aspect of integration. The second major novelty of his speech concerned the new conceptualisation of Greece's relationship with the EC: Pangalos castigated both the conception of the EC as a *vincolo esterno* and the notion that the EC is nothing but a 'cash cow'. Rather, membership offered a framework and a mechanism that could promote both the modernisation of the Greek economy and the long-standing objective of the Greek Centre-Left and the Left to emancipate the country from the influence of the USA. This required self-confident involvement in EC procedures, coalition-building and a move away from the perception of the EC as a mere transaction forum.

The combination of the relaunch of the single market project with the elevation of economic and social cohesion to the level of the EC's 'constitutional' objectives (coupled with the explicit political commitment to increase the flow of funds to less-developed regions) accounts for the Greek government's positive stance. While the trade-off between economic liberalisation (and re-regulation) on the one hand and the significant enhancement of the EC's redistributive capacity on the other was clear at the European level, and it accounts for the Greek government's decision to sign the SEA, this decision did not signal the adoption of a new economic policy paradigm at the domestic level, nor did it entail a new kind of relationship with the EC. This is so because PASOK's statism had roots that were as deep as those of populism.

Indeed, the Greek government was pursuing contradictory domestic policies. The significant increases in public spending that marked domestic economic policy during the first four years of socialist rule had been funded primarily by means of public borrowing. Papandreou was aware of the problem of public debt and sought to change economic policy by appointing Simitis to the Ministry of National Economy to stabilise the finances of a country that faced a severe current account crisis.[31] A key part of this effort was a loan from the

EC,[32] which, crucially, was presented to the public as the real reason for the domestic stabilisation programme[33] (interview with former PASOK Cabinet minister). This was an indication of both the defensive attitude of the government vis-à-vis the EC and its propensity to give in to the strong populist strand that permeated the party. Instead of presenting the loan (and the EC as a whole) as a key mechanism for the modernisation of the economy, the easy route of the 'politics of fear' was chosen, couched in the presentation of membership as an external constraint, despite the benefits that the country derived from it.

At the same time, the socialist government was pursuing the policy of 'socialisation' of ailing private firms by putting them under 'social' (essentially state) control in an effort to fight unemployment. In other words, while it had agreed at the European level to a process of gradual liberalisation of the economy, it was pursuing a completely different economic policy at the domestic level. Thus, the second half of the 1980s was marked by the remarkable tensions between strategic decisions of its leadership (especially the decision to keep the country in the EC) on the one hand, and the preferences of the majority of its cadres, many of whom occupied positions of power in the public sector (and its unions) and were the carriers of a mixture of populism and views inspired by the experience of the Eastern bloc.

The power of the advocates of these views, coupled with the predominantly defensive attitude towards membership of the EC, meant that the effort to rationalise the country's finances was short-lived. It became the victim of the rampant populism that permeated the party, as well as fears that the stabilisation programme pursued between 1985 and 1987 would lead to electoral defeat. The powerful populist section of the Cabinet (including ministers Tsovolas, Koutsoyiorgas and V. Papandreou) gave a hostile reception to Simitis's proposals to align (i.e. limit) incomes policy with inflation, but, after the meeting (and once Simitis had made a public announcement), Andreas Papandreou,[34] speaking in parliament in the debate regarding the budget, distanced himself from his leading minister who, as a result, resigned in November 1987. That was the end of the stabilisation programme. Populism and short-term electoral considerations had won, to the detriment of the first attempt actively to engage with the EC in an effort to improve the country's finances. At the same time, it highlighted the major credibility problem that Papandreou had in the European context.[35]

The transition to a new policy paradigm

Although PASOK was compelled to focus on its political survival as a result of the scandals of the end of the 1980s, the Maastricht Treaty and the decision to launch the process of EMU raised issues that the party could no longer avoid. The fact that it was in opposition undoubtedly facilitated the reflection process, but this remained confined to the party elite and was centred on prominent or ambitious members of its front bench[36] and their personal initiatives, rather than the party's formal institutions (interviews). In fact, the party itself did not engage in a meaningful and mature dialogue (interviews with former PASOK Cabinet members). The way in which the party leadership (specifically, Andreas Papandreou) dealt with the issue of the Maastricht Treaty is indicative of this (widely confirmed) absence of organised dialogue within the party (interviews). Aware of the issues raised by the Treaty, Papandreou dictated the party line: although PASOK MPs would vote in favour of the ratification of the Treaty, the rhetoric would highlight its deficiencies. For that purpose, he chose Gerassimos Arsenis, to make the main speech on behalf of the socialists in parliament.

Arsenis had worked for the UN Conference on Trade and Development and, while he was minister of national economy in the first PASOK government, he was the main exponent within the Cabinet of economic views that had been influenced by the experience of third-world countries. Unsurprisingly, he was also a left-wing critic of European integration; this is why he was chosen to represent PASOK on that occasion. In his speeches in parliament – both in the plenum and the economic affairs committee – Arsenis attacked, not only the Treaty's monetarist provisions regarding EMU, but also the democratic deficit of the entire EMU edifice, as well as the foreign policy- and defence-related provisions.

His criticism of the Treaty echoed the views held by many social democrats across Europe:

a)   EMU's institutionalised emphasis on monetarism radically reduces the capacity to fight against unemployment and promote redistribution.
b)   The institutional arrangements regarding the European Central Bank (ECB) actually increase the EC's democracy deficit.
c)   The provisions regarding the common foreign and (more specifically) security policy seem to promote the objective of turning the WEU (and the EU) into the European branch of NATO, instead of promoting the development of the EU's capacity to act in the international scene.

Arsenis's speech contains two noteworthy changes. On the one hand, it was the first explicit acknowledgement of the inability of individual states to deal with many of the major problems faced by citizens (Hellenic Parliament debate, 27 July 1992, 9). For a party and a country where the capacities of the state were often thought to be of Herculean proportions, this was a major change. The internationalisation of capital, argued Arsenis, means that its accord with labour and the state will have to be developed at a higher (regional, if not global) level. This is 'the one-way route' to a united Europe, as he put it, though it should involve the state as a key component, instead of seeking to eliminate it. On the other hand, it explicitly rejected the notion that non-involvement was a viable policy, arguing instead that non-participants would simply be compelled to implement the decisions that participants (even weak ones) would make – only by participating in the process of integration can one build 'political Europe' he said (Hellenic Parliament debate, 27 July 1992, 10).

Castigating the conservative government's passive stance in the negotiations, he highlighted the experience of the mid-1980s regarding the Integrated Mediterranean Programmes (IMPs), which demonstrated that the socialist government's active involvement in EC-level procedures had enabled it to promote the national interest. This is an important point that PASOK later turned into one of the main planks of its European policy (see *infra*).

Papandreou's speech on that occasion was remarkable. Placing the developments that led to the Maastricht Treaty in a wider international political and economic context, he pointed out the importance of (a) Germany's relationship to Europe and (b) the idea that the rapid enlargement of the EC was likely to promote the interests of the USA by undermining the process of European integration and turning the EC to a mere free trade area. He also acknowledged that Greece had no alternative. It had to follow the European route in an effort to promote the kind of Europe that PASOK preferred: a democratic Europe promoting redistribution and economic development through a robust European budget, full employment, the welfare state and the protection of the environment and territorial integrity from any external threat (Hellenic Parliament debate, 27 July 1992, 39–41). Finally, he returned to the familiar theme of Greek–Turkish relations by pointing out that the logic behind the Greek accession to the WEU had been undermined by the declaration whereby the members of the WEU reinterpreted the organisation's clause on mutual assistance.[37]

After PASOK's landslide victory in the general election of October 1993,[38] participation in the third stage of EMU became one of the government's main objectives (interview with former PASOK Cabinet minister). The credibility of this commitment was demonstrated by Papandreou's choice of Cabinet ministers. Indeed, the task of preparing the country for this process was entrusted to a group of moderate and experienced ministers, including centrists[39] and social democrats.[40] Mirroring the requirements of the Maastricht Treaty, the socialist government embarked on an orthodox programme of economic convergence (involving partial privatisations of state firms and reductions in public expenditure) similar to that followed by other member states in the 1980s (Tsakalotos 2001, 156–7).[41]

At the same time, PASOK's almost instinctive nationalism remained present in some aspects of the government's foreign policy. For example, it was evident in the conflict that opposed Th. Pangalos and George A. Papandreou, on the one hand, and K. Papoulias on the other (interview). Taking a hard line, the latter opposed EU efforts to resolve the problems that stemmed from the establishment of the former Yugoslav Republic of Macedonia as an independent state. By contrast the former supported it.

The Europeanist 'intermezzo'[42]

The risks created by the electoral sensitivities of the party's leadership, the instability created by Andreas Papandreou's poor health and the legacy of 1987, and the end of the first stabilisation programme meant that the continuation of this reform programme was far from guaranteed. Nevertheless, Costas Simitis's election as party leader and prime minister in January 1996 (confirmed after PASOK's victory in the general election of 1996) quickly dispersed these fears.[43] It marked the beginning of a new era that was characterised by the country's most successful involvement in the process of integration and the pursuit by the PASOK government of the clearest and most avowedly social democratic agenda for Greece and the EU as a whole.

Simitis – a man of conviction who had repeatedly clashed with the populist elements of PASOK's leadership and resigned twice from senior Cabinet posts and once from the party's Executive Bureau – saw the link between Greece and the process of integration as a potentially self-reinforcing tandem. Greece stood to gain from a strong EU, but only on condition of active and (above all) credible participation in the process of integration (Simitis 2005, 617). Simitis was determined to transform Greece into a reliable member of the EU's core group of states by accelerating the pursuit of the modernisation of the country and by taking an active interest in the major debates regarding the future of Europe. He turned membership of EMU into the core task of his government, but this was just a part of his own vision for the modernisation of Greece and the future of Europe as a whole. He was fully aware of the fact that the creation of the single currency would raise pressing and value-laden issues (including the major issue of political union) to which the social democrats ought to be able to respond (Simitis 2005).

His action while in power was underpinned by an explicit and highly developed understanding of the challenges that social democracy faces in the beginning of the twenty-first century. He believed that, in conditions of growing interdependence – in particular, in order to respond to the challenge of globalisation – the strategy of the Left should not be limited to the national level. Rather, a political response to the growing autonomy of the market brought about by globalisation is a necessity. This task is best carried out at the European level. Turning the EU into a powerful actor capable of promoting growth, economic and social cohesion, the modernisation of the European social model, peace, security and prosperity would give appropriate new meaning to the internationalism that characterised social democracy since its inception (Simitis 2005, 559, 563–4).

Simitis's vision regarding the future of Europe contained four key components that his government consistently promoted in the negotiations which led to the Amsterdam Treaty, the Nice Treaty and the Constitutional Treaty (Simitis 1995, 127–38; 2002a, 99–107; 2005, 126–7). First, integration must move beyond the economic sphere. The gradual transformation of the EU into a political union with strong and legitimate central institutions based on the federal model, with the Commission holding executive power, the EP legislative power and the Council as the second (upper) legislature representing states,[44] ought to be preferred to other existing models (including the Europe of concentric circles and Europe *à la carte*), because they do not rely on the rules and logic of democracy.[45] Second, although the Maastricht criteria do not attach sufficient importance to employment, and economic and social cohesion, they should not be abolished, because individual states (acting on their own) cannot cope with the challenges posed in an increasingly inter-dependent world. The real alternative is to (a) turn real economic convergence into a core component of an economic policy that will promote full employ-ment and (b) transform the Union into a leading actor in the management of the global economy. Third, the EU should promote the enhancement of the social dimension of integration in an effort to promote growth, as well as the protection of the European social model and its adaptation to new technological and demographic challenges. This should be combined with a more specific policy for the promotion of industrial competitiveness. In that context, the EU's redistributive capacity ought to be enhanced, and solidarity should replace the notion of *juste retour*. Finally, the Union will be incomplete as long as it does not possess the institutions and the policies that will enable it to play a more active and effective role in international politics, promoting the establishment of a multi-polar order based on international law, conflict prevention, crisis management and the protection of its own external frontiers on the basis of the principle of solidarity.

One major change – in comparison with the 1980s – was the leadership's (specifically Simitis's) willingness to make a positive case in public in favour of turning Greece from an awkward partner into a credible, confident and constructive one. For a party (and a country) that had been used to a rather confrontational attitude, marked by the government's Promethean role as the protector of the national interest, Simitis's attitude marked a radical break with the past. Simitis was willing to talk openly about the fact that (a) membership of the EU entailed opportunities as well as constraints (unlike his predecessors, who had often emphasised the latter in an effort to shift the blame for unpop-ular policies) and (b) one could not hope to turn the country into a credible partner capable of participating in core debates regarding the future of Europe without fulfilling the obligations that its governments had previously accepted. More importantly, unlike his predecessors, Simitis realised that the advent of the euro had the capacity to mobilise public opinion, which was tired of the scandals and the political turmoil that marked the end of the 1980s and the early 1990s. Unlike prominent members of the party leadership who advocated a slow adjustment to the criteria for the adoption of the euro (to a large extent because of electoral considerations), Simitis imposed the adoption of the euro (simultaneously with the core members of the euro zone) as the primary objective of his first government.

The economic programme that led to the adoption of the single currency as part of the first wave of member states that entered the euro zone reflected the need to fulfil the relevant formal criteria, but also the deficiencies of the Greek economy, as well as the need to ensure that the weaker social strata were protected from the negative effects of adaptation. In order to achieve these objectives, the government combined two sets of measures. The first entailed the more systematic, rapid and determined implementation of the orthodox[46] economic programme of the last Papandreou government. The more pronounced efforts to reduce inflation and public debt[47] were coupled this time with a more sustained fight against tax evasion and greater emphasis on market liberalisation. The second (and more innovative) set of measures entailed the reform of local government,[48] the establishment of autonomous regulatory agencies and, above all, an extremely ambitious programme for the modernisation of the country's infrastructure.[49] This programme was important for two reasons. On the one hand, it was designed to facilitate economic activity and improve standards of living. On the other hand, it was meant to create jobs and thus absorb a significant part of the pressures on employment created by the Maastricht criteria. These measures were coupled with the government's social policy, which was aimed at protecting the most vulnerable social strata.[50]

This happened as a result of a conscious decision to reduce defence spending.[51] In turn, this change was facilitated by the management of Greece's relations with Turkey on a multilateral (i.e. European) rather than a bilateral basis, itself a key innovation introduced by Simitis and pursued by his government. This entailed the pursuit of long-standing Greek views but in a way that highlighted the EU-wide stakes. Seizing the opportunity offered by the Turkish government's objective of full membership of the EU, the Simitis government ended the isolation of Greece that stemmed from the fact that successive Greek governments had vetoed efforts aimed at developing Turkey's relationship with the EU. Although this policy had its roots in Turkey's aggressive policy – exemplified by the Imia crisis that took place during Simitis's first days in office – it had also run its course.[52] Simitis realised that Greece stood to gain (at least in terms of reductions in defence expenditure) from transforming the role of the EU in that respect. This is why he sought to turn the EU from a forum into an active mechanism for the implementation of a long-term strategy that entailed the promotion of democratisation in Turkey and the accession of Cyprus to the EU (interview with former PASOK Cabinet minister).

His modernisation project and his ambitious Europeanism were also based on his belief that the statism that had informed PASOK's worldview and practice until 1996 had reached its limits (Simitis 2005, 561). Aware of the ability of special interests to penetrate the state, and the inability of the latter to defend itself (and society) against clientelism, Simitis was willing to break with his party's quasi-institutionalised statism and promote the *état-stratège*. The policy of (partial or total) privatisation of some public firms and the emphasis that he placed on a network of regulatory agencies were the direct consequence of his views.[53]

Another facet of his scepticism vis-à-vis his party's traditional conception of statism was reflected in his support for supranational institutions as well as the gradual extension of QMV, against PASOK's traditional attachment to unanimity on foreign policy issues. Though Simitis did not deny that the extension of QMV should not happen prior to the development (at EU level) of common principles, policy objectives and the mechanisms that would put them into effect, he was willing to state openly, unlike his predecessors, that unanimity had also been counter-productive for Greek interests.[54]

Although Simitis undoubtedly innovated in terms of both the policy that he pursued and the method that he employed, his tenure as leader of PASOK and prime minister was remarkably consistent with that of Andreas Papandreou in one key respect. It confirmed the pattern of presidentialism that permeates preference formation in PASOK since 1974. Simitis was a long-standing and vocal proponent of intra-party democracy. While he was party leader and prime minister, both party fora and Cabinet committees met regularly.[55] Thus, party members and officials, as well as government ministers, had the opportunity to express any dissenting views. Nevertheless, this did not happen for two reasons. First, there was no coherent alternative. Second, PASOK did not have an established tradition of internal political debate. Between 1996 and 2004, the party remained a passive observer of Simitis's initiatives, secure in the knowledge that his personal popularity ratings were extremely high and that he had the personal credibility that enabled him to win two consecutive electoral contests. Indeed, under Simitis, PASOK increased both its overall number and share of votes.[56]

Although his vision regarding the future of Europe and the position of Greece therein was undoubtedly shared by a number of senior and junior government ministers, his legacy does not appear to have taken root within the party. His successor, George A. Papandreou (the eldest son of Andreas), has chosen a different course of action.

After Simitis: PASOK's 'exodus'[57] from Europeanism

The pattern that emerged since George A. Papandreou's election as leader of PASOK in 2004[58] confirms the predominance of leadership as a key explanatory factor in preference formation on European integration. Nevertheless, it is important to divide this period into two distinct phases that reflect novel features in (a) the development of PASOK as a political party and (b) the nature of its preferences on European integration. The first phase commenced with Papandreou's elevation to the leadership of the party in February 2004 and ended with the party's seventh conference in March 2005. The second phase began with the Dutch and French referenda on the Constitutional Treaty (May–June 2005). The former is marked by the enduring presence of key traits of the Simitis era in terms of the party's formal ideological and programmatic platform and its internal organisation and leading team. The latter is clearly marked by the new leader's ideological and programmatic as well as personnel-related choices. Crucially, PASOK's presence in the opposition benches gave it the opportunity to revise its programme, strategy and tactics ahead of the next general election.

George A. Papandreou's elevation to the leadership of the party was the result of a novel process, both in terms of the party's history and the broader Greek political culture. As a result of plans that were afoot since June 2003

(Simitis 2005, 592), Papandreou met Simitis in the latter's private residence on 6 January 2004. In addition to Simitis's personal decision to hand over[59] to Papandreou the party's leadership and the responsibility for the election campaign,[60] they agreed to (a) revise the party's procedure for the selection of leader and (b) call an early election in March 2004. On Papandreou's initiative, the new leader would be 'elected' directly by party members and supporters (or 'friends'[61]), rather than the party conference, as had hitherto been the case. This required the reform of the party's charter. This reform was formally endorsed by the party's extraordinary conference held on 6 February 2004. George A. Papandreou was the only candidate. As a result, his 'victory' was entirely expected.[62] However, two key features of this process deserve to be highlighted, for they were politically consequential (see *infra*).

First, the participation of more than one million members and 'friends'[63] (PASOK 2004d) was both surprising and unprecedented. This process was not as democratic as it seemed at the time. Indeed, it was more akin to a referendum or a crowning than an election. The latter requires not only the participation of competitors but also explicit political platforms. Moreover, the fact that (a) Simitis had already designated George A. Papandreou (whose surname was – and remains – his major political asset in the eyes of many of the party's core voters) and (b) the party was about to face a general election after thirteen consecutive years in power effectively precluded the possibility of alternative candidatures and the oxygen of political contestation that they would provide. Nobody was willing to risk appearing to divide the party. Second, Papandreou's elevation to the leadership of the party was founded on an unspecified platform of 'radical change'. Indeed, his involvement in public meetings, party gatherings and election rallies was dominated by one slogan: 'George, change everything!', which he openly endorsed. The combined effect of these two facts gave Papandreou a personal, strong but unspecified mandate, which appeared to be the political equivalent of a blank cheque. Nevertheless, PASOK suffered heavy defeats, both in the general election of March 2004[64] and the European elections of June 2004.[65] As a consequence, both the party and its new leader, now in opposition, could begin to reassess its ideological and broader political position, as well as its internal organisation.

During the two electoral campaigns, PASOK's formal rhetoric on European integration remained remarkably consistent with the avant-garde left-wing federalism that characterised the Simitis era (PASOK 2004a; 2004b; 2004c). Most of these preferences were reaffirmed at the party's seventh conference held in March 2005 (PASOK 2005). More specifically, the party reaffirmed its strategic attachment to the country's European orientation (PASOK 2004b, 198) and the quest for 'a strong Greece in a potent and progressive Europe for the management of globalisation', i.e. two core components of Simitis's policy (Simitis 2005; 2007a, 24). Indeed, Simitis had explicitly and unequivocally linked the country's prospects and his government's social democratic policy with 'the debate on the future of Europe and its role in the world' (Simitis 2005, 125; 564).

The party explicitly construed the country's future as being part of Europe's political union, as 'a strong Europe will guarantee multilateralism and the democratic and peaceful governance of globalisation' (PASOK 2004a, 2), supported those who sought the rapid pursuit of a federal Europe equipped with its own constitution, defence and foreign policy (PASOK 2005, 7 and 31), and regarded Greece as being capable of participating in enhanced co-operation arrangements in defence (PASOK 2004c, 12).

In addition, the party formally endorsed the mainstream social democratic agenda of a social, environmentally sustainable and multicultural Europe, coupled with a powerful and democratically legitimate economic policy and institutions. It also reaffirmed its commitment to economic and social cohesion and the enhancement of the Union's redistributive capacity, including its budget. Finally, PASOK explicitly endorsed the 2004 enlargement, as well as the prospect of the accession of both Turkey and the countries of the Western Balkans.[66]

The lengthy process of internal reorganisation began in spring 2004 and culminated in the adoption of the new charter and internal structure at the party conference of March 2005. The aim of the establishment of the new, so-called 'open party', was to turn PASOK from an elitist and hierarchically organised party into a decentralised network of members and 'friends' – including immigrants and representatives of civil society – marked, in addition, by the participation of more women.[67] The internal reform of the party was aimed at promoting the principle and the means of participatory democracy[68] and improving the standard of its cadres, largely through the use of IT. In reality though, PASOK has remained a catch-all party, with a governmental vocation. The enhanced legitimacy of the new leader significantly increased his margin of discretion in terms of policy-making, as well as the appointment of the party's senior cadres and, of course, the front bench. George A. Papandreou's PASOK is decidedly presidential, and this had a direct impact on preference formation on European integration.

The ratification of the Constitutional Treaty by the Hellenic Parliament in April 2005[69] was the last significant event of the first phase of George A. Papandreou's tenure. Speaking during the parliamentary debate, not only did he reaffirm the party's Europeanism – explicitly drawing on his own role in (and the contribution of the Simitis government to) the Convention on the Future of Europe and the first stage of the subsequent IGC – but he also contrasted them to the conservative government's passivity and called for a referendum[70] (Hellenic Parliament debate, 15 April 2005, 7554–6). This demand was also supported by left-wing opposition parties and was later formally submitted to parliament. The proposal was debated in parliament on 12 May 2005, but the ruling conservative majority rejected it.[71]

Two events marked the commencement of the second phase of Papandreou's tenure as leader and the beginning of a gradual shift in his position (as well that of the party) on European integration, namely the negative outcome of the referenda in France and the Netherlands (May and June 2005) and his appointment as president of the Socialist International in January 2006. George A. Papandreou's political discourse (speeches, articles etc.) is indicative of the aforementioned shift and took even more specific form in the leadership's formal proposal (March 2007) submitted ahead of the conference, which defined the party's new programme.

Two key features stand out (Papandreou 2005, 4; 2006a). First, Papandreou abandoned the Constitutional Treaty just weeks after the referendum in the Netherlands. Later on, he made very vague references to the need for an EU Constitution comprising two parts – one on the principles and values of the EU and one on its decision-making mechanisms (Papandreou 2006b, 4) – without articulating a clear alternative for the crisis that permeated the EU. At the same time, he criticised the conservative government for failing to participate in the ongoing discussion on the future of Europe (Hellenic Parliament debate, 4 February 2007, 83). Both he and senior officials of his choosing openly supported the view that the debate on the institutions of the EU was irrelevant after the French and Dutch referenda, and that priority lay with the definition of policies that would concretely respond to citizens' needs and wishes (interviews). In other words, Papandreou clearly broke with Simitis's strategy, which directly linked the reform of the Union's institutions with the policies that they produce. Second, there has been a marked shift away from the European integration-centred frame of reference on which both he and the party had drawn until then. Instead, Papandreou consistently drew on more abstract cosmopolitan references and concepts, such as 'global governance', 'global democracy', 'global citizenry' etc.[72] In his discourse, European integration did not appear to be linked directly (or even principally) to the objective of the 'humanisation . . . and democratisation of globalisation', i.e. the main priorities of the new leadership.[73] Thus, Papandreou and the party gradually moved away from Simitis's project, message and strategy. Unlike Simitis, they opted for vague references to 'a strong Greece in Europe and in the world' (PASOK 2007).[74] Although this emerging frame of reference informed much of the party's literature that was published on the occasion of the seventh conference, it was obscured by the Europeanist discourse on which Papandreou had to rely during the debate on the Constitutional Treaty – a milestone in his tenure as minister of foreign affairs. The swift abandonment of the Constitutional Treaty and Papandreou's appointment as president of the Socialist International accelerated the transition from Simitis's left-wing federalism to what Papandreou calls 'global revolution' (Papandreou 2006a; 2007c), i.e. a cosmopolitan 'new internationalism' that promotes the democratisation of neo-liberal globalisation through the co-ordination of citizens' action. In other words, Papandreou increasingly identifies with, and refers to, his new role (Papandreou 2006c; 2007a), from which he tries to draw ideas and policies, as well as his personal political identity. Indeed, he has publicly argued that, today, PASOK 'has a global presence and can take initiatives and engage in battles across the globe via the Socialist International' (Papandreou 2007b, 7). Moreover, while he draws systematically on his role as president of the Socialist International in his rare appearances in meetings of the Party of European Socialists, he does not give the same prominence to his role as leader of a party of an EU member state in his much more frequent appearances and speeches in gatherings of the Socialist International.[75]

In terms of the *aims and the scope of integration*, PASOK's and Papandreou's 'new agenda' construes Europe as the country's natural strategic space. Although political union formally remains an objective (PASOK 2007, 100), it is rarely present in Papandreou's discourse. Indeed, in a statement issued on the occasion of the fiftieth anniversary of the signing of the Treaty of Rome, he opted for the more vague[76] term 'political Europe' (Papandreou 2007d). As regards the EU's international role, although frequent reference is made to the need for a more autonomous or stronger European voice (PASOK 2007, 100), the need for a multi-polar system based on international law, consultation and the peaceful resolution of conflicts, these statements remain quite abstract, while references to CFSP, ESDP and the development of the Union's political and military crisis management capabilities have disappeared completely from the terminology used both by the party leader and the party's official literature (ibid.). The increasingly abstract references to the EU's autonomous international role are deprived of an explicit statement of the instruments that could turn it into reality. So, they do little more than obscure George A. Papandreou's latent Atlanticism[77] or, at best, a preference for Europe construed as an *area*. Indeed, although he was very quick to abandon the Constitutional Treaty, he remained attached to the idea of further enlargement (Turkey and Western Balkans), which he dissociates from the Union's crisis (Papandreou 2006e, 4), despite the fact that 'enlargement fatigue'[78] was, arguably, a major contributing factor in the outcome of the French and Dutch referenda. In other words, changes that risk diluting the EU even further remain firmly on his agenda. Nevertheless, PASOK did not refrain from supporting the notion of deepening integration – e.g. by means of a larger common budget, support for policies on economic cohesion, R & D – and the expansion of the agenda of the ECB to include growth and employment, although the absence of references to a *gouvernement économique* or economic governance and the rebalancing of economic and monetary policy is striking.

Furthermore, the shift in emphasis in terms of *institutional reform* of the Union is both obvious and spectacular. Simitis's left-wing federalism (see *supra*) has been ostracised and replaced by abstract references to a 'democratic Europe' (PASOK 2007, 100). PASOK's and Papandreou's[79] silence on institutional reform is coupled with frequent references to the need for the country's active involvement in the relevant debate and 'the avant-garde of the countries that can and wish to go ahead' (PASOK 2007, 100). The combination of Papandreou's insistence on further enlargement – despite the significant and vocal opposition to it both in Greece and in other member states – and the abandonment of Simitis's emphasis on institutional reform leads to the conclusion that Papandreou appears to espouse an Anglo-Saxon agenda and rejects Simitis's more balanced and holistic strategy.

These remarks reflect the platform (approved by Papandreou) on the basis of which the party's new programme was effectively adopted at the conference of May 2007 (PASOK 2007). This text was subsequently presented *verbatim* as the party's manifesto and remains to date the most important point of reference. In that respect, five key points deserve to be highlighted. First, this political platform that was meant to channel and inform the debate within the party is PASOK's first and only text issued since 2005.[80] Second, it has been personally approved by Papandreou. Third, it bears striking resemblance to Ségolène Royal's *Pacte présidentiel*, in terms of its form (i.e. a mere list of objectives and policy proposals), the basic concepts and keywords – including participatory democracy, proximity to the citizen, decentralisation, fair society – that it utilises (Moschonas 2007) and the parallel debates that it has generated (on the cost of these proposals and the origin of funding). Fourth, after the conference, the text reappeared in the form of PASOK's government programme, although it refers to the Constitutional Treaty even after the meeting of the European Council in Brussels in late June 2007. Finally, it is permeated by a pronounced cosmopolitan element, highlighted by extensive references to a 'global agenda' and the role of socialists (be they Greek or not) in promoting it, while its European component is remarkably feeble and almost entirely buried under vague and ambiguous statements. Indeed, less than one of the document's 123 pages is dedicated to European integration construed as both an objective and the means to an end (i.e. PASOK's preferences under Simitis). The 'new', 'patriotic' and 'internationalist' PASOK construes Europe, not as an *actor* that plays 'an autonomous, powerful and progressive' international role promoting peace, co-operation, development and security (PASOK 2005, 31), but as a mere *area* of peace and co-operation (PASOK 2007, 98) that ought to be enlarged.[81]

These changes in PASOK's preferences reflect the broader political context in which they occurred. Numerous opinion polls indicated that PASOK lagged behind the ruling conservative party and appeared to be incapable of reversing this trend. Papandreou's tactics and his capacity to lead the party were widely and openly questioned and criticised (*The Economist*, 7–13 April 2007, 43). As regards European affairs specifically, Papandreou often berated the conservative government and the prime minister personally for (a) undermining the country's status within the EU, (b) their inability to manage and increase the structural funds earmarked for Greece and (c) their policy on Cyprus and Turkey's accession bid (e.g. Hellenic Parliament debate, 2 November 2006, 767). On the other hand, neither the reform of the Union nor domestic issues with a pronounced EU dimension were used as part of PASOK's opposition tactics.[82] Rather, Papandreou argued that the conservative government and the EU had colluded in an effort to promote 'harmful solutions' in pension reform in exchange for ending the supervision of the country's public finances under EMU rules (*Eleftherotypia*, 12 May 2007).

Papandreou's elevation to the leadership of the party on a radical internal reform platform highlighted (a) the lack of trust in traditional leading party figures, as well as Simitis's modernisers and (b) the new leader's wish to rejuvenate the party in terms of personnel (politicians and cadres).[83] In addition, both during the process of the party's reorganisation (May 2004 to March 2005) and since the establishment of the 'new', so-called 'open' party (March 2005), numerous overlapping committees and task forces were established within the party in an effort to define party policy and tactics. The establishment of these bodies was often advertised with great fanfare, but they failed to produce any meaningful output (interview). Indeed, their operation revealed a serious lack of co-ordination[84] – both because there was no visible, coherent front bench and because the party essentially lacks a clear frame of reference and convincing programmatic beliefs, coupled with the corresponding tactics (interview). As a result, internal strife, insecurity and incoherence ensued, as exemplified by frequent public and bitter internal disputes. This, in turn, further accelerated the pace of PASOK's presidentialisation and the personalisation of the party's leadership. Papandreou's leadership is couched in the constant but incoherent use of 'surprise tactics', whereby the leader suddenly announces in public the party's position on political issues that dominate the national agenda. In other words, a new, aristocratic-authoritarian[85] and ultimately unconvincing presidential style has emerged. It is founded, not on democratic control, but on the tactical use of uncertainty and the surprise effect. The most telling (without being the only) example of George A. Papanderou's authoritarian style was the former party leader and Prime Minister Costas Simitis's expulsion (between June 2008 and March 2009) from the parliamentary party owing to his public disagreement with the party's proposal to hold a referendum for the ratification of the Treaty of Lisbon.[86]

Under George A. Papandreou, PASOK's exodus from the Europeanism of the Simitis era appears to entail an aristocratic-authoritarian style coupled with a cosmopolitan message inspired by the new leader's Atlanticist instincts. Papandreou combined an autonomous style of operation (beyond any collective body or procedure) and a vague, elitist and seemingly normative conception of global politics that is devoid of any reference to either specific forms of government or methods leading to 'global democracy'. This is unsurprising as – with the notable exception of the Simitis era – the entire Greek political class has developed a habit of simply reacting (as opposed to contributing) to the EU agenda. The latter defines the range of the domestic political debate on Europe. Paraphrasing Simitis, we argue that, if 'the others' do not produce a vision for Europe, 'we' are deprived of a sense of direction in 'our' debates. However, as Simitis rightly argued, no meaningful political vision can be bestowed or 'donated'; rather, it can only be the result of active civic engagement in political strife, coupled with a critical assessment of the status quo (Simitis 2007a, 16). This is why PASOK entered the September 2007 general election campaign deprived of a vision for Europe at a time when the debate on the new treaty was being actively relaunched.

In addition to the gradual and subtle, though manifest, shift to the afore-mentioned new kind of rhetoric, Papandreou effectively began downplaying the importance of the ongoing debate regarding the future of the EU. This is exemplified by his reluctance even to raise the issue or comment on important developments. In contrast, in the past he could have been expected to make a statement (at least in his capacity as president of the Socialist International) on the occasion of an event of EU-wide importance – such as the meeting of the European Council in Brussels in June 2007, which drafted the mandate and decided to convene the formal IGC that led to the Treaty of Lisbon – to make a statement and express his views. However, this did not happen, even on the occasion of the conclusion of the Treaty of Lisbon in October 2007. His silence (and that of his party) was deafening.[87] Equally telling was his (and his party's) limited interest in a substantive debate, both in parliament and Greece as a whole, on the occasion of the ratification of the Treaty of Lisbon a year later.[88]

More importantly, despite the debate and the conference that endorsed the new programme in May 2007, the party did not fight the general election of September 2007 on that basis. Rather, Papandreou decided to fight the election on the basis of a campaign focused on two persons, namely himself and the prime minister. PASOK's heavy defeat in that general election[89] triggered a leadership challenge. In that context, the main challenger (Ev. Venizelos, a former academic lawyer and Cabinet member) fought the leadership election largely on a platform that drew inspiration from Simitis's strategy and objectives on European integration. The leadership campaign revealed that senior frontbenchers disagreed with Papandreou's views. Indeed, based on a sophisticated analysis of the tensions between (a) European integration on the one hand and (b) the distinction between the Left and the Right, Venizelos supported, not only the explicit politicisation of European integration, but also the pursuit of Simitis's entire left-wing federalist agenda (including, for example, the transformation of the EU into a pillar of a multi-polar international system), even before the leadership campaign had kicked off (Venizelos 2006). This demonstrated clearly the EU-related political consequences of the party 'referendum' of 2004. Dissenting voices were silenced, and the exigencies of retaining (or regaining) power shifted attention away from Europe, even within a self-proclaimed 'pro-European' party. Nevertheless, even this incident proves the main argument put forward in this chapter: the leader rules. Papandreou comfortably won the leadership election of 11 November 2007.[90]

Finally, it is worth noting the confusion and contradictions that characterise the party think-tank's (ISTAME 2009) proposals that were issued ahead of the 2009 European elections. This is ISTAME's first text on Europe[91] after the leadership election and can therefore be said to fully express the party's new leader.[92] Although the authors of the text make a clear attempt to provide answers to the major isues that confront the EU – on the basis of the key question: how much and what kind of Europe do we want? (ISTAME 2009, 4) – and rely on mainstream Europeanist terminology and old (EMU, political union) as well as new concepts (such as 'politicisation'[93]), they also make confusing and unclear (as to the desired result) proposals including (a) the direct election of the president of the Commission or even the president of the European Council,[94] and (b) the limitation of the Commission's exclusive power of legislative initiative, which, if implemented, would deal a major blow to the Community method[95] etc. Finally, while the authors of the text pay lip-service to the wish to see the EU become 'a stabilisation force within its geo-political sphere and a strong pillar in the new international architecture as a peaceful and democratic step towards a new multi-polar world' (ISTAME 2009,41–9), no reference whatsoever is made to the means that would make this happen, and the reference to the objective of a common defence and security policy is at best vague – even in comparison with the Union's *acquis*; rather, the option of the development of the EU into a 'soft power'[96] is presented axiomatically (ISTAME 2009, 46).

Despite having initially under-estimated the 2009 European election's political stake, both PASOK and George A. Papandreou, subsequently turned the contest into a referendum regarding the popularity of the conservative goveernment (Papandreou 2009a). The slogan 'we vote on Europe, we decide on Greece' that they deployed (Papandreou 2009c) is indicative in that respect. In electoral terms this was a successful strategy, with the electoral result[97] paving the way for PASOK's (and Papandreou's) major victory in the early general election of 4 October 2009.[98]

Interests, institutions or ideas?

Unlike the other four cases examined in this volume, where (as the other contributions reveal) several independent variables have – over time – come to play a role in preference formation on European integration, and, as a consequence, a more significant dose of nuance is required, the case of PASOK can be summarised in a manner that highlights one key variable that has played (and still plays) a decisive role during the party's almost four decades in Greek political life. The primacy of the leader is the single most important and enduringly influential factor in the making of the party's preferences on European integration. The leader of the party chooses the broad direction, scope and content of the party's preferences on European integration, as well as the strategy and tactics used to pursue them. From Andreas G. Papandreou, through to Costas Simitis and even George A. Papandreou, the leader of the party is both a substantial actor within the party and a figurehead whose actions (when the party is in office) and rhetoric (when the party is on the opposition benches) exemplify what the party (and the government) as a whole stands for on the central issue of European intgeration. However, this does not mean that the content, clarity and specificity of these preferences do not vary over time. Rather, only between 1996 and 2004 (i.e. when the party and government were led by Costas Simitis) did the party have a clear objective and strategy with regards to the future of European integration, indeed ones that were founded on core social democratic values coupled with an explicit belief in federalism, i.e. what we called 'left-wing federalism'.

Variation over time is directly linked to the primacy of the leader (as the content of the party's preferences and strategy changes when the party chooses a new leader) but cannot conceal the influence of (nor can it be completely separated from) other independent variables mentioned in the introductory chapter.

Electoral, economic and geo-strategic interests have played a role in preference formation in this case, but their impact has been mediated by the leader's role. The two Papandreous have linked European integration and domestic electoral considerations, calling for referenda aiming at making political capital against the ruling conservative ND. Less ephemeral has been the influence of economic and geo-strategic interests. Both Andreas G. Papandreou and Costas Simitis have sought – in different ways – to enhance the EU's redistributive capacity, because they were aware of the exigencies of the Greek economy and (in Simitis's case) the medium-to-long-term implications of this mechanism for the process of integration as a whole. Finally, geo-strategic interests have (implicitly or explicitly) influenced preference formation, though the outcome has, again, been mediated by the leader's views as well as the development of the EU. This is exemplified by the party's (more accurately, the government's) stance on Greek–Turkish relations and the role of the EU therein. Whereas, under Andreas Papandreou, the EU was seen as little more than just another forum where Greece had to defend its interests, the development of the EU, the realisation of the limits of this strategy and Simitis's belief that the EU could become the means for the protection of the national interest have led PASOK formally to accept Turkey as a candidate whose accession prospects would rely on progress made in bilateral issues as well as the issue of Cyprus.

The primacy of the leader also reflects the impact of domestic political culture. The two main parties (PASOK and ND) have traditionally been top-heavy and very centralised. Far from fostering a culture of internal debate (found in other social democratic parties such as the Swedish SAP),[99] the primacy of the leader reflects the broader weakness of civil society in Greece (Mouzelis and Pagoulatos 2002). When Costas Simitis was in charge, he created numerous opportunities for internal debate, but he could not create his interlocutors as well.

Finally, in terms of ideas, populism, initially, and modernisation along social democratic lines in the second half of the 1990s have also been found to have had an impact on preference formation. Populism has been a useful electoral tool during the tenure of the two Papandreous as party leaders, but even they differ from each other, in that Andreas was striving to make a coherent party (papering over the genuine differences that existed therein) out of a diverse protest movement in the immediate post-junta period, whereas George's insistence on a referendum appeared in a mature democracy. On the other hand, Simitis's left-wing federalism has been explicitly (and deliberately) associated with a modernisation agenda, in part as an effort to overcome resistance to change (in terms of domestic, European and foreign policy) by depicting it as archaic and outdated. The content of this modernisation agenda also reveals the influence of the policy paradigm, which entailed a change of focus from (a) the 'state' to the 'public' and (b) the 'national' defined along domestic lines to a definition that links it inextricably to the 'European'.

Conclusion

Two sets of conclusions can be drawn from the preceding analysis. First, the case of PASOK provides no support for either the obfuscation or the dependence theses. As regards the former, support for European integration has not been used by PASOK in an effort 'to compensate for failure and retrenchment at the national level', nor was it a vehicle for the mobilisation of support by the party, 'despite the absence of substantive social democratic policy output' (Bailey 2005, 14). Indeed, membership of the EU has generated concrete evidence to indicate that action beyond the nation state can promote a social democratic agenda. Moreover, in this case, there is no link between continued membership and active engagement on the one hand, with a fear of national exclusion on the other (Haahr 1993, 263). By contrast, this case indicates a degree of support for the instrumental view of European integration (Sassoon 1996, 734). Integration has been used as the means to achieve the regulation of markets (at the supranational level) as well as the modernisation of Greece – a country whose political elite openly acknowledges the weaknesses of the nation state. However, this begs the question: *how* did this come about? In other words, was this choice (a) enduring and (b) linked to interest-based, institutional or ideational factors?

Evidence clearly indicates that PASOK did not perform the U-turn that has been ascribed to it. Rather, its initial robust rhetoric has obscured the party's more nuanced but real position: the *terms* of membership mattered[100] because Greece was facing specific economic, political and geo-strategic issues. Although electoral considerations and the diversity of the ideological orientations of its leading elite were undoubtedly important factors in shaping the party's initial rhetoric, the decisive role of the leader cannot be concealed. In Andreas Papandreou's early PASOK, electoral considerations provided an important motive, while the absence of a clearly defined and articulated *positive* ideological platform deprived the party of a yardstick against which existing alternative views could be assessed. In that historically defined context, the party leader effectively acted as a *primus solus*. In fact, this is the dominant and enduring feature of preference formation on European integration within PASOK.

Focusing exclusively on this institutionalist explanation can be misleading. After all, political institutions reflect the balance of power that characterises the context in which they are created. Indeed, the party as such has never been actively involved in policy-making, either when it was in opposition or – even more so – when it was in power. In that sense, the top-heavy PASOK exemplifies Greek political culture, which is marked by the absence of the ethos of debate on major issues.[101] This does not promote joint 'ownership' of party preferences, which inevitably become short-lived. This also indicates the decidedly elitist nature of the party (and preference formation within it), as well as the shallow nature of the apparent 'Europeanisation' of the Greek political class. 'Europe does not sell', one is told. How will it (irrespective of its precise meaning) 'sell', when no one dares speak about it?

Appendix: list of interviewees

Gerassimos Arsenis, former PASOK MP and Cabinet minister, Athens, 11 July 2006.

Paraskevas Avgerinos, former PASOK MEP and Cabinet minister, Athens, 13 July 2006.

Panos Beglitis, PASOK MEP, Athens, 27 March 2006.

Anna Diamantopoulou, PASOK MP, former European Commissioner and junior minister, Athens, 10 July 2006.

Pantelis Economou, former PASOK MP, Athens, 30 March 2006.

Yiorgos Floridis, PASOK MP and former Cabinet minister, Athens, 12 July 2006.

Yannis Kapsis, former PASOK MP and deputy minister of foreign affairs, Athens, 28 March 2006.

Yiorgos Katiforis, former PASOK MEP, former member of the Praesidium of the Convention on the Future of Europe and former economic adviser to Prime Minister Andreas G. Papandreou, Athens, 11 July 2006.

Paulina Lampsa, PASOK cadre (international affairs secretariat), Athens, 12 January 2007.

Apostolos Lazaris, former PASOK Cabinet minister, Athens, 30 March 2006.

Andreas Loverdos, PASOK MP and former junior minister, Athens, 13 July 2006.

Vangelis Papachristos, PASOK MP, Athens, 30 March 2006.

Alexandros Papadopoulos, PASOK MP and former Cabinet minister, Athens, 12 July 2006.

Yannos Papantoniou, PASOK MP, former MEP and Cabinet minister, Athens, 13 July 2006.

Christos Papoutsis, PASOK MP, former European Commissioner and Cabinet minister, Athens, 27 March 2006.

Yiorgos Romeos, former PASOK MP, MEP and Cabinet minister, Athens, 28 March 2006.

Yannis Roubatis, PASOK cadre and former MEP, Athens, 30 March 2006.

Panagiotis Roumeliotis, former PASOK MEP and Cabinet minister, Athens, 10 July 2006.

Dimitris Stefanou, PASOK cadre and adviser to George A. Papandreou, Athens, 7 March 2006.

Nikos Themelis, former aide to Prime Minister Costas Simitis, Athens, 14 April 2006.

Grigoris Varfis, former European Commissioner and PASOK junior foreign affairs minister (European affairs), Aegina, 31 March 2006.

Evangelos Venizelos, PASOK MP and former Cabinet minister, Athens, 11 January 2007.

Notes

1 We are grateful to several PASOK MPs, MEPs, party and government officials, Cabinet members and former European Commissioners who gave confidential interviews for the purposes of this project (see Appendix). The interviews were conducted between March 2006 and January 2007, i.e. when the party was in opposition. The list that appears in the Appendix indicates the interviewees' institutional role or position at that point it time. Dionyssis G. Dimitrakopoulos gratefully acknowledges the financial support provided by the School of Politics and Sociology, Birkbeck College, University of London, and Maria Zampara's contribution to tracing obscure publications from the Greek book market.
2 The EEC and NATO are the same syndicate.
3 Despite its rhetoric, the party (and its leader) was, at least since 1977, in search of a policy platform that would manage to reconcile contradictory demands stemming from the party's diverse social basis, its activists and competing members of its leadership.
4 It obtained just under 14 per cent of the votes in the general election of November 1974.
5 As Susannah Verney appositely notes:

> The attempt to attract support across a broad section of the political spectrum was indicated by PASOK's attempt to trace its origins to the triple roots of EAM (the wartime National Resistance Front), the 1960s *Anendotos*, and the 1973 Polytechnic uprising against the Junta . . . It thus sought recognition as the heir of all the historic anti-Right struggles, laying claim simultaneously to the traditions of the Left, the Centre, and the anti-dictatorship student movement.
>
> (Verney 1994, 296)

6 Papandreou was conscious of this diversity and has been (rightly) credited with turning it into one of the strengths of the political movement that he led (Pangalos 2004, 26).
7 Greece belongs to the Greeks.
8 Greece belongs in the West.
9 As Verney rightly argues (1994, 304), 'claiming to be socialist in a country where the Left had always been communist-dominated distinguished the party from the communist movement with its "sinful" Civil War past and allowed PASOK to present itself as something new.'
10 For example, a 'certificate of national probity' was a formal requirement for the provision of a driver's licence. Also, in 1962, there were 1,350 political prisoners (Tsoukalas 1969, 145–6).
11 Accession was mentioned in the Association agreement of 1961 as a formal and mutually agreed objective.
12 Political considerations initially covered both domestic and international issues, but, in the run-up to its accession to power in 1981, the former had become the main focus of PASOK's rhetoric (see *infra*).
13 The Simitis era is the only notable exception in the sense that, under his leadership, references to political integration were at least as prominent.
14 This is what it was at the point of its establishment (Spourdalakis 1998, 23).
15 This is so 'because they understood its aim was to make Greece's post-war orientation to the West irreversible' (Verney 1987, 257).
16 It is important to distinguish between the public statements that Papandreou made in his capacity as a (rather mainstream) academic economist (especially in the 1960s) and the statements that he made as a political leader.

17 In his public statements, Papandreou rejected both Western capitalism and the Soviet model. This was part of a strategy that was meant to expand the party's appeal. Indeed, Papandreou's virulent criticism of the West combined references to the inherent monopolistic tendencies of capitalism on the one hand, with the rejection of European social democracy that he portrayed as the genteel mask of capitalism, on the other. He also rejected the bureaucratic socialism of the Soviet model (Verney 1994, 304–5). Both were designed to make PASOK more attractive to segments of the non-communist Left and the Centre.

18 Karamanlis's correct tactical decision mirrored the primacy of the political benefits of membership as well as the weaknesses of the Greek economy.

19 This was already present in PASOK's rhetoric, but it gained greater prominence after the 1977 general election.

20 No to monopolies' Europe; yes to peoples' Europe.

21 One good example is provided by the government's decision to present the new agreement with the US, as a result of which the most important US military bases remained on Greek soil, although, while in opposition, PASOK had pledged to do the opposite.

22 This was an important decision because Simitis was expected to boost the pro-EC camp within the Cabinet while he was dealing with the crucial issue of maximising the benefits of Greek agriculture from the CAP. CAP funds were a major factor in the reduction of the intensity of the conflict with PASOK's left wing (interview with former senior Cabinet member).

23 He had been president of the Republic since 1980.

24 The first Greek presidency (July–December 1983) did not end with the traditional joint statement/presidency conclusions. This has been ascribed to the unwillingness of the French government to accept a compromise and was in line with Papandreou's opinion that the conclusions of the presidency ought to be drafted in a way that would enable European citizens to understand and accept them (Varfis n.d.). It should be noted that, during that presidency, Theodoros Pangalos, then a junior trade minister, had successfully promoted the establishment of a new formation of the Council of Ministers dealing with consumer protection issues (Pangalos 2003).

25 The Commission explicitly argued that IMPs were a response to many of the demands outlined in the (Greek) memorandum.

26 Taking advantage of the latter required the active engagement with EC processes instead of the frequent denouncement of other governments' (often assumed) intentions.

27 The Constitution of Greece stipulates that deputy ministers are members of the Cabinet.

28 While Simitis and Pangalos were major pro-European figures, the Cabinet also included ministers who harboured either caution or downright hostility vis-à-vis European integration.

29 Papandreou did not hesitate to side with the conservative prime ministers of Britain and Denmark at the European Council meeting of Milan in 1985 in an effort to block this decision. The Italian presidency's ingenious procedural decision to rely on qualified majority voting enabled the circumvention of their opposition but confirmed both Papandreou's willingness to take on the majority as well as his fears regarding the impact of membership of the EC on national sovereignty. Nevertheless, it also served the purpose of reminding other member states (and the Commission) that Greek interests could not be ignored within the context of the IGC, whose successful conclusion required a unanimous decision.

30 See, for example the statement made in parliament by Mihelogianis, a socialist MP (Hellenic Parliament debates, 14 January 1987, 2614).

31 This change has been ascribed to the influence exerted by Jacques Delors and Mitterrand's economic policy U-turn of 1983 (interviews with PASOK MEP, Athens, 27 March 2006 and former senior Cabinet member, Athens, 11 July 2006).

32 The Greek government submitted this request in October 1985, i.e. during the IGC. The Greek government had one additional source of lending, namely the IMF. Given its vehement criticism regarding the role of this institution, the Greek government was keen to avoid this option (Kazakos 1987, 439).

33 The current account problems faced by the Greek government in 1985 had turned the loan into a necessity. The programme entailed currency devaluation, a tight incomes policy and an attempt to bring the ballooning public deficit under control (Tsakalotos 2001, 144). It had received the explicit and concrete backing of Jacques Delors, then president of the European Commission.

34 Though Papandreou, speaking to one of his close collaborators, angrily cited the need to convince the party (a near impossibility at the time) about Simitis's proposal, it is more likely that he merely used it as an excuse to justify the decision to execute this U-turn; after all, he was the party's undisputed leader (interview with former PASOK MEP, Athens, 11 July 2006).

35 Despite the government's decision to embark on a spending spree that the country could not afford, PASOK lost the 1989 election.

36 These included Simitis, Pangalos, V. Papandreou, George A. Papandreou and Y. Papantoniou.

37 As prime minister during the second half of the 1980s, Papandreou was reluctant to pursue the idea of membership of the WEU, although the organisation's then Secretary General was very positive about this prospect. As a result, Greece ended up joining the WEU a few years later (under the conservative ND government), but in a manner that effectively diluted the concrete benefits that were expected. Indeed, on the occasion of the accession of Greece, other member states declared that, in case of a conflict between a member (such as Greece) and an associated member (such as Turkey), the clause of mutual assistance would not apply.

38 It won 46.9 per cent of the votes and 170 out of a total of 300 seats in parliament.

39 G. Yennimatas and, after his death, Y. Papantoniou were ministers of national economy, A. Papadopoulos was minister of finance.

40 Simitis was minister of trade and industry and Pangalos was deputy foreign minister in charge of European affairs.

41 Unlike similar efforts made by the conservative governments of 1990–3, this stabilisation programme (and the one followed by the Simitis government in the second half of the 1990s) does not seem to have had a negative impact on the real economy, leading, instead, to 2.4 per cent growth rate in 1995. This contrasts markedly with the -1.6 per cent growth rate of 1993 (Tsakalotos 2001, Table 1, 146). In addition, although this programme differs markedly from the economic policies that PASOK implemented in the 1980s, PASOK's efforts in the 1990s entailed an 'attempt to share the burden of adjustment more fairly and to shelter, to some extent, the most vulnerable sections of society' (Tsakalotos 2001, 158).

42 An intermezzo is, according to the *New Oxford Dictionary*, 'a short piece for a solo instrument'.

43 Simitis was a long-standing vocal supporter of the acceleration of the country's constructive engagement in the process of integration.

44 The process of the gradual transfer of legislative power from the Council to the EP ought to start from the areas that directly affect individual citizens, such as consumer protection, health, human rights and the protection of the environment (Simitis 1995, 131).

45 The looser models entail fewer rules. This gives greater freedom to larger egocentric states and threatens the coherence of the union. Moreover, differentiated

integration should not institutionalise divergence; rather, it should be designed to help weaker participants catch up (Simitis 1995, 130).

46 As Kevin Featherstone rightly argues:

> The shift to 'sound money and sound public finances' in Greece was clearly inspired by the EU and the discipline of the single currency. A different policy paradigm was imported: one that owed more to the German monetary policy tradition than to the traditional Greek electoral cycle.
>
> (Featherstone 2003, 931)

47 Speaking in parliament in 1999, Simitis rightly claimed that the effort to reduce public debt was totally in line with PASOK's long-standing objective of national emancipation as, the more you owe to third parties, the more you depend on them (Simitis 2002a, 152).

48 This major reform entailed the merger of a large number of local authorities into a small number of viable bodies.

49 This concerned the transport and energy infrastructure (including new motorways, the modernisation of national railways, the new airport and underground of Athens and a large number of new ports and marinas), as well as infrastructure that affects the quality of life, such as new hospitals, the modernisation of the water infrastructure in major urban centres and the biological treatment of sewage (Simitis 2005, 252–3).

50 This policy involved, inter alia, increased social security benefits (especially for low-income pensioners), increased unemployment benefits and the expansion of free health care to cover all registered unemployed people (Simitis 2005, 265).

51 For many years, Greek defence spending was one of the largest (in terms of GDP share) among members of NATO.

52 This policy had often allowed other national governments to hide behind what was often perceived as Greek intransigence. This was no longer a viable strategy. The new Greek policy on the matter forced them (and EU institutions) to deal with the realities of Turkey's bid.

53 Simitis maintains that ownership is nowadays not as important as the actual operation of public firms and objects to the primacy of ownership (over their effectiveness) of the means of production (specifically the presence of public firms) as the key criterion for the definition of a progressive economic policy (Simitis 2005, 554–8).

54 Speaking in parliament in March 1996, Simitis pointed out that one member state (Britain) had prevented the adoption by the EU of a statement in support of the Greek view on the Imia incident (Simitis 2002a, 63).

55 The exact opposite pattern marked Papandreou's tenure.

56 PASOK obtained 41.49 per cent of the votes in 1996 and 43.79 per cent four years later.

57 According to the *New Oxford Dictionary*, the term 'exodus' is mentioned in the second book of the Bible, 'which recounts the departure of the Israelites from slavery in Egypt, their journey across the Red Sea and through the wilderness led by Moses, and the giving of the Ten Commandments'.

58 This happened thirty years after his late father played a major role in the establishment of the party.

59 The terminology used in Greece on that occasion ('the handing-over of the ring') clearly reflects the imagery of aristocratic circles. However, the remainder of the process was effectively designed in an explicit effort to disconfirm this notion. Simitis's decision to name his successor took many by surprise, not because he sought to dissociate himself from what seemed to be an almost certain electoral defeat, but because of his consistent fight against his own predecessor's authoritarian practices.

60 Simitis justified his choice (2005, 589–95) by referring to George A. Papandreou's popularity within and beyond the party, his work while he was minister of foreign affairs and the likelihood of a new political and electoral dynamic that this decision was likely to generate.

61 The party's charter stipulates that the party's friends have the right to vote and can contribute to party policy-making, but they cannot run for party office (art. 20).

62 The family name carried significant weight, especially with large segments of older generations of PASOK voters and sympathisers.

63 This is roughly one-tenth of the country's entire population.

64 PASOK's share of the vote dropped to 40.5 per cent, but the party lost just over 5,000 votes compared with the general election of 2000.

65 This was a major defeat. PASOK won 34.01 per cent of the vote, i.e. nine percentage points fewer than the conservative ND (43.03 per cent). The corresponding difference in the European elections of 1999 was just 3.1 per cent.

66 This was in line with the views expressed by virtually all Greek political parties on the matter.

67 Forty per cent is the target.

68 This was to be achieved through internal consultation and accountability, referenda, an ombudsman etc.

69 PASOK and the ruling conservative ND supported the ratification (268 votes in favour), while seventeen left-wing MPs voted against (Hellenic Parliament debates, 19 April 2005, 7712).

70 This was in line with the decision of the party conference of March 2005.

71 The proposal was supported by 123 PASOK and left-wing MPs, but it was successfully opposed by 151 conservative MPs (Hellenic Parliament debates, 12 May 2005, 8455). Various opinion polls published a month later recorded, inter alia, (a) the public's support for a referendum (80–3 per cent) and (b) the fact that – although the public felt that they knew little about the content of the Constitutional Treaty (73 per cent), the debate in parliament and its outcome (65 per cent) – there was a majority against ratification (40–6 per cent against, 30–2 per cent in favour), which, the public felt, had not been affected by the result of the French referendum. The surveys also revealed another important finding: among PASOK voters, a majority (38–52 per cent compared with 28–9 per cent) was prepared to vote against the ratification of the Constitutional Treaty, while 20–32 per cent refused to express an opinion. ND voters supported it (38–40 per cent in favour, 32–6 per cent against), whereas Communist Party voters opposed it – 5–12 per cent in favour, 13–27 per cent against (*Ta Nea*, 1 and 2 June 2005, *Avgi*, 1 June 2005; *Eleftherotypia*, 2 and 5 June 2005).

72 On these notions, see Vertovec and Cohen (2003) and Archibugi (2004).

73 This is a good example as Papandreou appears to equate the EU to classic international organisations such as the IMF and the World Bank (Papandreou 2006d, 3).

74 The same logic underpins his recently (February 2009) announced five national objectives, the first of which refers, inter alia, to the country's 'equal participation in Europe and international affairs'.

75 For instance, he has argued that, 'now we must reinvent Europe as peace in a globalising world, as a socialist project of humanising globalisation' (Papandreou 2008a), while, in a speech in New York, he gave a different meaning to the EU:

> Now, no one can do this alone, not the US, not China, not the European Union, not others. But the US will have to play a leading role, for three reasons. First of all, it has its huge responsibility in creating, if not fully creating itself, but very much responsible for a large part of the mess, the crisis we now see. Secondly, not even the US can escape interdependency.
>
> (Papandreou 2008b)

76 This echoes the switch of the French *Parti Socialiste* from references to the 'socialist' to 'social Europe' (Marlière, this volume, pp. 63–5).
77 This is expressed through an eagerness (also encountered in New Labour) to refuse to give to the EU (or at least the prospect of joint action at that level) the prominence that he ascribes to other actors – such as the US – when it comes to dealing with major international issues – including the financial and economic crisis – despite the fact that the EU is the largest single market on the planet and a major trading bloc. In other words, unlike his predecessor, who saw the EU as the 'natural' context within which Greece should define and pursue its objectives (while contributing to the process of integration), George A. Papandreou relies on a much more diffuse conception that inevitably privileges the status quo and the hegemonic position of the US therein.
78 There is broad consensus within the Greek political class in support of enlargement (to Turkey and Western Balkans). The government's policy on Turkey's accession bid subsequently became an additional point of divergence between George A. Papandreou and Costas Simitis (Simitis 2008).
79 In his attempt to find a 'third way' between the Franco–German and the Anglo-Saxon models, Papandreou supported novel but incoherent proposals, such as the enhancement of the EU's legitimacy through the use of EU-wide referenda and the direct election of the 'President of the European Union' (Papandreou 2006f, 2).
80 Mimis Androulakis's 70+1 'theses' that were subseqeuntly endorsed by the party at its 8th conference in May 2008 have – just like the conference itself – been completely forgotten (Hassapopoulos 2008).
81 Deepening is also mentioned, though only in policy terms.
82 One good example is the debacle regarding the compatibility of domestic legislation (including the Constitution), which regulates the links between public procurement on the one hand and mass media ownership on the other, with EU law (Dimitrakopoulos 2008b, chapter 5). George A. Papandreou's PASOK was remarkably quick to retreat from the defence of the idea that membership of the EU entails both rights *and* duties (and thus do away with the image of the EU as a mere 'cash cow'). Papandreou had a major opportunity to buck the trend and show that active engagement in the EU is the only meaningful way to define and promote the 'national interest', and that a provincial attitude was both counter-productive (in the long term) and ineffective (in the short term), but he avoided it, sensing the trend of Euroscepticism that permeates Greek public opinion, as indicated by the opinion polls mentioned earlier (see *supra*). This is unsurprising since, as a PASOK cadre put it, 'Europe does not sell nowadays', and senior PASOK politicians who can talk about it, refrain from doing so (interview).
83 The choices he made when he defined the party's list for the European elections of June 2004 bear testimony to this intention.
84 The same applies to PASOK's MEPs, whose selection was George A. Papandreou's first major personnel decision (interview).
85 The expulsion of Y. Papantoniou (a senior member of Simitis-led Cabinets) from the parliamentary party is a good example of this leadership style. Papantoniou went against George A. Papandreou's declared populist line on the issue of the privatisation by the conservative government of a major state-owned bank by declaring (rightly) that this was also the policy of the previous PASOK government.
86 As T. Pappas (2008) appositely put it, 'Europe is the fateful word that for three decades casts its shadow on Simitis' relations with the Papandreous'.
87 This might seem to be a rather harsh criticism but it is not. Indeed, Papandreou did find the time to make a public statement regarding the suicide attack against

Benazir Bhutto in October 2007, but said nothing about the Treaty of Lisbon that was agreed on just a few days earlier.

88 For example, in his speech in parliament, he focused on the government's 'absence' from negotiations in Brussels and the request for a referendum (Hellenic Parliament debate, 11 June 2008, 1086–90).

89 It won 38.1 per cent of the votes and 102 out of a total of 300 seats in parliament. In comparison with the previous general election, PASOK lost 276,678 votes and fifteen seats.

90 Approximately 738,078 members and 'friends' of PASOK voted, including 16–18-year-olds, immigrants and nationals of other EU member states. George A. Papandreou won 55.9 per cent of the votes, Ev. Venizelos 38.1, and Costas Skandalidis 5.7 per cent.

91 It is worth noting a text authored by Simitis's close collaborators (ISTAME 2006) that inevitably reflects the ideas and objectives of the Simitis era. An updated version of the same text was subsequently presented as the think-tank's 'study' on the occasion of the fiftieth anniversary of the Treaty of Rome (ISTAME 2007). This was a desperate effort on the part of the think-tank's leadership to conceal the total absence within the party of any effort to problematise the issue of European integration.

92 This text arguably reflects the views of George A. Papandreou's closest collaborators (be they elected or not, within the party or elsewhere), whose role in the making of European policy seems to be significant but has not been systematically researched (interview with PASOK cadre).

93 Despite the intensive debate within academia and among politicians on this notion, the authors of this text do not indicate what they mean. Politicisation is the development of public political contestation both (a) on the definition of the EU's agenda and the policies that exemplify it and (b) on the operation of the EU's institutions, which involves (but is not limited to) the distinction between Left and Right (Hix 2008).

94 See ISTAME (2009, 14) for proposals that he had mentioned in the past and subsequently chose to re-use, arguing that they are a response to 'stich-ups be they for Barroso or anybody else' (Papandreou 2009b).

95 See ISTAME (2009, 14). These proposals are probably destined for the domestic audience, as they were not included in the same think-tank's contribution to the debate between similar organisations attached to sister European parties during the preparation of the 2009 European election manifesto of the Party of European Socialists (European Network of Social Democratic Foundations 2008, 15–17).

96 On the debate as to whether (a) the EU should (or should not) be confined to the role of a 'soft power' and (b) this option is 'progressive', see Hettne and Soderbaum, where 'soft imperialism' is construed as the use of soft (non-military) power 'in a hard way, that is an asymmetric form of dialogue or even the imposition or strategic use of norms and conditionalities enforced for reasons of self-interest rather than for the creation of a genuine (interregional) dialogue' (2005, 539).

97 Twenty-two MEPs are elected in Greece. PASOK won 36.7 per cent of the votes (and eight seats); the conservative ND won 32.3 per cent (eight seats); the Communist Party won 8.4 per cent; and three smaller parties (including the extreme right-wing LAOS and, for the first time in European elections, the Greens) also won seats. The turn-out rate was 52.63 per cent.

98 PASOK won (43.92 per cent) comfortably (more than ten percentage points of difference vis-à-vis conservative ND, which came second). Thus PASOK has a confortable majority in parliament (160 of the 300 seats).

99 Even when debates do take place, they are very rarely, if at all, couched in written contributions. This is what A. G. Passas (2008) calls 'the culture of spoken word'.

One of the main problems we encountered during our research for this chapter was the very limited number of written party documents. As a result, we had to rely on politicians' speeches, books and several interviews (as well as written testimonies) provided by our interlocutors.

100 At least in Andreas Papandreou's mind (cf. PASOK (1976, 16), where – even with C. Simitis's seal of approval – the party explicitly rejects the options of membership, 'as well as membership under certain conditions').

101 Indeed, this applies not only to the party's European policy but also its switch to a new policy paradigm.

6 Swedish social democracy and European integration

Enduring divisions

Karl Magnus Johansson and
Göran von Sydow

> Nothing is as mentally demanding to a party leader as when the party is divided
> into two groupings equal in size on an important matter, such as the
> relationship to the EU. Before the [2004] election to the EU parliament the
> antagonism blossomed anew and I was again struck by the gloomy feeling that
> the internal strategies were mainly about forming a majority and running over
> the minority.
>
> (Persson 2007, 382)

Introduction[1]

The Swedish Social Democratic Party (*Sveriges socialdemokratiska arbetareparti*,
SAP), one of the most successful political parties anywhere, is deeply divided
over European integration. In fact, the party's own supporters were almost
evenly split between the 'yes' and 'no' camps in the 1994 referendum on EU
membership. A faction within the party opposed membership but was unable
to prevent the party leadership – and the government – from going ahead with
the application. The SAP contested the extraordinary European election in
1995 with lists including candidates from both camps. The opponents of
membership, mainly at the grassroots level, apparently sought revenge from
the party elite for accepting Swedish membership in the first place. Since the
country's accession, Sweden's approach to economic and monetary union
(EMU) and most notably its third stage, that is, currency union, led to further
tensions inside the party as well as in the government. It was a divided party
that fought the 2003 referendum on the euro. Influential actors within the SAP
and the electorate saw EMU as a threat to the Swedish welfare state. The
negative outcome weakened the authority of the party leader and Prime
Minister Göran Persson. For several years, he was playing a waiting game and
tried, at least rhetorically, to appease the Eurosceptics (Fichtelius 2007, 385–410;
Persson 2007, 360–9). Strategically, his priority was to avoid a decision of the
party's congress against full EMU membership, just as his predecessor, Ingvar
Carlsson, was concerned not to provoke the party congress into ruling out
prospective EC/EU membership back in 1990. Accordingly, and more generally, the political strategy aimed at maximising the leader's freedom of action.

In any event, the party leadership failed to mobilise support for European integration among the rank-and-file of the party. This has been most evident in European elections, with low turn-out and considerably poorer SAP results than in national elections. Arguably, 'Europe' has reinforced the social democratic grassroots' tendency to be disloyal to the party leadership, which, in turn, has contributed to increasing apathy among traditional SAP supporters and to party–voter de-alignment. During the entire post-war period, until the leadership's re-orientation, both Sweden's policy of neutrality and the concept of the welfare state prevented the SAP from supporting Swedish participation in the process of European integration. These were central components of the SAP's identity. Thus, it was very difficult for the party leadership to change its attitude towards European integration without challenging party cohesion and party–voter congruence.

Irrespective of the views vis-à-vis the EU in the internal, electoral and parliamentary arenas (cf. Sjöblom 1968), the SAP – the sole party in government between 1994 and 2006 and the largest Swedish political party – must position itself on major EU issues. In that respect, the interplay between the party and the government is of central importance. The political leaders have been trapped into a delicate balancing act between basic support for membership of the EU, the wish to honour the membership application and to retain credibility as loyal partner within the EU on the one hand, and anti-EU views inside the party and among Swedish public opinion more broadly, on the other hand.

All three independent variables outlined in the introductory chapter – interests, institutions and ideas – come into play in the relationship between Swedish social democracy and European integration. The three independent variables provide potential explanatory factors and sources of social democratic party preferences in relation to European integration. One of the main purposes of this chapter is to specify those variables in the case of the Swedish Social Democrats. It is assumed that there is a causal nexus between those three sets of variables and the key dependent variables (scope, aims and institutions of integration). As was noted in the introductory chapter, these three variables reflect the key dimensions of party preferences on European integration. So, what kind of Europe does the SAP want, and, above all, what enabling and constraining factors account for party preferences in relation to European integration?

In seeking to identify the origin of the SAP's preferences on European integration, our aim is also to shed light on how such preferences are formed more generally (see, e.g., Dimitrakopoulos and Kassim 2004a; Johansson 2002a; Moravcsik 1998). Haahr's comparative study (1993) of the European policies of the British Labour Party and the Danish Social Democratic Party (SDP) is useful in this respect. It analyses how these two parties abandoned their previous sceptical approaches to European integration and became increasingly pro-integrationist since the mid 1980s. Haahr examines the internal and external determinants of the parties' EC policies and their re-orientation.

He uses the neofunctionalist approach to regional integration and identifies instances of spillover. Haahr (1993, 324) argues that the two social democratic parties changed their European policies from the mid-1980s onwards mainly because of the increased relevance of the EC (see also Ladrech 2000). The Danish SDP was subject to a learning process, for example in relation to the party's acceptance of the strengthening of the EC institutions, notably of the European Parliament, and to EMU (Haahr 1993, 254–7). Although domestic factors must be taken into account, Haahr (1993, 258) emphasises that concerns for the party's future electoral prospects and future in government cannot explain the actual *content* of SDP policies on the EC's development. It does seem as if it can be explained, at least partly, by learning processes and transnational elite interaction and socialisation. The SDP (leadership) worked in the framework of the Confederation of Socialist Parties of the European Community (CSPEC) – the forerunner to the Party of European Socialists (PES) – and through representatives in the European Parliament (Haahr 1993, 257).

The Swedish Social Democratic Party can be placed alongside its sister parties, primarily the Danish SDP. The long-standing links between these two parties have been forged and developed both bilaterally and through Nordic co-operation, most notably the Joint Committee of the Nordic Social Democratic Labour Movement (SAMAK). Furthermore, the SAP had observer status in the CSPEC. The re-orientation of the Swedish social democratic government on EC membership in 1990 coincides with the (further) re-orientation of the policies of the Danish and British sister parties on European integration. The background conditions may well have been similar, if not exactly the same. As the EC became more relevant and was changing, social democratic elites increasingly looked upon European integration as a central element in the broader renewal or modernisation of social democracy.

This chapter is based on material from a number of sources, including archival documents and elite interviews.[2] In addition to a few formal elite interviews, a significant number of informal conversations with interlocutors, as well as material provided by the international department at the SAP's central office, were particularly useful. Hence, this chapter is based on 'hard' as well as 'soft' data sources. Hard primary sources used for this analysis include government documents and party documentation compiled through archival research, which was undertaken at the Labour Movement Archives and Library.[3] The SAP's annual activity reports (1989–2004) have also been used. As regards secondary sources, this chapter draws especially on research on corporatism (e.g. Rothstein 1996) and Sweden's relation to Europe, most notably the abrupt U-turn on membership in 1990 (e.g. Aylott 1999; Gustavsson 1998; Ingebritsen 1998; Kite 1996; Luif 1995; Miles 1997; 2000; 2005). Moreover, our understanding of Swedish social democracy and its relation to European integration has benefited from memoirs and biographies.

The remainder of this chapter is organised along the following lines. The first section focuses on Sweden's relationship to European integration over the years. This overview provides the background to, and contextualises, the SAP's preferences. The second section deals with the set of dependent variables, namely the scope, aims and institutions of integration. The third section analyses the independent variables (interests, institutions and ideas) and their impact on preference formation in the case of the SAP. In the concluding section, we summarise the main findings and draw out the major implications for the development of theory and for future research on (social democratic) party preferences on European integration.

Sweden and European integration

This section examines the key historical developments in Sweden's stance vis-à-vis the European integration process, with particular reference to the role of social democracy. Special attention is given to the turning point in this relationship in the context of the decision on membership in 1990.

Staying apart

For a long time, Sweden stayed aloof from European integration. The federalist underpinnings of the European project found limited support in Sweden, an established nation state that enjoyed strong support and legitimacy among its citizens. Moreover, after the end of World War II, Sweden was in a position to manage its economy on its own and was not in need of being rescued (Gustavsson 1998; cf. Milward 1992), for it had once again escaped the horrors of war and remained a stable democracy.

Two objectives guided Swedish foreign policy throughout the post-war period, namely to establish an international presence in order to protect national interests, and to preserve national autonomy as much as possible. To that end, Sweden would not accede to supranational organisations such as the European Coal and Steel Community (ECSC) and the European Economic Community (EEC). These organisations were believed to represent an unacceptable constraint on national sovereignty, especially in light of Swedish neutrality and the far-reaching ambitions the SAP harboured for the construction of a welfare state.

During the debate on the creation of the Council of Europe in the late 1940s, Sweden had sided with Britain in arguing that this arrangement should be based on intergovernmental principles and methods. As a result, Sweden was not part of the group of states that preferred another kind of order and established the ECSC in 1951. Indeed, Swedish participation was never considered, and, at that stage, the Swedish government did not believe that this form of co-operation would turn out to be very successful (af Malmborg 1994).

Evidently, Swedish decision-makers, just like their British counterparts, under-estimated the underlying dynamics of the European integration process in the 1950s. However, as this process continued, it was vital not to stay entirely on the sidelines but instead to reach some kind of partnership. The

Swedish position became more complicated with the establishment of the EEC in the late 1950s. There was a fear, not least among leading industrialists, that Sweden would be deprived of full access to some of its most important export markets.

Once the British government declared that it would apply for membership in 1961, the issue of Sweden's relationship to the EEC became politicised and the national consensus that had prevailed during the 1950s was challenged (Bergquist 1970). In particular, representatives of non-socialist parties and industry emphasised the risk of isolation from important trading partners.

The government's position was presented in a speech given by the social democrat prime minister (1946–69), Tage Erlander, in August 1961, at the conference of the Swedish Steel and Metalworkers' Union. In his speech, Erlander described how he understood the EEC and spelled out in some detail why Sweden could not become a member. Later dubbed 'the Metal Speech', this statement would leave an indelible mark on the subsequent Swedish debate on Europe. Erlander couched his decision to reject EEC membership both in foreign and domestic policy considerations. Membership on the basis of the Treaty of Rome was incompatible with Sweden's policy of neutrality. Sweden was militarily non-aligned, whereas the six founding EEC member states were also members of the North Atlantic Treaty Organization (NATO). According to Erlander, the Treaty of Rome was a step on the road to a real federation. He argued that members effectively give up their sovereignty to a supranational body governed by majority decisions in areas such as economic policy, social policy, taxation, labour market, agriculture, movement of capital, tariffs etc. The Swedish government would stick to its policies, notably in social affairs, which were embraced by most Swedes and had won Sweden international renown. Erlander therefore said that it is 'not surprising that we should have doubts about acceding to international agreements that can be expected to restrict our chances of pursuing this policy considerably' (Erlander 1962, 122). Here, Erlander portrayed Sweden as a pioneer in the construction of the modern welfare state. He mentioned Sweden's successful policy against the crisis of the 1930s, claiming that this would not have been possible if Sweden had at that time been constrained by a treaty subordinating the individual countries' economic policies to a supranational European body. Erlander even said that countries on the European continent at the time conducted a completely different policy of a traditional, conservative kind. Erlander placed special emphasis on labour market policy, alongside social policy. In addition to these two main arguments related to Sweden's foreign and domestic policy, Erlander criticised the EEC for its high tariffs against developing countries. Although Erlander had little positive to say about the political ambitions and vision of the EEC, he emphasised that Sweden needed a commercial agreement with it. An application for association to the EEC was submitted in December 1961. However, negotiations were never initiated. When French president de Gaulle declared in January 1963 that he would veto British entry, the whole issue of enlargement was removed from the agenda.

A new attempt to reach an agreement with the EEC was initiated in 1967. It was triggered by the second British application for membership. The Swedish government submitted an 'open application'. The government wanted to initiate negotiations over the material content of an agreement and leave the form of accession for a later date. Sweden's new approach was partly a concession made in order to achieve a national consensus on the issue, at a time when opposition parties had called for an initiative. Meanwhile, the new approach reflected changes that had taken place within the EEC. The Luxembourg Compromise of January 1966 helped allay fears regarding the supranational aspects of the EEC and their impact on 'vital national interests'. Moreover, the French withdrawal from NATO's central military command appeared to have weakened the previously obvious connection between the EEC and the Western military bloc.

These changes gave the Swedish government hope for the dilution of the supranational dimension of European integration. However, once again, this reflected a tendency among Swedish decision-makers to engage in wishful thinking. In 1970, the Werner and Davignon reports proposed strengthened co-operation between the EC member states in economic and foreign policy, respectively.

Against this background, Prime Minister Olof Palme, in March 1971, declared that the Swedish government no longer viewed membership as a viable option. Citing especially the Davignon report, Palme argued that Swedish participation in this type of co-operation would have consequences for the credibility of the policy of neutrality (Ekengren 2005, 128). Moreover, testimonies from Cabinet meetings subsequently revealed that this was only part of the picture: the traditional fear of losing control over domestic policy was still crucial. However, unlike Erlander in 1961, Palme chose to downplay this in public statements. Rather than emphasise the unique features of the Swedish welfare system, Palme asserted that other states as well had tried to find interesting solutions to social problems.

In the end, Sweden, together with the other EFTA member states, and the EC negotiated a free trade agreement, which was signed in 1972. The outcome did not satisfy the Swedish government, which had preferred a customs union as well as access to numerous other attractive areas of Community co-operation. However, at that point in time, the agreement could solve the most pressing trade-related problems.

During the 1970s, the issue of membership more or less disappeared from the political agenda in Sweden. As long as the Cold War continued, Sweden was bound to its traditional policy of neutrality, which provided the key constraint on Swedish foreign and security policy. Neutrality and non-alignment remained incompatible with Swedish membership of the EC. Within those constraints, Sweden could and should co-operate as closely as possible with the EC. This was the line of successive SAP leaders (first Olof Palme and his successor – since 1986 – Ingvar Carlsson). This policy line was clearly expressed by Palme in a speech in November 1981, in which he also expressed sympathy for President Mitterrand's notions of giving the EC a new, distinct social profile, by creating an *espace social européen* (Palme 1981). This was certainly an ambition with which Swedish social democrats could identify.

Closer co-operation

In 1986, the EC member states signed the Single European Act, which laid down the rules for the internal market and the four freedoms of capital, services, goods and labour. This triggered considerable activity on the part of the Swedish social democratic government and the prime minister. In addition to numerous meetings with individual government leaders, Ingvar Carlsson established a close relationship with Jacques Delors, the Socialist president of the European Commission. They met in Stockholm in early June 1986. On this occasion, Carlsson said, with reference to Palme's 1981 speech mentioned above, that Sweden could take part 'in all fields except foreign policy and security matters' (Carlsson 1986). It is also noteworthy that Carlsson emphasised that Delors was convinced that 'the economic and social dimensions are interwoven'.

The social dimension of the internal market would play an important role in the re-orientation of Swedish social democracy, or at least of its leadership, on European integration, along the lines followed by the Danish and British sister parties (see Haahr 1993). Carlsson returned to the subject of the social dimension in several subsequent statements and speeches. He drew attention to Delors's address in the European Parliament in January 1990 and to the European Council meeting in Strasbourg in December 1989, where the EC's Charter of the Fundamental Social Rights of Workers was adopted.[4] Rhetorically, Carlsson placed much emphasis on social goals and the creation of a true citizens' Europe (*medborgarnas Europa*). Thus, the perceived bias towards market integration was to be balanced by adding more emphasis to the social dimension, both at the national and the European level. This permeated the Europe-related discourse of the SAP leadership. Again, social democratic grassroots and the party faithful could identify with this aspiration.

The revival of the integration process in Western Europe by the mid-1980s meant that the European question returned to Swedish politics. With the relaunch of the internal market project in the mid-1980s, and the entry into force of the Single European Act in 1987, the EC had manifested itself as the obvious centre for economic and political co-operation in Western Europe. Swedish decision-makers started to worry about Sweden's isolation from continental Europe, especially in commercial terms. In light of the changed circumstances, the Swedish government presented an extensive European policy bill to the *Riksdag* in the autumn of 1987. Sweden was to adopt a vast range of unilateral adjustment measures. This strategy was to be combined with a new joint EFTA initiative, with the intention of negotiating a new institutional structure with the EC. After three months of negotiations in the *Riksdag*, a broad national consensus emerged in the spring of 1988 around the government's proposal. The pro-European opposition parties to the right of the ruling Social Democrats agreed not to raise the question of membership.

From 1989 onwards, the international political situation entered a state of flux. The fall of the Berlin Wall and the end of the Cold War fundamentally changed the international environment and had a catalytic effect on Swedish decision-makers, including their attitudes to the question of European integration and prospective Swedish membership of the EC. At the time, the SAP's leadership stressed the new opportunities opening up for social democracy in Europe, East and West. In short, these opportunities had to be seized.

However, the institutionalised policy of neutrality remained – at that point in time – a constraint on Sweden's relationship to the EC. The social democratic government wanted to discuss the prospect of deepened and broadened co-operation with the EC in all policy areas where this was compatible with the policy of neutrality.[5] Foreign and defence policies were the only exceptions.

Membership considered

In 1990, EC membership was discussed in influential circles in Sweden. At the time, the government struggled with problems related to the economy. The government was in turmoil and in February 1990 Sweden experienced a rare government crisis and even a ministerial resignation.[6] Ingvar Carlsson formed a new government. However, popular support for the Social Democrats had declined. Opinion polls in 1990 showed that support for the SAP fluctuated around 25–30 per cent, the lowest level ever recorded since the introduction of opinion polls in Sweden. Meanwhile, polls also showed an increasing support for the EC among Swedes. As non-socialist parties were in favour of membership, the SAP stood the risk of being seen as negative on this issue while the next general election was only a year away.

At this stage, the question of EC membership re-entered the Swedish public debate. It involved interventions by politicians, academics and others on the subject of Sweden's relationship to the EC. Another factor triggering the discussion in Sweden was the Austrian application, submitted in July 1989, for EC membership. An op-ed article in the leading daily newspaper, *Dagens Nyheter*, by Prime Minister Ingvar Carlsson, which was published in late May 1990, provided the focus of attention. Carlsson stuck to the position that membership was not an issue, but he did not rule out the option of reconsidering this position at a later stage. This would depend on national security considerations, as well as on the outcome of the European Economic Area (EEA) negotiations.

The prime minister's article was widely interpreted, or misinterpreted, as a rejection of membership and left him somewhat politically isolated. In an interview with Swedish Radio (10 June 1990), which raised the issue of Sweden's relationship to the EC, Carlsson said that all depended on developments in Europe that would determine if neutrality would be necessary or not. If not,

Sweden could become a member of the EC. Carlsson said he was hoping for such a development. However, membership would be impossible if the EC were to become a political union, with co-ordination in foreign and defence policy. Unlike the other 'sovereignty questions' that had played a role in the past but had become irrelevant, now only neutrality stood in the way of membership.[7] Those questions were no longer construed as an obstacle to membership. This was interpreted as a more flexible approach as far as the prime minister was concerned and appeared to indicate that supranationalism was accepted in areas other than foreign policy. Moreover, this approach differed from that of the leader of the Centre Party, who defined neutrality as freedom from supra-nationalism and placed strong emphasis on independence and sovereignty. The prime minister's statement was interpreted as a move – albeit a cautious one – towards membership. The outcome of the EEA negotiations would determine if membership would become an issue in the 1991 election campaign. It could be a difficult debate for the SAP.[8] The party was internally divided, but the government could come out in favour of an application for membership in due course.

The foreign minister, Sten Andersson, was reportedly more open and not as categorical as the prime minister on the issue of membership. However, Andersson too argued that Sweden should concentrate on the EEA negotia-tions.[9] In his view, there was no need to hurry. He pointed out that Sweden should wait and see what the EC political union actually meant.[10] After all, he believed that a decision on membership would not have to be taken until 1992.[11]

Traditionally, the SAP and trade unions had maintained a close relation-ship (see *infra*). The position of trade unions on the issue of EC membership was therefore likely to have an impact on how the party positioned itself. In the aforementioned radio broadcast, it was noted that trade unions were also moving in the direction of membership and that this, in turn, would influ-ence the politicians. However, trade unions were far from being united on the issue. The chairman of the peak organisation representing white-collar workers, the Swedish Confederation of Professional Employees (*Tjänstemännens Centralorganisation*, TCO), was reportedly close to the position of the Liberal Party, that is, in favour of membership. Also, the chairman of the Swedish Trade Union Confederation (*Landsorganisationen*, LO) was in favour of membership. However, in an op-ed article, two of LO's economists argued strongly against membership and urged the prime minister to say 'no' (*Dagens Nyheter*, 24 June 1990). Their main argument concerned the goal of full employment. They argued that EC membership threatened the Scandinavian model. With a seat in the SAP Executive Committee, LO could also exert influence from within the party. So, by mid-1990, Europe had become a salient issue for the party. The issue of European integration was raised at the Executive Committee meeting on 1 June 1990 (Carlsson 2003, 395–6).[12]

Carlsson, with his collegial style of decision-making, was concerned about the potential effect of EC issues on the party's unity. He and other leading

Social Democrats were well aware of the negative impact of the same issue on the Norwegian sister party back in the 1970s (Carlsson 2003, 402–3). Carlsson – a cautious politician – was convinced that he had to be careful. For him, too, timing was of the utmost importance. Beyond the concern with the party, as prime minister he had to take broader (national) considerations into account, and he was keen to retain his freedom of action. This priority is clearly evident in his op-ed article published in *Dagens Nyheter* in early July 1990. Though membership was not an issue at that point it time, he argued that it could be in the future. It was therefore essential that the September 1990 SAP conference left open the question of EC membership (Carlsson 2003, 406–7). The conference followed suit. At the conference, Ingvar Carlsson drew attention to the new developments in Europe and said, once again, that he wanted a citizens' Europe and stressed the importance of welfare and the fight against unemployment.[13]

U-turn on membership

As it turned out, the re-orientation was to come both sooner than expected and under different circumstances. Faced with a big outflow of capital and a balance of payments/currency crisis, the government, on 26 October 1990, adopted an economic austerity package, which contained measures intended to restore confidence in the Swedish economy. As the first item in this statement, which was presented by Prime Minister Ingvar Carlsson and Finance Minister Allan Larsson, the government declared that it wanted a new *Riksdag* decision that 'more distinctly and in more positive terms clarifies Sweden's ambition to become a member of the European Community' (quoted in Gustavsson 1998, 66). In fact, this statement was prepared by a small group of government ministers and the prime minister's close advisers. At the same time, the prime minister sounded out the parliamentary group as well as the Party Board about this decision (Andersson 1996, 562; Carlsson 2003, 413). Interestingly enough, however, the government's decision, a collective decision under the Constitution, was communicated to Helsinki and Oslo even before the parliamentary group and, apparently, some ministers had been informed.

Significantly, EC membership was framed as an economic issue. The finance minister announced the decision together with the prime minister, whereas the foreign minister, Sten Andersson, and the minister for trade and European affairs, Anita Gradin, evidently were on the margins of decision-making. In short, the foreign minister was bypassed (Gustavsson 1998; see also Lewin 2002; 2004). However, previous research has not been able to show exactly how Andersson dealt with this situation. In an author interview, he said that he 'protested' when Allan Larsson, speaking in a Cabinet meeting, presented this as an economic issue (interview, Stockholm, 13 June 2006). Andersson considered resigning but came to the conclusion that he could not do so for the sake of party unity. He wanted to postpone the decision in order to give the party more time. Andersson said that you cannot 'run over' the party – a 'people's movement' – and argued that a big party 'must hold together'. However, as a former Secretary General of the party (1963–82), he felt he could not resign: 'the price was too high, I could have torn the party apart'. Andersson said there was something of a panic about the decision. The prime minister had to handle an economic crisis. However, this was not how he used to take decisions. He was usually careful to 'anchor' his decisions. Andersson said that Carlsson 'must have been influenced by others' (interview, Stockholm, 13 June 2006).

Apparently, the prime minister counted on the loyalty of his foreign minister. At the same time, however, a way around Andersson had to be found, as he had recently argued against membership, at least in the short term. In his statement during a debate on Europe in the *Riksdag* on 10 October 1990, Andersson argued that 'today [it] is wrong and unwise' to raise the issue of membership and take a snap decision that was 'unnecessary and really premature'. This was so, he argued, for a number of reasons. One reason was, predictably, neutrality. Moreover, he felt that the government should pursue the option of negotiations for the EEA. EC membership was not a goal for the ongoing negotiations, though this could change in the longer run, depending on security considerations. Andersson also said he wanted consensus among the Swedish political parties, both regarding the issue itself and the timetable. For him, membership was above all a question of timing. He was not against membership in principle, and even pleaded for future membership in his speech at the party conference in September 1990.

Andersson noted that his statement in the *Riksdag* had been 'approved by the prime minister's office' (interview, Stockholm, 13 June 2006). Only a couple of weeks later did the prime minister, in tandem with his finance minister, announce the decision to apply for membership. In the midst of EEA negotiations, the government made a U-turn or 'volte-face' (Aylott 1999) on the issue of membership. Carlsson declared that the conditions underpinning Sweden's traditional objection to membership had ceased to exist, and that becoming an EC member was in the country's national interest. This was a radical re-orientation and policy change. For the first time ever, a Swedish government had come out in favour of full participation in the West European integration process.

In a way, the Swedish re-orientation on EC membership in October 1990 shows that central political decision-makers were victims of unforeseen events. The decision was taken during an acute economic crisis, while the country was under pressure from capital markets, and can be seen as an instance of political and economic crisis management. There are strong indications that the situation was running out of control. This interpretation suggests that the decision, or at least the timing, was more or less accidental. At the same time, however, the crisis and the unfolding events opened a 'window of opportunity', and this was instrumental for individual decision-makers, most notably the finance minister, Allan Larsson, and the prime minister and SAP leader, Ingvar Carlsson (Gustavsson 1998; see also Aylott 1999; Lewin 2002; 2004; Lundgren Rydén 2000).

In his memoirs, Carlsson (2003, 408) writes about the 'dilemma' that the government was facing. There was a need for 'cautiously opening up for a change', while defending the existing foreign policy line. Carlsson strongly argues against the 'myth' that this decision was a kind of coup and challenges a number of arguments used to explain his decision (2003, 373), including the following:

a)   acute economic problems gave Sweden no other possibility than to become a member;
b)   the prime minister, that is, Carlsson himself, together with the finance minister, Allan Larsson, compelled the foreign minister, Sten Andersson, 'to submit to our will';
c)   the Liberals and the Moderates put the SAP under pressure to make this concession;
d)   the decision was made because of a threat of losing the election (due in September 1991).

According to Carlsson, such theories are 'completely unreal'. It was not a 'panic decision' (Carlsson 2003, 374). Rather, European issues had been managed within his office for a long time (Carlsson 2003, 412). His closest political aides – above all his state secretary, Kjell Larsson, and chief foreign policy adviser, Hans Dahlgren – were in favour of an initiative (Carlsson 2003, 408). Looking back, Carlsson points out that he did not feel alone or isolated in his view that the situation and the conditions for Sweden were about to 'change radically'. On the contrary, 'central decision-makers' regarded membership of the EU much more positively. The finance minister, Allan Larsson, was certainly in this group.

The former Norwegian prime minister, Gro Harlem Brundtland, writes in her memoirs (1999, 162–3) that Ingvar Carlsson had said, at the SAMAK meeting in Copenhagen in November 1990, that the Social Democrats had tried to take control of this important issue by seizing the initiative themselves, and that Swedish industry was facing major difficulties, citing investment in particular. The EEA negotiations between the EC and EFTA would continue, with the aim of the treaty coming into force on 1 January 1993. Carlsson also indicated that Swedish public opinion was clearly in favour of EC membership (unlike in Norway, in the context of the 1972 referendum, which had had such serious effects on the Labour Party). The party risked getting into trouble for appearing to be negative, said Carlsson: 'Public opinion is ahead of LO, and LO is ahead of the party.' According to Carlsson, recent changes in Europe had facilitated a much more positive judgement on the prospect of Swedish EC membership. After the fall of the Berlin Wall, in November 1989, a new situation had arisen.

Obviously, the prime minister and his finance minister were keen to send a positive signal to the electorate and, in the short term, primarily to various markets so as to restore confidence in the Swedish economy at home and abroad. The business community, including leading industrialists, was pushing for membership. Such an interest-based interpretation suggests that material interests were predominant (see, for example, Ingebritsen 1998). At the same time, however, the role of ideas and ideology should not be under-estimated. It was argued that the welfare state could be preserved by closer European co-operation. Carlsson, who maintained contacts with other leading social democrats in Europe and was influenced by such personal contacts, portrayed the EU as a political instrument that had to be used in order to secure the labour movement's traditional values. He would repeat this message time and again, not least during the referendum campaign in 1994.

Although neutrality was weakened as the prime argument against closer Swedish involvement in European integration, a number of arguments relating to sovereignty, autonomy, the welfare state and the societal model remained obstacles to the legitimisation of membership. In the public debate, the consequences in terms of sovereignty were summarised as a loss of *formal sovereignty* but an increase in *real sovereignty*. The conclusions became known as the *calculus of sovereignty*. This conceptual innovation entailed a reinterpretation of popular sovereignty, as stipulated by the Swedish Constitution, as well as of democracy, implying that efficiency was emphasised more than procedural democracy (Jacobsson 1997). Increased economic and political interdependence had created a situation where independent political decisions were seen as ineffective. This reasoning struck a chord among political elites, including the SAP leadership. The experience of the economic crisis in 1990, along with the lessons from the economic policy change of the French Socialist government in the 1980s, affected the previous conception of sovereignty and autonomy among social democratic elites.

Ingvar Carlsson pointed out that experience had shown – not least in France in the 1980s, but also in Sweden in the early 1990s – that 'the nation state is no longer sufficient' (interview, Stockholm, 22 October 1997; see also Johansson 1999, 90). Carlsson later recalled that he strongly linked the employment issue to the EU and membership thereof (interview, Stockholm, 29 August 2005). One of the main reasons why he supported Sweden's membership of the EC was that it is impossible to handle employment policy (or, for instance, the Baltic Sea environmental issues) in isolation from other countries. Sweden, therefore, ought to be brought closer to the process of European co-operation and integration.

Referendum and membership

After the U-turn on the issue of membership, the Social Democrats had to decide whether to hold a referendum. The party has traditionally been reluctant to use referenda. On the issue of EU membership, leading Social Democrats had memories of the disruptive and serious effects of the 1972 Norwegian referendum on the Labour Party (Carlsson 2003, 402–3). They were reluctant to call a referendum before the completion of the accession negotiations.

However, by January 1991, just a few months after the U-turn, all parties except the SAP had publicly declared that they wanted to resolve the issue of membership through a referendum. The SAP leadership was thus forced to follow suit. The split within the party and the electorate made it impossible to handle the issue in a general election (Carlsson 2003, 417–18). The risks and potential losses were far too big. Even though the major political parties and interest groups supported the application, public opinion seemed less convinced.

The referendum took place on 13 November 1994. After intense campaigning, 52 per cent of the voters voted 'yes'. Given the strong standing of the Social Democrats in Swedish politics, the victory was facilitated by the SAP's victory in the parliamentary election that had taken place two months earlier. As in the other Nordic countries, the social democratic constituency was a key determinant of the final verdict on the issue of membership. In the end, the SAP 'barely managed to scrape together a majority of their own followers to vote for membership' (Svåsand and Lindström 1996, 212).

Sweden, along with Austria and Finland, became full members of the EU on 1 January 1995. Sweden joined at a time of economic recession, and the government implemented a tight fiscal policy, involving cuts in social security provisions, during the early years of Swedish membership. These political circumstances strengthened Euroscepticism in Swedish public opinion, which, in turn, restricted the freedom of action of Swedish decision-makers. European integration became a new dimension of conflict in Swedish politics. It generated factionalism in traditionally very disciplined and cohesive Swedish political parties. Overall, the pattern of party support and opposition to the EU reflects the positions in the 1994 referendum. The SAP remains divided on EU-related issues, and the party has only cautiously clarified what kind of Europe it wants.

What kind of Europe?

Since the somewhat dramatic circumstances under which the Social Democratic government reached a decision on membership, the party has had to define its European policy. As neutrality and non-alignment, as well as reluctance to lose sovereignty over core policy areas, had been the main obstacles to Swedish membership, the SAP needed to rethink its discourse and policies, as well as its basic ideological orientation.

Scope of integration

The SAP basically construes European integration first and foremost as *intergovernmental* co-operation aimed at delivering political results in areas where the nation state is no longer effective as an institutional framework. The EU is perceived as a means to address some of the consequences of globalisation. For the SAP, it is obvious that political decision making has not been internationalised at the same pace as the markets. Through the deregulation of capital markets and the development of a global market, a political and legal vacuum has appeared . . . The European Union is a natural platform for common action in the global economy.

(Socialdemokraterna 2000, 8–9)

The EU is perceived as a way of increasing the *real sovereignty* of a small state with an internationalised market. In the same document, it is argued that:

faced with the choice between possible ameliorations for the benefit of EU citizens and formal national decision making power that cannot change the living conditions of the people, we choose the first.

(Socialdemokraterna 2000, 9)

The *calculus of sovereignty* is here translated into the language of the SAP. The result, defined in terms of better conditions that pooled sovereignty can bring about, is the central source of legitimisation of supranational decisions. In its programme, the party argues that:

when it comes to the question of what decisions ought to be taken in the EU, two extreme positions often stand against each other: to transfer almost all decisions to the EU or to oppose all common (supranational) decisions. Instead, we – Social Democrats – start from the issues at stake: which questions are suitable for the national (or local) level and which ones are suitable for the supranational level?

(Socialdemokraterna 2000, 9)

Against this background, the SAP has not, despite its hesitations about the EU, been especially keen on limiting the scope of integration. The main principle has been that the EU should essentially deal with policy areas that have truly cross-border implications. The prime example of this kind of issue is the environment. However, in its statements, the SAP often tries to strike the delicate balance between controlling central welfare state functions at the national level and highlighting the importance of EU co-operation in these policy areas.

One area where the SAP has stressed the need for more co-operation in the EU is employment policy (Johansson 1999; Johansson and Svensson 2002).[14] The party has been firmly behind the Lisbon Process and even contributed to the establishment of the Open Method of Co-ordination, which relies on benchmarks and political commitments rather than legal acts.

Enlargement is another issue of great importance for the Swedish Social Democrats. As argued above, the change in party preferences on European integration was from the outset related to enlargement. It was one of three priority areas – along with employment and the protection of the environment

– of the Social Democratic government during the Swedish EU presidency in 2001. There is broad consensus in Sweden, among all political parties, in favour of EU enlargement. This is also one of the few issues where public opinion in Sweden is more positive than in other member states, according to the Eurobarometer. There is a clear tendency to favour widening of the geographical scope of the EU rather than deepening of integration. This holds, not only with regard to the previous enlargement process, but also to the question of Turkish membership of the EU (Langdal 2006).

The internationalist profile of the party has been a key feature of the SAP throughout its history. International solidarity, combined with an activist foreign policy paradigm, was prominent when Olof Palme was party leader (1969–86). In relation to the EU, the SAP has been very keen to safeguard national sovereignty in the area of welfare state institutions, while construing the EU – and especially enlargement – as part of a broader peace project.

In the run-up to the 2004 enlargement, a debate emerged on the transition rules and openness of the domestic labour market. In a statement made in November 2003, Prime Minister Göran Persson warned that there was a fear that the opening-up of labour markets after the enlargement might lead to a sort of 'social tourism'. There was a fear that citizens from the new EU member states would exploit Swedish welfare benefits (Swedish News Agency, 21 November 2003).[15] This statement provoked a long debate about whether or not Sweden should, like other member states, introduce transitional arrangements concerning the free movement of labour. The Swedish Trade Union Confederation, LO, did not share the government's position and proposed an alternative solution that focused more on reforms of the labour market regulations and not so much on the social security system. In the end, the proposal for transition rules was rejected (Eriksson 2006).

More recently, the debate in Sweden on EU-related issues has focused on the challenges to the country's model of industrial relations and collective wage bargaining, after the European Court of Justice issued its ruling in the Laval case in December 2007. The court found that Swedish construction workers, organised in the Swedish builders' union (*Byggnads*), were not justified in blockading a building site in Vaxholm near Stockholm, run by a Latvian building company, Laval un Partneri, that failed to pay the locally agreed wage rate. The Laval ruling intensified tensions in the EU over balancing workers' ability to move across borders with labour and trade union rights, and in Sweden over the system of collective bargaining. The issue has been highly politicised and has remained contentious during and beyond the 2009 European elections. The SAP's manifesto for this election emphasised this issue (Socialdemokraterna 2008).

Aims of integration

The aim of integration is closely related to the way in which the SAP has legitimised accession in the first place. The overarching aim is to deliver results, through joint problem-solving with other countries. The party has adopted a very pragmatic strategy. The main objective is to achieve peace and prosperity. In the SAP's view, the EU is also a means to protect a small and interdependent country from globalisation. The EU can in this way be understood as a means to strengthen national autonomy. The contestation within the party over European integration has been about the loss of national sovereignty versus a redefined understanding of national autonomy and decision-making capacity. This, in turn, is intimately connected with diverging understandings of the nature of the welfare state in conditions of internationalisation. The critics within the party claim that the EU is a threat to the Swedish welfare state and labour market model, whereas the party leadership has argued that the EU can serve to protect the welfare state from globalisation.

Traditionally based on a Keynesian paradigm, the SAP faces a challenge on how to manage macro-economic policy. As mentioned above, a central reason for the decision to join the EU was the perceived necessity of co-operation as a means to strengthen the political capacity for action. The key problem concerns the choice between the EU as a market-correcting or market-making mechanism. In this regard, the SAP does not have distinct preferences other than that competences over welfare state policies should remain within the realm of the nation state. The party has repeatedly rejected proposals for (a) tax harmonisation at the EU level and (b) the expansion of the Union's redistributive competences.

Institutions of integration

As a governing party during the first decade since Sweden's accession to the EU, the SAP has been involved in successive rounds of treaty reform (leading to the treaties of Amsterdam, Nice and Lisbon). The party has therefore been forced to indicate its preferences on EU institutions. This has not always been straightforward. The party has often been criticised by its political opponents for neglecting matters related to institutional reform. In the 1996 IGC, the government's positions reflected earlier attempts to steer the debate away from institutional questions towards a focus on issues thought to be less controversial and of more direct relevance to citizens (Johansson and Svensson 2002, 345–6). This clearly remained a strategic priority for the government. This approach must be seen in the context of internal party divisions, and it is directly related to the predominant understanding of the EU as a basically intergovernmental form of co-operation aiming at delivering results in some policy areas.

In a government report published in 2000 on the so-called 'Amsterdam leftovers', it is argued that:

> there are no reasons for changing the constitutional basis of the EU. It should continue to rest on an intergovernmental agreement where in certain areas the member states delegate decision making powers to supranational bodies. Any amendments to the treaties should continue to be made the same way as before.
>
> (Swedish Government 2000, 4)[16]

Here, the basic understanding of European integration as a form of inter-governmental co-operation between sovereign states, as well as a normative goal of continuing this arrangement, is emphasised. Despite the emphasis on intergovernmentalism, the party still considers supranational institutions to be legitimate. The party even stresses that the independence and functions of those bodies (European Commission and courts) need to be secured, as those bodies can protect the smaller member states. Therefore, the Social Democratic government has argued in favour of the principle of one commissioner per country – even more fiercely than it did in the negotiations regarding the voting rules in the Council. This may seem rather paradoxical when the intergovernmental status of the EU has been so central to the party. However, the SAP has strongly objected to increased parliamentarisation at the European level that would enhance the Commission's accountability to the European Parliament.

During the negotiations that led to the adoption of the Constitutional Treaty, the Social Democratic government maintained the view – shared by a majority of the *Riksdag* – that the institutional balance in the EU should remain unaltered (Swedish Government 2002; Swedish Parliament 2002).[17] Nevertheless, the government supported the proposal for a permanent president of the European Council, as well as the proposal to abandon the pillar structure, which implies an extension of areas subject to QMV in the Council and the enhancement of the role of the European Parliament. In October 2001, Göran Persson stated that he supported the extension of QMV in the Council in areas such as 'labour market and social affairs, as well as in asylum and immigration matters' (Persson 2001, 8).

In the final phase of the process leading to the Lisbon Treaty in 2007, the SAP, now in opposition, supported the non-socialist government's priorities and kept a rather low profile. The need to keep the bulk of the Constitutional Treaty's provisions, while removing symbols such as references to the flag and hymn, was a position shared by many, including the SAP.

Having sent somewhat mixed signals, the opposition Social Democrats voted with the centre-right parties of the ruling coalition in favour of the ratification of the Lisbon Treaty by the *Riksdag* in November 2008. Although none of the SAP's members of parliament voted against, eight abstained (including two ex-ministers). In that context, the Social Democrats placed a strong emphasis on the Swedish labour market model, with its system of collective bargaining and agreements, while, in the past, individual politicians of the party had argued that the Lisbon Treaty should not be ratified until the issues relating to the Vaxholm or Laval case (see *supra*) had been resolved.

Preferences and preference formation

This section examines the link between the explanatory factors specified in the introductory chapter and the preferences of the SAP. Some of these factors vary over time, whereas the influence of others is enduring. It is therefore difficult to apply the questions these factors raise to the entire time frame. The section focuses mainly on the preferences of the SAP in the period 1994–2009, that is, after the U-turn on membership and the referendum.

Interests

Economic interests

The ties of the SAP to the trade unions, especially the blue-collar workers' union LO, have been very strong throughout the twentieth century. The Swedish labour market model, with centralised bargaining and significant powers delegated to the social partners, is a distinctive feature of Swedish corporatism. The labour market organisations have also been closely involved in various stages of the policy-making process. The overlapping interests of the LO and SAP were core ingredients in what became key components of the Swedish model, with its compromise between capital and labour from the 1930s onwards (Rothstein 1996). The organisational ties between the LO and the SAP are so close that they are considered two wings of the same movement. Until the early 1990s, LO membership automatically entailed membership of the SAP.

As already noted, the Swedish industry is highly export-oriented, and the interests of union branches predominantly representing workers in the export industry were, at the outset, different from those of public sector workers in relation to European integration. The traditional Swedish labour market has been dependent on solidarity between different branches of the LO. The re-emergence of European integration as a core issue has challenged the unity of the labour movement. The coalition between different branches of the labour movement was therefore under pressure. The trade unions representing workers in the export (metal and paper) industries favoured membership, whereas those mainly in domestic or public sectors (municipal workers, retail workers) opposed it. The LO centrally decided not to support any of these positions. It is often stressed how important the LO has been in (a) mobilising support for the SAP and (b) legitimising decisions of the government. In order to preserve unity, the LO had to remain neutral (Aylott 1999, 152). The split between the branches of the LO reflected diverging material interests in relation to the expected effects of full membership of the EU. Whereas some unions perceived it as a threat, others saw it as an opportunity. This division also came to the fore in the voting patterns in the referendum, as well as in subsequent polls. It also shows how deeply split the whole labour movement was on the issue of European integration. It follows that the SAP could not expect the same support from the LO on European integration as on other issues.

Vote maximisation and political competition

Swedish political life has been dominated by the outstanding success of the Social Democrats. The average Swedish government is a one-party, Social

Democratic minority government with support in the *Riksdag* from the small Left Party. Between 1998 and 2006, the Social Democrats needed, and received, the support of the Left Party and the Greens in the *Riksdag*. This differed from earlier instances of co-operation, as the two supporting parties were invited to reach political deals before the proposals had reached parliament. Co-operation included all issues apart from foreign and security policy and matters related to the EU, on which the government relied mainly on the political support of the Centre Party or other non-socialist opposition parties. Indeed, the Euroscepticism of the Greens and the Left Party prevented them from forming a formal coalition with the Social Democrats (Fichtelius 2007, 171; Persson 2007, 236, 327, 398). Although the direct influence of the Left Party and the Greens on EU matters was limited, their position has affected the SAP. As there are high levels of Euroscepticism among SAP voters and members, the party fears that they might turn away and vote for the sceptical parties. In election campaigns, the pro-European parties seek to avoid the European issue, whereas the two sceptical parties try to increase the salience of the issue, but without any major success. The pro-EU parties have strong incentives to keep party competition along the established left–right axis. This strategy was clearly expressed in the SAP platform ahead of the 2009 European election, where it was stressed that the election concerned 'a typical conflict between right and left' (Socialdemokraterna 2008, 3). In that electoral contest, the Eurosceptic share of the vote went down substantially, but this did not help improve the SAP's score in comparison with previous electoral contests. One would have expected the party to benefit from not being in government at the time of the election, but the result was identical to that of 2004.

The continuous split between the party's elite and supporters has been demonstrated in the European elections and the two EU-related referenda. The gulf between the official party position and the views of the party's supporters is most significant in the case of the SAP, although the Centre Party and the Christian Democrats have encountered similar problems. In the context of national elections, no clear connection can be established between the SAP's share of votes and the party's preferences on European integration. However, the Greens and the Left Party may have gained from their scepticism towards the EU by attracting disappointed SAP voters. This has been the case especially in European elections. The SAP obtained 28.1, 26.0, 24.6 and 24.4 per cent of the votes in successive European elections from 1995 to 2009, compared with 45.3, 36.4, 39.9 and 35.0 per cent in national elections between 1994 and 2006.[18]

In most matters related to European integration, the SAP has looked for support among the non-socialist parties. New patterns of competition and collusion within the party system have emerged. On the one hand, there was closer collaboration between the SAP and its partners (the Greens and the Left Party) than previously. On the other hand, these parties have exerted little or no influence on EU policy, an area where the SAP has much more in common with non-socialist parties. The fact that Swedish parliamentarism is negative[19] substantially curbs the veto power of the two Eurosceptic parties. This has allowed the SAP's minority governments to shape EU policy, often with the support of non-socialist opposition parties.

In recent years, the Greens have adopted a more positive stance vis-à-vis the EU, and, in the aftermath of the 2009 European election, a debate within the Left Party on abandoning its clearly Eurosceptic position was emerging. An eventual change in this regard would make the SAP–Green–Left alliance a more cohesive government alternative and would make it easier for the SAP to draw up party strategies and formulate EU policy.

Party cohesion

Party cohesion has probably been the most central aspect restricting the party leadership's room for manoeuvre during the period examined in this chapter.[20] The party was already suffering severely from internal dissent after the application for membership. Sub-groups, such as Social Democrats against the EC, were formed, and the party leadership had to strike a difficult balance between accommodation and confrontation. Aylott (1999, 152) has argued that the 'issue-management strategy implemented by the Social Democratic leadership can be summarised as accommodation of opposition, combined with steadfastness about the leadership's objectives. In many ways, it can be considered a success.'

Nevertheless, this successful management of internal divisions cannot be said to have lasted. The party leadership has been unable to convince its rank-and-file to support the views of the leadership. As already mentioned, the party leadership tried to accommodate the sceptics in the 1995 extraordinary European election by launching two different lists. Arguably, this strategy of accommodation did not result in greater unity. Ahead of the referendum on the euro, the division within the Cabinet became even greater when individual ministers campaigned against the adoption of the single currency. All the social democratic governments from 1994 onwards included ministers who were prominent on the 'no' side but the divisions were even greater on EMU. This undermined the authority of the prime minister quite severely and meant that European policy was downplayed even more after the referendum on the single currency in September 2003. In this context, uniting the fragmented party became an urgent need. The appointment of the Eurosceptic minister of culture, Marita Ulvskog, as Secretary General of the party in 2004 was a direct attempt to appease the Eurosceptics within the SAP (Fichtelius 2007, 103). This appointment was significant in that it 'illustrated the enduring influence of the party on European policy' (Aylott 2007, 182). The same can be said of the decision to make Ulvskog the party's top candidate for the 2009 European elections – a decision that also must be seen in light of party competition to attract the Eurosceptic vote.

From a historical point of view, the inability of party leadership to convince the rank-and-file is indeed a novelty. These tensions have remained in place, and the party's position has not been reconciled with the views of party members and voters. This indicates the depth of these splits. The degree of dissent within the party has certainly limited the leadership's room for manoeuvre. The party's strategy on EMU and in all elections since 1990 shows that the party has tried to avoid the European dimension of party competition. As Aylott (2002) puts it, the party has adopted a strategy of 'let's discuss this later'. The distance between party and voters on the issue, as well as the severe internal divisions, have all led to the conclusion that the European dimension could, in a worst-case scenario for the Social Democrats, lead to realignment. Hence, it had to be excluded from the domain of political competition, especially in national legislative elections.[21]

When it comes to preferences on European integration, three points can be noted in relation to party cohesion, namely, the unwillingness to include EU themes in the field of political competition; the interpretation of the EU as a form of limited intergovernmental co-operation between sovereign states; and, finally, the quest for an understanding of the EU that is consistent with the party's own ideology, coupled with explicit support for the EU in areas marked by high levels of congruence between the leadership, the members and the voters (employment, enlargement, environment, gender equality and openness/transparency).[22] All these central features of the SAP's European policy can be understood as ways of coping with dissent in the internal arena and with the party–voter incongruence.[23]

Institutions

National political culture

The academic discussion on the degree to which Swedish political culture is best described in terms of conflict or consensus has been long-standing. Scholars have offered varying interpretations, which to some extent depend on the design of the studies in terms of time period, policy focus, the actors or structures studied and focus on ideology or strategy. The government usually seeks national unity or consensus in the foreign and security policy domain. Central actors have held the view that consensual decision-making strengthens the foreign policy of a small country. As seen in previous sections of this chapter, a new coalition pattern on the political scene took shape when the pro-EU front in the 1994 referendum campaign included the leader of the conservative Moderate Party and the leader of the SAP. Alongside them were the Liberals, the Centre Party and the Christian Democrats, many trade unions and business associations. This created an image of consensual preferences that were in line with traditional foreign policy. Initially, the EU was mainly perceived and treated as part of foreign policy. Therefore, it is not surprising that much of the parliamentary decision-making on the EU was made in a spirit of traditional foreign policy.

It is hard to ascertain the influence that this factor has had on the SAP's preferences on the EU. On the one hand, it may have restricted the party's capacity to form its own vision of the EU. On the other hand, the party has been very keen on highlighting alternative visions of the EU. After Sweden's accession to the EU, the leadership has been eager to convince the SAP's supporters that the party's vision and agenda for the EU differ from that of the right-of-centre parties and especially the Moderates.

Party policy-making

The party itself is an institution that constrains decision-making, also when the SAP is in government. In addition to internally elaborated opinions, there are external links to the trade unions, most notably to LO, and to the broader civil society. The party chairman may face constraints stemming from various internal bodies, such as the Party Board and Executive Committee. In addition, the parliamentary party is another important player. Overall, the need for party discipline and the nature of decision-making vis-à-vis the EU imply that members of parliament exert quite marginal influence when the party is in government. Their influence on party preferences increases when the party is in opposition.

After the party's electoral defeat and the election of a new party chairman in 2007, a new and smaller EU group was set up. The 'Reference group for EU affairs' serves as a body for deliberations between the party organisation, the parliamentary party, the delegations in the European Parliament, the Committee of the Regions and the European Trade Union Confederation (ETUC). The group is also a point of reference for the party's representatives in the presidency of the Party of European Socialists and working groups. The group offers an arena for meetings and provides support to the Secretary General of the party on EU-related matters (interview with Susanne Eberstein, Stockholm, 14 November 2007).[24]

Over the years, the EU group has been assigned additional tasks related to European elections and intergovernmental conferences. Initially, the main task of the group, which was formally established by the SAP Executive Committee in January 1995, was to prepare positions for the 1996 IGC. The group served as a reference group for the SAP's representative in the PES working group on the IGC. After the end of the IGC, the group focused on enlargement-related issues. It continued to serve as a reference point for the SAP's representatives in the PES. The group was also asked to present proposals to the party's Executive Committee and the Party Board before the 1998 national election, the 1999 European election and the Swedish EU presidency during the first half of 2001. In addition to representatives of the party, the groups in the European Parliament, the *Riksdag* and the Trade Union Confederation (LO), the group also used to include officials from the Ministry for Foreign Affairs, the prime minister's office and some senior politicians, including ministers and state secretaries.

Party–government relationship

When the SAP is in government, there are potential conflicts between the representatives of the party who hold public office, the party's headquarters and the party's grass roots (cf. Mair 1994). As regards Swedish EU policy, Miles (2005, 93) observes that:

> it is also necessary to recognise the importance of formal centres of decision-making power which influence national EU policy that lie outside the formal structures of government. One of the most important of these is the vital role of members of the executive committee of Sweden's largest (and usually governing) political party – the Social Democrats. Without the support of the elite of the Social Democratic Party in Sweden, the political will to push forward ambitious European-orientated solutions barely exists. For example, the government's policy on EMU has been the subject of intense debate within this select group of leading Social Democrats influencing the attitude of the premier on when to hold a future public referendum on joining the Euro.

However, in the case of the Social Democrats, 'EU policy has increasingly been led by the prime minister himself' (Miles 2005, 143).

There are clear indications that the party chairman, especially when heading the government, has become more detached from the party organisation since Sweden joined the EU. EU business adds significantly to the attention that heads of governments in EU member states have to pay to matters related to international or supranational co-operation and decision-making. The growing importance of EU policy-making has substantially strengthened the power of the national core executive (Johansson and Tallberg 2010; Moravcsik 1994), especially when the logic of intergovernmental relations/negotiations prevails in the context of the EU. Poguntke and Webb (2005a, 13–14) argue that, where issues are dealt with via intergovernmental negotiations, 'this shifts power to the heads of governments and some of their key advisers or governmental colleagues. Increasingly, parliaments and even cabinets can only ratify the decisions which have been taken elsewhere.'

National chief executives have been strengthened by their informational advantage over parliaments and over other parts of the government. The international trend of presidentialisation or chief executive empowerment applies in Sweden too (Aylott 2005; Johansson and Tallberg 2010). In addition to more general factors, presidentialisation in Sweden is usually explained by the contingent personality factor of Göran Persson, who took office in 1996. However, this tendency can be traced back to earlier times and has to do with the centralisation of policy co-ordination more generally, as well as with institutional and structural factors.

In the EU, the prime minister is the principal representative of Sweden at European Council summits. He chaired the European Council during the first half of 2001. The Swedish EU presidency was directed from the prime minister's office, whose role in EU policy subsequently increased. The state secretary for EU affairs, Lars Danielsson, was especially instrumental in (a) providing political advice on European matters, (b) formulating Swedish negotiating positions and (c) ensuring consistency and coherence in national positions in the EU (Johansson 2008). In this connection, it is essential to combine an understanding of both Swedish national interests and domestic political concerns and priorities, including the views of intra-SAP groups.

When he was prime minister, from March 1996 until October 2006, the party leader Göran Persson gradually became more comfortable with political activities at the European level. According to his state secretary and close political aide in international and European affairs, Lars Danielsson, Persson perceived the EU mainly as a political *arena* (Danielsson 2007, 122). As prime minister, Göran Persson devoted on average about half of his working hours to international and EU affairs, about half of which related to the EU (interview with Lars Danielsson, Stockholm, 28 September 2005; see also Persson 2007, 175). The time spent on EU affairs naturally increased during the Swedish EU presidency in 2001 (Ruin 2002). EU summitry in particular takes up a significant portion of time for the prime minister of an EU member state. In October 2003, Persson said, at a press conference in the context of a summit, that he meets his colleagues in the European Council more often than the SAP's Board back home. Arguably, this is a sign of prime ministerial detachment from the political party. More generally, it has been argued that 'leading Social Democratic ministers have indeed become more independent of their party, thanks to the logic of EU policy-making' (Aylott 2007, 184). However, the strengthened role of the prime minister is the most striking feature of this Europeanising impact on the Swedish system of government and on party–government relations.

Transnational party links

As was noted in the introductory chapter, institutional influences on preference formation also stem from participation in the process of European integration. Transnational links have been suggested as one of several factors that could explain party responses to European integration (Johansson and Raunio 2001).[25] Gatherings within transnational EU party families may socialise party officials and politicians in a manner that affects subsequent political choices (Ladrech 2000, 399). Transnational party federations can be seen as institutional fields and mechanisms of socialisation, with potential Europeanising effects. However, it is not easy to establish the actual influence of transnational relations on party preferences. One difficulty stems from the elitist and informal nature of transnational party co-operation. Transnational activity involves primarily party leaders and party officials. Therefore, any wider influence presumably has to come indirectly from Europeanising influences on elites percolating down through party structures. This is a fairly difficult area to research.

There were transnational sources of party (leadership) preferences in the context of the EEA negotiations and the EC membership application in 1990. There was an element of elite socialisation and socialised preferences, as the party leader/prime minister was involved in the network of European Social Democrats and cultivated relations with individual politicians. It is beyond doubt that he was inspired by conversations and meetings with other leading European social democrats, including the Spanish prime minister, Felipe González, the Austrian chancellor, Franz Vranitzky, and European Commission president, Jacques Delors.

The SAP leader and selected party elites, including party officials, have continuously been involved in other transnational networks as well, including the regular meetings of the Nordic labour movement (SAMAK). In the wider context of European party co-operation, it is interesting to note that the SAP became an observer of CSPEC as early as the late 1970s, and a full member of the PES in November 1992.

As was noted above, the EU group inside the SAP serves as a reference point for party representatives in the PES. The party is represented in meetings of party leaders, the presidency as well as the co-ordination team, which is composed of the heads of international departments of PES member parties. Whether in government or in opposition, a party such as the SAP can draw on PES membership when forging links to sister parties in other EU member states as well as in accession countries. Specifically, noteworthy examples include the meetings of the PES that precede meetings of the European Council and the group of 'sherpas', that is, the personal representatives of party leaders in government. These representatives prepare European Council meetings and are engaged in inter-state EU policy co-ordination.

The SAP hosted the PES Conference held in Malmö in June 1997, which brought together a majority of EU heads of government a week before the meeting of the European Council in Amsterdam, and exactly a week after her election as party chairman in March 2007, Mona Sahlin took part at the PES leaders' meeting in Berlin before the EU summit to mark the fiftieth anniversary of the Treaty of Rome. In her address, the new SAP chairman placed emphasis on 'social Europe', in line with the PES declaration adopted on the occasion. She was subsequently appointed to lead the 'Save our planet' discussions inside the PES as an input to its manifesto for the 2009 European elections. A Swedish Social Democrat and former minister of finance, Pär Nuder, had a key role in the process of drafting the manifesto.

Ideas

As the historical overview demonstrates (see *supra*), several main currents in the basic ideology of the SAP find it difficult to accommodate supranational co-operation. It may even be argued that 'the ideology of Swedish Social Democracy is less compatible with the concept of supranational integration than most brands of European social democracy' (Aylott 1999, 183).

The development of the Swedish model has been so closely linked to the SAP that the policy legacy of the party has, to a large extent, become the national legacy. The focal points of sovereignty, welfare state expansion and neutrality have all been central in the making of the social democratic project. This project has indeed been a national project. The so-called *folkhemmet* – literally the people's home – has reinforced the tendency for welfare nationalism (Aylott 1999; Stråth 1992; Trägårdh 2002; Westberg 2003). Even though the Swedish welfare state model has attracted considerable interest elsewhere, it is primarily a *within-nation* programme of solidarity, and the SAP has been successful in preserving 'a sense of social democratic distinctiveness in Sweden' (Berman 2006, 198), not least because of the *folkhemmet* idea.

Core aspects of the SAP's ideology were challenged by the rapprochement to the EU in the early 1990s. The arguments against accession focused on how the EU undermines national sovereignty and, in that sense, also democracy. It was argued that the member states differ from the Swedish model in terms of the organisation of the welfare system. The old argument regarding the incompatibility of European integration with the Swedish policy of neutrality was strongly invoked by those who opposed membership. These were core aspects of social democratic ideology. All had to be addressed by the party leadership; all had to be reinterpreted in a way that made it possible to reconcile the policy legacy of the SAP with EU membership. This was a challenge for the joint LO–SAP group that prepared the platform for the 1990s. The platform stresses the importance of social issues and the need for employees across Europe to work together for better conditions (Lundgren Rydén 2000, 210). Westberg (2003, 202) argues that, in this process, the party leadership and the LO abandoned the national version of the 'people's home' without abandoning the overall theme of the 'people's home' from party discourse. The general aims of the paradigm were still present, emphasising participation, employment, welfare, working conditions and equality. These traditional goals retained their major mobilising potential. It was owing to its effort to achieve these central goals, at a time of severe economic crisis, that the SAP finally opted for the 'European rescue'.

For most of the period examined here, the two ideological and policy paradigms of (a) the 'people's home' and (b) neutrality have served as constraints on SAP's policy on European integration, thus offering very limited scope for policy alternatives. The SAP's ideology and narrative had been closely related to a model of society so fiercely defended and legitimised by the party during almost the entire period since the parliamentary and democratic breakthrough in Sweden. This is why it became so difficult for the party leadership to convince activists and voters to break with their old worldviews and convictions and instead endorse the leadership's re-orientation.

Conclusion

The enduring internal divisions are central to the understanding of the constraints under which the SAP has developed its preferences on European integration. The capacity of the party leadership to maintain loyalty among its members and voters has remained a cumbersome task. The risks of splits, defection, de-alignment and realignment constitute real challenges for the party leadership. The understanding of the EU as a form of primarily inter-governmental co-operation, the pragmatic focus on results rather than visions, as well as the argument as to how the EU can shelter the (national) welfare state in the era of globalisation all bear hallmarks of the traditional, reformist worldview of the SAP.

For example, the priority themes of the SAP government during the EU presidency of 2001 – enlargement, employment and environment – were all issues where,

a)   there are relatively high levels of congruence between the party leader-ship, party members and party voters;
b)   public opinion is more positive about EU involvement; and
c)   Swedish national interests are not challenged by European integration.

Since the country's accession to the EU, the SAP has prioritised pragmatism and results at the European level, while trying to increase its political autonomy at the national level. Nevertheless, unity within the party and congruence with voters on EU matters has not been achieved. Answering the question as to why a party that is traditionally characterised by high levels of internal unity, strong organisation, strong ties with trade unions and an unprecedented success in the electoral and governmental arena fails to achieve unity and to subsume a newly emerged conflict in traditional cleavage terms remains a challenge.

The explanations could point to elements of a changing internal decision-making style, the loss of social support (with declining membership rates as the prime indicator) or the weakening of union–party ties. Explanations could also be based on changes of a more systemic character, such as the changing economic structure, changes in individual orientations and the weakening of belief in political authorities. It can still be argued that the internal division and the lack of party–voter congruence are important for our understanding of SAP preferences on European integration. The party leadership's room for manoeuvre, as well as the preferences of the party, indicates that the party seeks a balance between maximising its respective goals in the internal arena (party cohesion), the parliamentary arena (influence) and the electoral arena (votes). Reconciling the strategies that correspond to each of these three arenas is not always easy. As with EMU, where party loyalty was even questioned by Cabinet ministers, the picture is dominated by European integration as an issue that cuts right through the party. The attempts to interpret European integration in terms of existing cleavage lines, entailing a projection to the European level of conflicts established in the national arena, have still not been successful enough to create unity within the party or between the party and its core voters.

One difficulty with interpreting the European preferences of the SAP is that the strategies adopted by the party have involved 'silencing', 'downplaying' and compartmentalising EU-related issues. This must be seen in light of internal party divisions. The constraint provided by intra-party factionalism is particularly salient. One issue for further research is how economic developments have affected unity within the labour movement as a whole and the creation of changing opportunity structures for different groups. This could also account for the difficulties encountered by the party leadership in maintaining loyalty among voters and members. In this connection, internationalisation and Europeanisation challenge traditional social democratic ideals and policies.

Another implication of this study concerns the development of party organisation. Transnational party links have been emphasised as one of several factors affecting party preferences. It does seem that party elites are socialised into certain ways of thinking, and an element of learning and socialisation results from transnational networking and international contacts more generally. At the same time, the SAP chairman became more detached from the party organisation and was unable to mobilise support for European integration and strengthen party cohesion in matters related to the EU. There are two possible explanations of this phenomenon. First, the conflict over European integration goes deeper than other internal disputes. Second, the party organisation itself has lost some of its powers to foster discipline. These two explanations are not mutually exclusive and could be starting points for further research into party preferences on European integration.

Appendix: list of interviewees

Sten Andersson, former SAP minister for foreign affairs, Stockholm, 13 June 2006.
Ingvar Carlsson, former prime minister and SAP chairman, Stockholm, 22 October 1997 and 29 August 2005.
Lars Danielsson, former state secretary to Prime Minister Göran Persson, Stockholm, 28 September 2005.
Susanne Eberstein, MP, chairman of the SAP Reference Group for EU Affairs and deputy chairman of the Committee on EU Affairs in the Swedish Parliament, Stockholm, 14 November 2007.

Notes

1 This chapter has benefited from comments made by participants in the workshop and the conference on social democratic parties and European integration held at Birkbeck College in December 2006 and April 2007. We should like to thank Dionyssis G. Dimitrakopoulos, Paul Heywood, Hussein Kassim and Paul Taggart for specific and useful comments. All translations are our own.
2 Karl Magnus Johansson has conducted the interviews and the archival research.
3 In particular, the personal archives of Ingvar Carlsson (SAP chairman between 1986 and 1996 and prime minister between 1986 and 1991 and 1994 and 1996) and Sten Andersson, foreign minister between 1985 and 1991, on matters European, including statements and speeches by Carlsson in 1989–90, have been used.

4 In January 1990, Carlsson met Jacques Delors in Brussels and the then leaders of the Nordic social democratic parties in Copenhagen (Carlsson 2003, 393).

5 See, for example, the statements on government policy (*regeringsförklaringen*) delivered by the prime minister in parliament on 3 October 1989 and 7 March 1990. Sweden was discussing 'a deeper and broader co-operation with the EC in all societal areas where this is compatible with the policy of neutrality.' The ambition was to take part 'as far as possible' in the emerging internal market. However, membership was not an issue in the ongoing talks with the EC.

6 The finance minister, Kjell-Olof Feldt, resigned from the government and was replaced by Allan Larsson, who was subsequently instrumental in the Swedish government's re-orientation on EC membership (see Gustavsson 1998).

7 The historian Bo Stråth (1992, 235) has argued that the policy of neutrality was redefined during the spring of 1990 and that this redefinition took place exclusively at the elite level.

8 It was noted that it could be difficult for the Centre Party too. At the time, in June 1990, there was a clear division between this party and the other two non-socialist parties in parliament. The SAP could be tempted to exploit this split for electoral purposes, as it had done in the past.

9 The formal EFTA–EC negotiations over the EEA commenced in 1990. At the time, Sweden held the presidency of EFTA. In mid-June 1990, the EC–EFTA summit took place in Gothenburg. The Swedish prime minister had a separate meeting with the Austrian chancellor, Franz Vranitzky.

10 Political union was on the agenda of one of the two IGCs that resulted in the Maastricht Treaty.

11 This timetable was the same as the one announced by the Norwegian Labour Party. This was hardly a coincidence. The two parties co-operated closely with each other, both on a bilateral basis and in the framework of Nordic institutions. Moreover, Sten Andersson and the Norwegian foreign minister (1987–9 and 1990–3), Thorvald Stoltenberg, were personal friends and held regular meetings.

12 The chairman of the party's youth wing, Anna Lindh, a future foreign minister, came out in favour of membership.

13 The leader of the Danish Social Democratic Party, Svend Auken, was a guest at the SAP conference. In his talk, Auken pleaded for Swedish membership and advised the SAP not to delay its decision (Aylott 1999, 124; Carlsson 2003, 406).

14 In the 2006 election manifesto, the only reference to the EU indicates that, 'through EU membership, Sweden has greater capacity to influence developments in Europe. Today we have an enlarged EU that is more responsible for employment, social justice and sustainable development than was conceivable ten years ago' (Socialdemokraterna 2006, 11).

15 Shortly before, Persson had given an interview in which he argued against transition rules. This change of opinion has been interpreted as the result of the influence exerted on Persson by a television documentary in which the issue of social tourism was raised (Eriksson 2006).

16 In a speech delivered at Humboldt University in 2001, Göran Persson (2001, 7) reiterated these views: 'I would not be prepared to accept that a transfer of competence from the national to the European level could be made without ratification by national parliaments.'

17 In the party manifesto for the June 2004 European election, there were no references to institutional issues, the Convention or the Constitutional Treaty (Socialdemokraterna 2004).

18 On European election results, see Oscarsson and Holmberg (2006, 13).

19 This means that a government can be installed as long as it is unopposed by a majority in parliament. Hence, it does not need the active support of a majority. This is why minority governments are so common in Sweden.

20 In the Chapel Hill expert survey, national experts ranked party positions on European integration and the degree of internal dissent over European integration. From very low levels of internal dissent in the two first observations (1984 and 1988), the SAP is among the most divided of all political parties in Europe after the change in the leadership's position. According to the expert survey, the SAP has become increasingly divided over time (Ray 1999).

21 This echoes the analysis of Steenbergen and Scott (2004).

22 In his closing speech at the party conference in 2004, Göran Persson said that 'the voice of Europe is necessary to counterbalance the world's sole superpower. First of all, we have to become better at co-ordinating our foreign policy' (Persson 2004).

23 The newly elected leader, Mona Sahlin, announced in her inauguration speech in March 2007 that she will place more emphasis on European integration. She also announced that the then Swedish Commissioner, Margot Wallström, and the former foreign minister and senior diplomat, Jan Eliasson, would chair the party's working group on foreign and European affairs. This group should provide input to the party's manifestos for the European election in 2009 and the national election of 2010. In her speech, Sahlin said it was time to move away from the 'yes' and 'no' camps on European integration, and that the party will 'raise the level of mobilisation, engagement, development of policy in the run-up to the European parliamentary elections and the next general election' (Socialdemokraterna 2007, 20).

24 The group has been assigned a special role in the run-up to the European elections in 2009 and the national elections in 2010.

25 The other factors suggested are basic ideology, public opinion, factionalism, leadership influence, party competition and the development of integration.

7 Conclusions

Dionyssis G. Dimitrakopoulos

Introduction[1]

The aim of this chapter is threefold. First, it seeks to identify the points of agreement and disagreement between the five parties in the immediate post-Convention period. Second, given the enduring diversity of these parties' preferences on European integration – a finding that refutes the argument that associates European integration with convergence – it discusses the sources of the diversity of their preferences. Finally, it draws some broader conclusions regarding the nature of social democracy in Europe and the challenge that it faces in the beginning of the twenty-first century. More specifically, the first section of this chapter (a) categorises the current preferences of these parties in terms of the scope, aims and institutions of integration and then (b) discusses the extent to which they have changed over time. The second section examines the extent to which interests, institutions and ideas affect preference formation on European integration in these parties. Drawing on the material presented in the five substantive chapters of this volume, the final section of this chapter outlines the broader implications of this study for our understanding of the nature of social democracy in Europe and the challenges it faces in the early twenty-first century.

What kind of Europe? The resilience of diversity

The five case studies examined in the country-specific chapters reveal two major findings regarding the preferences of these parties in the immediate post-Convention era, i.e. at a time when the focus of the political debate has shifted to the new question: what *kind* of Europe do we want? First, there is a remarkable degree of agreement between these parties as regards the scope, but they disagree on the aims and the institutions of integration (Table 7.1). Second, once the issue of participation in the process of integration had been resolved, these preferences remained, by and large, stable.[2]

The question of the *scope of integration*, i.e. the policy areas that the integration project should (or should not) cover, was at the heart of the 'old debate' that pitched the supporters against the opponents of integration. In that context, segments of the democratic Left construed integration as a zero-sum

Table 7.1 Social democratic preferences on the future of Europe (post-Convention)

	Scope	*Aims*	*Institutions*
SPD	Extensive	Political union	Federal
Parti Socialiste	Extensive	Political union	Federal
Labour Party	Extensive	Area, EMU	Intergovernmental
PASOK	Extensive	Area, 'political Europe'	Position in flux
SAP	Extensive	Area, EMU	Intergovernmental

game. In other words, they believed that the pursuit of European integration inevitably entailed the commensurate reduction of national sovereignty, at a time when state action and the corresponding state capacity were *sine qua non* requirements for the pursuit of the social democratic agenda at the national level. Although, in the past, social democrats had become entangled in the debate regarding the principle of the EU's involvement in more or fewer policy areas – an issue that had divided them – in the post-Convention era, there is consensus about what has become a reality: the EU is, in fact, involved (though in varying ways) in virtually all areas of public policy. Instead of concentrating on the principle of the EU's involvement in a given policy area, social democrats are more concerned about the *nature* and outcomes of this involvement. This constitutes a remarkable and revealing change in these parties' preferences since the years that followed the establishment of the European Communities. This change reflects (a) the long-term limits of the national strategies pursued in countries such as Britain and Sweden – where social democrats interpreted participation in the nascent European Communities as running counter to the pursuit of their domestic agenda – as well as (b) the inability of the alternatives devised at the European level (specifically, the European Free Trade Area) to counterbalance more advanced forms of economic integration, i.e. those pursued within the EC.

To be sure, two groups of social democrats can be identified among the parties examined in this volume. Whereas the first group – comprising the PS and the SPD – sought the expansion of the scope of integration as an objective worthy of being pursued in its own right, others – especially the Labour Party and PASOK – sought (in the late 1970s and early 1980s, respectively) to enhance the redistributive capacity of the EC, but they did so as a result of purely *domestic* considerations, i.e. without a real interest in the broader (intra- and extra-European) implications of this development. This attitude, in turn, is indicative of the difference between a *normative* and an *instrumental* conception of European integration. Whereas the former is couched in an understanding of integration as both an instrument *and* an end in its own right, the latter reflects the pursuit of European integration exclusively as a means to resolve domestic policy problems. However, the capacity of the more reluctant of these parties to affect collective decisions regarding the scope of integration has been influenced, not only by domestic factors – especially access to power – but also by the timing of their countries' accession to the EC/EU. Indeed, the British Labour Party was in opposition when the Single European Act and the Treaty on European Union were adopted – i.e. the two treaties that did so much to extend the scope of European integration – while Sweden had chosen to remain outside the EC/EU until 1995. These parties' – especially New Labour's – acceptance of the extended scope of European integration and their subsequent pursuit of a policy of active involvement therein do not reflect real programmatic or ideological convergence with sister parties, nor should the 'pro-European turn' be conflated with it.

In terms of the *aims of integration*, the five preceding chapters reveal a significant degree of divergence between social democrats. In fact, there is support for the conception of Europe as (a) an area and (b) an actor, though it is important to note that this does not always apply to the pure versions of these alternative models. In other words, whereas the PS and, mainly, the SPD support[3] the establishment of political union, each of the other three parties supports a mixture of the pure version of Europe construed as an area and elements of more advanced forms of economic integration – a sign of their manifest pragmatism. Another reason why political reality currently defies neat categorisations is the fact that PASOK appears to be moving away from the advanced left-wing federalism that characterised the party's preferences when Costas Simitis was party leader and prime minister. Nevertheless, the diversity of these preferences is instructive, for it reveals, in addition to pragmatism, the impact of domestic considerations and historically defined policy paradigms on party preferences (see *infra*).

In contrast, for the SPD, the EU is much more than an economic area. It is a community underpinned by democratic and social values, a response to globalisation and a vital element in the quest for a multilateral world – a vision that is shared by the French PS (PS/SPD 2007), despite the problems created by the result of the national referendum of May 2005. Indeed, the German Social Democrats go as far as explicitly to support the establishment of a European security and defence union, entailing the gradual creation of a European army whose use ought to involve parliamentary legitimacy (SPD 2007).

The SAP and the British Labour Party are closer to the other extreme of the continuum. Both parties favour a looser conception of Europe, i.e. one that construes the EU primarily as an area/market – though officially they also support, in principle, Economic and Monetary Union,[4] as well as the development of CFSP. Two caveats are necessary here. First, their preferences differ from those of the PS and the SPD primarily in terms of the *manner* of the EU's involvement in the areas of foreign, security and defence policies. Indeed, the SAP and Labour favour the intergovernmental method (see *infra*), whereas the SPD and, to a lesser extent, the PS declare their support for federal arrangements. Second, the Swedish Social Democrats explicitly[5] draw on the principle of solidarity (SAP 2005) and reject membership of NATO, but pragmatically support co-operation with it. This distinguishes them from the Atlanticism that – as Hussein Kassim shows in his contribution to this volume

– appears to be 'hard-wired' in the Labour Party. Finally, PASOK occupies a position between these two extremes. Having moved away from the explicit Europeanism and support for political union of the Simitis era, under the leadership of George A. Papandreou the party's rhetoric and official literature remain emphatically in favour of further enlargement,[6] while expressing tepid, at best, support for the vague notion of 'political Europe'.

Diversity in terms of the *institutions of integration* is the direct consequence of these parties' diverging preferences on the aims of integration. Thus, whereas the SAP and the Labour Party are ardent supporters of intergovernmentalism, the SPD and, perhaps less enthusiastically, the French PS[7] support the federal model. Finally, PASOK's preferences appear to be in flux. References to 'democratic Europe' and 'political Europe'[8] cannot conceal the party's move away from Simitis's left-wing federalism. The place and role of the state within the EU's institutional architecture were – and remain – key and divisive issues for the social democratic parties examined in this volume. Despite the frequent critiques against various aspects of the operation of the EU's institutional architecture – including the democracy deficit – both the SAP and the Labour Party have been keen on preserving or enhancing the intergovernmental structures,[9] in part because of domestic hostility (be it perceived or real) to 'supranational' or federal arrangements. As a result, they have failed to take on those of their domestic rivals who actually oppose integration but use debates on (inter alia) institutional issues as a smokescreen. In that sense, these parties have been much more concerned about the short-term management of political realities than they have been about the implications of reform of the institutions of the EU. The unwillingness to explicitly discuss the implications of key institutional choices is not limited to these two parties. Indeed, there is a mismatch between the declared support of both the PS and the SPD for political union and their willingness to be explicit about the concrete implications of the adoption of this model for the autonomy of the nation state.

The second major finding of this project concerns the remarkable *stability* of these preferences (to the extent that they have been explicitly articulated) on European integration, though it is important to add two caveats to this conclusion. First, in the cases of the Labour Party and the SAP, this stability became clearer only since the mid-1990s – i.e. after the issue of participation in European integration had been resolved.[10] Second, PASOK is an exception, because its preferences have changed since the accession of Greece to the then EC in 1981. Both points deserve further discussion.

Both in Britain and in Sweden, the issue of membership was settled by means of a referendum. This contributed to a debate that took a 'gladiatorial' or polarising style. This was understandable because, ultimately, the question of membership would be answered by a simple 'yes' or 'no'. Nevertheless, in both countries, the debates that took place *within* the Labour Party and the SAP were indicative of the preferences that prevailed once the issue of membership had been settled. For example, in both cases, the predominance of the economic logic and the frailty of the political dimension of integration can be traced back to the corresponding debate regarding accession.

Finally, PASOK is the most volatile – and, therefore, least typical – case. Once the issue of membership had been resolved, the party adopted a defensive stance in support of intergovernmentalism, quickly followed by the de facto approval in the early 1990s of the prospect of EMU and political union. In turn, this was replaced by the considered, credible and systematic support for the left-wing federalist option under Simitis. This has recently been replaced by George A. Papandreou's ill-defined, vague and often contradictory views. No other party examined in this volume can claim to have covered such a vast conceptual ground in such a short period of time.

The preceding country-specific chapters are based – like the framing chapter – on the belief that preference formation is a complex *process* that unfolds over time and is affected by a whole array of factors. The next section of this concluding chapter seeks to assess the relative importance of interests, institutions and ideas in this process.

Preference formation: driven by interests, institutions or ideas?

Interests

Given the prominence of the economic facet of integration, it would be counter-intuitive to expect economic interests to play a minor role in prefer- ence formation. However, the impact of these interests on preference formation varies across the cases examined in this volume, owing to (a) varying levels of economic development and (b) different policy paradigms.[11] Whereas the domestic exigencies of economic development have led PASOK consistently to support the enhancement of the EU's collective redistributive capacity, they have had a different impact in the cases of New Labour and the SAP. These parties tolerate the enhancement of the EU's redistributive capacity, preferring instead to construe the Union as an area where free trade offers opportunities for economic development, with rather limited funds being channelled to the least developed regions or states. Both of these parties opt for the latter, despite the diverging economic interests of their constituency. This is particularly relevant in the case of the SAP, where – as Johansson and von Sydow demonstrate in their contribution to this volume – blue-collar and white-collar workers have diverging interests that affect preference formation by enhancing the role of party leadership as an arbiter (see *infra*).

Interests are influential also when defined in terms of vote maximisation. As Egle and Marlière demonstrate in their contributions to this volume, the historically defined conception of European integration as a peace project that was meant to reconcile France and Germany has significantly constrained the SPD and the PS. It did so by setting a boundary beyond which criticism or rejection of integration would deal a severe blow to these parties' credibility and prospect of accession to power. As Dimitrakopoulos and Passas indicate, the link between acceptance of membership and credibility (or ability to be seen as a serious contender for power) was evident (albeit implicitly) in the case of PASOK in the late 1970s. In that sense, vote-seeking overlaps with office-seeking, but this line of reasoning does not shed light on the *kind* of Europe that these parties prefer. A more fruitful point of entry into this discussion is offered by linking vote-seeking and two sets of domestic concerns. On the one hand, social democrats have been affected by (often short-term) electoral concerns because of the competition that they faced from other parties, but the origin of this contagion varies across countries and over time. There is evidence of left-wing contagion in the cases of PASOK (until the country's accession) and the SAP (before and after accession). In contrast, contagion from the Right is an enduring factor in the SPD's case. There is evidence of contagion from both the right and the left side of the political spectrum (though at different points in time) in the cases of the PS and Labour.

On the other hand, the analysis of preference formation in New Labour and the SAP since the mid-1990s also reveal the limits – or, at best, the epiphenomenality – of Euroscepticism as an interest-based, explanatory variable. These two parties operate in countries with comparable levels of economic development and apparently high levels of Euroscepticism, but Swedish Euroscepticism relates largely to concerns regarding the potential impact of European integration on the *folkhemmet* – 'a within-nation programme of solidarity' (Johansson and von Sydow, this volume, p. 183) – whereas in Britain it is closely associated simultaneously with a rhetoric that highlights the centrality of the nation state (in reality as an agent that promotes the constant expansion of the autonomy of the market) and a determined effort (under both Tony Blair and Gordon Brown) to stifle attempts to regulate capitalism at the European level.[12] In other words, whereas the former is protective of the domestic *acquis* of the democratic Left, the latter seeks to prevent its extension to the European level of governance. In both cases, the decision stems, not from Euroscepticism per se, but the party leaders' calculated effort to promote their preferred policy paradigm and avoid addressing these issues at the European level.

In the British case, this is indicated by New Labour's determination to maintain its business-friendly[13] profile, rather than actively engage in social and economic regulation at the European level (as well as EMU), after the landslide victories in the 1997 and 2001 general elections that it won against the Conservatives, who run explicitly Eurosceptic campaigns.

In the case of Sweden, the SAP's willingness to protect the Swedish welfare state is not incompatible with other continental European social democrats' efforts to regulate capitalism at the European level – for example, in a manner that would at least seek to avoid developments such as the European Court of Justice's (ECJ) rulings in the Laval and the Viking cases (ECJ 2008a; 2008b) – nor is its support for the Open Method of Co-ordination – which is couched in 'soft' policy instruments such as (competitive) benchmarking – in and of itself more conducive to the aforementioned objective than EU legislation made with the direct involvement of supranational institutions.

Furthermore, the individual contributions to this volume – except the case of the SAP – confirm Delwit's argument regarding the *effet d'opposition* (Delwit 1995, 258), but an important distinction ought to be drawn between (a) critiques of government action and, to a lesser extent, (b) critiques of aspects of European integration per se. The discussion of preference formation in terms of the *effet d'opposition* reveals that the parties examined in this volume – except the SAP – have engaged in the quest for a 'different Europe' while they were in opposition, although it is important to note that this was often the by-product of the process of their programmatic reform.

Policy legacies were another powerful influence on preference formation. In Britain, Greece and Sweden, i.e. countries where membership has been – at certain points in time – politically contentious, policy legacies have played a powerful role in shaping party preferences (especially in economic affairs) in two ways. On the one hand, policy legacies have provided the basis for explicit criticisms of either government action or specific developments in European (economic) integration.[14] On the other hand, social democrats have relied on their domestic experience in an effort to articulate their own vision for the future of European integration. For example, the statist tradition has been particularly influential in shaping the preferences of the PS and, until recently, PASOK.[15] Policy legacies have been influential, not only by means of the electoral implications of policy change – i.e. through the logic of vote maximisation – but also as a concrete expression of prominent ideas (see *infra*).

Finally, geopolitical considerations have been found to have affected party preferences regarding the aims and the institutions of integration. One common thread that links these parties is their support for enlargement and the often explicitly held belief that it is positively correlated with security. Nevertheless, it has not led to a unique outcome, nor is it correlated with the size of the country in question. Indeed, these parties favour a multi-polar international system, except for New Labour, which has remained faithful to Atlanticism, despite support in Britain for a common foreign policy among the members of the EU towards other countries and a common defence and security policy (50 and 59 per cent, respectively) (Eurobarometer 2005, 45–6).

Institutions

The significant impact of the autonomy of the party leaderships – 'innovation from above' in Kitschelt's terms (1994, 213) – on preference formation on European integration is a major common feature of the five cases examined in this volume. Unlike other explanatory factors discussed in this chapter, the influence of the party leadership concerns both a party's stance on the issue of membership and the kind of Europe that a party prefers. The examples found in the five cases abound. Neither Kurt Schumacher's initial stance, nor the change that occurred in the 1960s was determined as a result of a collective process of decision-making within the SPD. The same is true of Guy Mollet's and François Mitterrand's key decisions in the French context. The same argument also applies to the changes brought about by Neil Kinnock, John Smith and Tony Blair in the case of the Labour Party, Ingvar Carlsson in the case of the SAP, and Andreas G. Papandreou, Costas Simitis and, more recently, George A. Papandreou in PASOK's case. This does not mean that leaders were (or are) independent of the party. Rather, the party can (and does) constrain the autonomous leadership (Johansson and von Sydow, this volume), but the key decisions on the broad orientation of a party's preferences on Europe are made by the leadership (see also Featherstone 1988, 310–12), especially when the Social Democrats are in government. In other words, not only has European integration 'increased the autonomy of party leaderships to drive party policy', especially in governing parties (Aylott, Morales and Ramiro 2007, 208), as recent research on the 'Europeanisation' of national political parties (both of the Left and the Right) has found, but party leaders *actually* use this autonomy to shape party references.

This phenomenon does not relate to national patterns of political development (especially the issue of intra-party democracy). Rather, it is the product of the combined effect of three major factors, namely (a) the multi-faceted nature of European integration, (b) party type and the related issue of party cohesion and (c) the impact of policy legacies. Despite their origins, both elite parties and mass parties have to devise – on behalf of complex societies – answers to issues that concern an increasingly complex world marked by the presence of an evolving European Union. As a result, party leaders are faced with the challenge of pursuing the often-conflicting interests of broad coalitions of voters. This frequently entails trade-offs between the short-term costs and the medium- or long-term gains of change. While these parties are in opposition, these trade-offs can be obscured by intra-party deliberations based on first principles.[16] However, when the Social Democrats are in power, the need for these trade-offs is more acute. The party leadership (unlike ordinary members) has (a) privileged access to information (including the desirability and likelihood of trade-offs between actors at different levels of government or between government and its interlocutors in civil society) and is therefore able to shape the agenda and (b) the power to impose, de facto, its decisions.[17] Furthermore, the EU offers multiple venues (such as the European Parliament) where dissent can be voiced – thus operating like a safety valve – without necessarily affecting the leaders' decisions. The autonomy of the party leadership is also increased by the complexity of the specific content of European integration (which remains largely construed as an elite issue) and the difficulties of engaging in a transparent, overall cost-benefit analysis.[18] Moreover, instead of fostering competition between alternative options for the future of Europe – a possibility that several social democrat leaders rejected de facto in 2009 – European elections have remained second-order elections. They are fought over *domestic* issues that, more often than not, have little or nothing to do with European integration. National elections are fought over an array of issues that often obscure European integration. This is mirrored by debates in party conferences,[19] even in parties where there is a tradition of substantive internal political debate. All of these factors facilitate the task of increasingly autonomous party leaders who, in their effort to maximise electoral support for these catch-all and internally differentiated parties, can (and often do) opt for vague formulations or, when integration is a politically contentious issue, adjust the pace of change while keeping its direction intact.

The five cases examined here do not provide evidence indicating that formal institutions such as the national constitution, electoral system, national parliament or the structure and operation of the national executive have influenced the process of preference formation on European integration. The opposite can be said of national political cultures and party systems. This influence has been channelled through the deployment of discourse that sets boundaries beyond which social democrats have been either unwilling or unable to go. The case of Britain is a good example. The combination of the gladiatorial logic of the Westminster model, the exigencies of the two-party system and the logic of the first-past-the-post electoral system are not conducive to the use of the kind of political discourse that could reflect the numerous nuances of European integration. The institutionalisation of a discourse that is couched in references to winners and losers (or even 'traitors'), 'red lines' and the defence of the so-called national interest bring about enduring consequences. This is achieved, in part, by making – at best – selective references to reformism, internationalism, solidarity and the belief in the primacy of politics – i.e. the cardinal ideological traits of social democracy (see *infra*).

Finally, the development of the EU as an institution has affected preference formation in two distinct ways. On the one hand, it has forced these parties to move beyond general and abstract statements of principle. Rather, they have had to define increasingly specific preferences on the scope, aims and the institutions of integration to such an extent that recourse to abstract notions can be legitimately claimed to provide evidence of a hidden agenda. On the other hand, two of the cases examined here – namely PASOK and the SAP – provide evidence of the socialisation effect brought about by involvement in European integration.[20] In PASOK's case, this is linked mainly to ministerial participation in meetings of the Councils. In the case of the SAP, this can be traced back to (a) the party leader's personal contacts and (b) the arena of the Party of European Socialists (Johansson and von Sydow, this volume).

Ideas

As stated earlier, interests and party leaderships are direct determinants of these parties' preferences, but their impact is also indirect, for it is mediated by the party leaders' chosen frame of reference. The decisions of the party leadership and their framing have enduring consequences, in terms of both preference formation and the nature of the debate on European integration at the national level, because certain terms confer more legitimacy to some of the available options and thus render some outcomes more likely than others (Berman 2001; Dimitrakopoulos 2005). In addition, the terminology used exemplifies the frame of reference on the basis of which party leaders make the inevitable *arbitrages*. Mitterand's references to a social – rather than a socialist – Europe, described in Marlière's contribution, is a good example. The same argument can be made with regards to (a) PASOK under George A. Papandreou, who speaks of the hazy notion of 'political Europe' while consistently avoiding his immediate predecessor's clear references to federalism and political union, and (b) New Labour under both Blair and Brown and their references to an 'open' and 'flexible' Europe, which differ from the terms used by John Smith.[21]

More importantly, the chosen frame of reference reflects the direct link between party preferences on European integration and the policy paradigm pursued at the domestic level. Indeed, the former can be seen as an extension of the latter, in terms of both policy content and institutional arrangements. In other words, the basic link between preferences concerning these two levels of government (Marks and Wilson 2000) is confirmed. More specifically, their preferences on European integration are inversely correlated with their attitude vis-à-vis the neo-liberal paradigm. The parties that are more willing to work within it are also unwilling to promote regulated capitalism at the EU level, whereas those that are less willing to do the former are more willing to pursue the latter. This is an indication of a clear change in comparison with the late 1980s.[22]

More specifically, the advent of the neo-liberal policy paradigm has divided the parties examined here into two categories, namely (a) those who (like the PS and PASOK) ascribe to the EU a causal role in that process and (b) the rest, who independently espoused this paradigm (or core aspects thereof). As a result, the former are much more vocal[23] than the latter in their criticism of the institutional architecture (especially its political deficit) and the overwhelmingly monetarist focus of EMU (which does not adequately take into account the need to promote growth) – so much so that, in France, this criticism has contributed to the negative outcome of the national referendum of May 2005. In both cases, these preferences are reflective of these parties' moderation and their propensity to converge towards the centre of the political spectrum (see *infra*).[24]

As regards the intensity of the relative continuity between domestic policies and preferences on European integration, New Labour and the French PS occupy the two extremes of this continuum. New Labour supports the single currency in principle, but offers no evidence of the voluntarism that is required for its adoption, or indeed, the regulation of capitalism at the European level. Its initial acceptance of the EU's *acquis* in that domain has enabled the party, at least initially, to make significant political capital on the domestic political front against the Tories, but has subsequently been coupled with:

a)   unwavering support for measures that promote the autonomy of the
     market (including the limitation of the EU budget and the Bolkestein
     Directive), free trade and enlargement to countries likely to bolster (at least
     in the short term) the neo-liberal camp;
b)   staunch opposition to tax harmonisation (matched by toleration of tax
     havens), as well as proposals regarding the regulation of financial services
     at the European level (even after the onset of the most significant crisis
     since the 1930s) in line with the policies that it so doggedly pursued at
     the domestic level when Gordon Brown was Chancellor of the Exchequer;
c)   intergovernmental institutions (see *supra*), so as to keep – as much as
     possible – policy development under control; and
d)   Atlanticism.

These preferences reflect both New Labour's domestic policies, where
significant elements of socio-economic regulation (such as improved workers'
rights) originated in the EU even prior to the party's victory in 1997 and have
been coupled with the full use of all forms of flexibility, an emblematic
example of which is the individual opt-out enshrined in the Working Time
Directive, and its Atlanticist foreign policy.

In turn, the SAP shares New Labour's support for limiting the EU budget
(precisely because solidarity is construed primarily as a *within-nation* project),
enthusiasm for enlargement, opposition to tax harmonisation and the non-
use of opportunities to promote the regulation of capitalism at the European
level. The SAP is also in favour of EU policies that promote sustainable
development. Its support for intergovernmentalism reflects the wish to defend
its domestic *acquis* and an effort to avoid 'increased parliamentarisation at
the European level that would enhance the Commission's accountability to the
European Parliament'[25] (Johansson and von Sydow, this volume, p. 174).

The SPD's willingness (under Schröder) to limit recourse to chequebook
diplomacy (in line with the country's historically defined attachment to low
inflation and balanced budgets) is as telling as its drift towards flexibility in
the labour market (mirroring the deeply unpopular Hartz reforms pursued at
the domestic level) and emphasis on supply-side economics (Egle and Henkes
2004), despite occasional populist punctuations aiming to appease its domestic
constituency, rather than promote socio-economic regulation at the European
level. Importantly, the SPD (while in a 'grand coalition' government with the
Christian Democrats) called for the re-regulation of European and global
financial markets, a crackdown on tax havens and – despite its unwavering
support for the Stability and Growth Pact – 'a better European co-ordination
in economic policy' (Egle, this volume, p. 39). It also shares New Labour's
enthusiasm for enlargement (though for reasons that bring it closer to the SAP,
namely the conception of European integration as a peace project), but not its
Atlanticist instincts, in line with broader German foreign policy that, for
example, involved opposition to the Iraq war.

Under Simitis, PASOK's domestic and foreign policies were even more tightly linked to each other, precisely because of the country's and the party's major credibility problem. Domestic policies involved spending (domestic as well EU) programmes on major infrastructure projects, while attempting to 'balance the books' at home, against the background of chronic economic problems (partly, though not exclusively, due to the unsustainable profligacy of several previous governments) and a political class (including several leading figures within PASOK) that consistently relied on populism and corruption to gain or maintain power. Against this background, the Stability and Growth Pact took the form of an opportunity to improve the country's public finances as well as its credibility, while Simitis – as prime minister – genuinely supported socio-economic regulation at the European level. At the same time, under Simitis, PASOK fervently supported enlargement (including Turkey's bid to become a candidate) and took bold steps to foster a *rapprochement* with Turkey on the bilateral as well as the European level (Dimitrakopoulos and Passas, this volume), in the belief that echoed the SPD's and the SAP's understanding of European integration as a peace project. This was coupled with active support for a genuinely common foreign and security policy, away from the Atlanticist camp led by New Labour.

Finally, the PS has consistently lent its support to the expansion of the EU's budget and socio-economic regulation (including tax harmonisation) at the European level and has criticised the monetarism of the Stability and Growth Pact in line with domestic policies that involved spending on:

a) job creation in the context of the switch to the 35-hour working week;
b) work experience programmes in public and not-for-profit organisations; and
c) the expansion of health care to low-income groups (Marlière, this volume, p. 81), coupled with the promotion of labour market flexibility (a key element of the Aubry laws of 1998 and 2000).

However, this conclusion – i.e. the continuity that marks their preferences on the domestic and the European fronts – also reveals the equally significant and striking fact that social democratic party elites have failed systematically to draw on three core traits of social democracy – namely solidarity, inter-nationalism and the primacy of politics (Bernstein [1899] 1969). This failure is an indication of their veritable transformation, i.e. the erosion of fundamental social democratic principles and the outcome of social democracy's ideological and programmatic decline since the 1970s (Berman 2010). It is even more striking in the light of the opportunities offered in conditions of complex interdependence and it is a common characteristic of the five parties examined here – although its intensity varies.

PASOK and the PS explicitly invoke solidarity within the Union (construed, for example, in terms of a larger common budget, improved workers' rights and the reform of the Stability and Growth Pact)[26] and claim to support the transformation of the EU into a powerful international actor and promoter of a multi-polar international system. However, they remain remarkably silent on the issue of solidarity beyond Europe. Concern with domestic agendas and the logic of vote-seeking have prevented these parties from developing new ways of reconciling domestic with European and broader international considerations. Selectivity is also present in the SAP's internationalism and use of solidarity. The prevailing conception of these core notions 'has reinforced the tendency for welfare nationalism' (Johansson and von Sydow, this volume, p. 183) and is often geared more to extra- rather than intra-EU concerns. New Labour uses a reformist discourse based on the international impact of EU policies (especially the CAP) predominantly as a tool for the promotion of the reform of these policies. The SPD was (under Schröder) keen to limit the EU budget and have Germany move away from 'chequebook diplomacy'. Yet, its new basic programme, adopted in Hamburg in October 2007, explicitly endorses the principle of multilateralism and rejects the notion of pre-emptive war (SPD 2007), and Kurt Beck (then leader) objected to American plans to establish a 'missile shield' in Europe and called for the EU to speak with one voice on this issue (*Bild*, 19 March 2007). These statements could hardly be expected to be found in formal policy documents of New Labour.

On the nature of social democracy in the integrating Europe

European integration is much more than a sectoral or narrow issue. Rather, it entails the redefinition of the way in which public authority is exercised. This is why the examination of the factors that shape party preferences on European integration can shed light on the nature of social democracy, as well as the challenges that it faces in the beginning of the twenty-first century. Sheri Berman concludes her incisive account of social democracy and the making of Europe's twentieth century by arguing, rightly, that twenty-first-century social democrats must reaffirm their loyalty to the primacy of politics and rediscover the value of 'communitarianism' (Berman 2006, 214). This argument can be extended to their contribution to the development of the European Union, but this entails action that has often proved to be beyond their capacities or political will.

First, narrow conceptions of internationalism and solidarity have lost much of their credibility. In an increasingly interdependent world, there is no a priori reason why they ought to be limited to either the nation state, or extra-European considerations (such as the needs of the developing world). Although the reduced emphasis (both in terms of political discourse and policy output) on a more inclusive conception of solidarity and internationalism may well stem from legitimate (e.g. electoral) considerations, social democrats – especially their leaders – face the challenge of recognising and dealing with the negative consequences that this stance has generated. It has contributed to the institutionalisation of short-termism, as evidenced by the propensity of a number of leaders to either (a) shift to the EU the blame for decisions to which they have contributed, or (b) avoid standing up for it when it is unduly criticised.

Second, although the emphasis on incrementalism is another core trait of social democracy, the evidence that appears in some of the preceding chapters indicates that it has either obscured the need for medium-to-long-term thinking, or it has often been ignored when social democrats engage in public debates on European integration.[27] Engagement in these debates (especially *within* parties) risks being counter-productive as long as European integration is not presented just as what it is, i.e. a process, not an event.[28] Thus, when reform is required, it will not come about without sustained action that reflects a coherent and comprehensive political project.

Third, technocracy – as exemplified by the role played by the European Commission – has made a major contribution to the process of European integration and remains an essential part of governance in an increasingly complex and interdependent world. However, it was not meant to replace politics or leadership ad infinitum. Both leadership and the explicit acknowledgement of the fact that the reform of the Union requires active political engagement are needed in the political struggle against populism and the opponents of European integration.

Finally, as political leadership needs to combine vision with tactical awareness, the social democrats risk either being seen as supporters of the status quo, even when reform is needed, or as once again surrendering European integration to their political rivals, as long as they do not seek to change the terms of the debate on European integration.

As Sheri Berman rightly asserts,

> [t]o the extent that the nation state – the instrument that social democrats have traditionally relied on to manage capitalism – has lost some of its autonomy and power, social democrats must now shift their attention to the international arena . . . The logical place to begin would be with the European Union.
>
> (Berman 2006, 214)

For social democrats this requires an active engagement in the politicisation of European integration, given the end of the 'permissive consensus' that has underpinned this process until the end of the last century. Yet, in the 2009 European elections, they suffered a major defeat. Far from reflecting the end of social democracy in Europe, this singular defeat – right at the heart of the most devastating financial and economic crisis since the 1930s, which proved beyond doubt the limits of neo-liberalism – highlighted a paradox. Indeed, the social democrats were not defeated by the supporters of neo-liberalism,[29] but by parties that openly adopted views that used to be associated with social democracy, such as the need for robust regulation of markets and the 'humanisation' or 'moralisation' of capitalism. This indicates that, in order to recover – at least in electoral terms – they will need to return to the objectives and strategies that motivated the social democratic movement in the first place (Berman 2010).[30] This is a Herculean task. Their divisions (and, in some cases, their faith in neo-liberalism) were so deep that they failed to answer reformist calls (Dehaene *et al.* 2008; Gonzalez *et al.* 2009) to name (ahead of the elections) a common candidate who would then compete for the presidency of the European Commission, thus providing – in addition to a genuinely common programme – a focal point for the political debate that the EU needs, and clear choices to citizens, many of whom understandably struggle to understand what is at stake (Hix 2008). The leaders of the Spanish PSOE and the Portuguese Socialists[31] and the Brown-led New Labour broke ranks with the Party of European Socialists and explicitly supported the incumbent (and candidate of the European People's Party), despite the efforts of the French Socialists[32] and the leader of the PES (*Le Monde*, 28 March 2009, online edition). In other words, they opted for a deal behind closed doors, deliberately depriving European citizens of the oxygen of genuine political contestation. Nevertheless, meeting in Prague in the context of the 8th Congress of the PES six months later, they stated that:

> giving face to a political platform is imperative in today's politics, especially in such difficult elections as the European ones. To make this election relevant, citizens must know that their vote can shape the executive and change policies. We therefore make the commitment of choosing a PES candidate for the European Commission Presidency for the next European elections.
>
> (Party of European Socialists 2009, 7)

Whether this is a genuine return to the primacy of politics remains to be seen.

Notes

1 I am grateful to the contributors to this volume for their constructive comments on an earlier draft of this chapter. The usual disclaimer applies.
2 PASOK is a partial exception.
3 The latter does so more enthusiastically than the former.
4 Indeed, the Labour Party officially supports the UK's accession to the third stage of EMU, which entails the replacement of sterling by the euro, but retains an open mind as to the timing.
5 For example, the party's international programme indicates that,

> the EU is developing into an actor with the scope of instruments needed to meet the multifaceted threats in today's world. This is positive. The solidarity that exists between the countries of Europe means that it would be unthinkable for Sweden to adopt a passive stance if another member country were to be struck by a serious crisis.
>
> (SAP 2005, 27)

6 PASOK's current leadership favours enlargement despite the risk that it entails for the cohesion of the EU and, as a consequence, its ability to act autonomously in the international arena.

7 The PS is much less explicit than the SPD on the institutional aspect of political union.

8 The abstract and, in many respects, primitive nature of these references mirrors the party's rhetoric regarding the aims of integration.

9 One good example is the initial reticence of the New Labour and SAP governments to agree to the establishment of the Convention on the Future of Europe after the debacle in Nice (Dimitrakopoulos 2005).

10 It is important to note that the degree of specificity of these preferences has changed as a function of the development of the European Union and its predecessors.

11 For a discussion of the impact of policy paradigms, see the third sub-section.

12 Examples abound, ranging from Peter Mandelson's statement – 'I don't think there is an appetite either here or in the rest of the European Union for great integrationist steps forward' (*The Independent*, 5 May 1997) – just days after New Labour's electoral victory of May 1997, the same government's handling of the reform of the Working Time Directive, involving what to an insider looked like 'the biggest diplomatic effort outside war' he had seen to keep the individual opt-out (interview with trade union leader, Brussels, 19 January 2009), to the post-2008 effort to protect the UK-based financial services industry from co-ordinated efforts to enact EU legislation in that area.

13 After years in opposition, the leadership of the party had defined a business-friendly stance as one that hardly ever involved policy initiatives that domestic business organisations would oppose. The introduction of the minimum wage is the exception that confirms the rule.

14 The threat to the welfare state is a good example.

15 In the latter case, this influence extends to the domain of foreign policy.

16 The British Labour Party accurately exemplified this phenomenon between 1979 and 1983.

17 Thus, it is not surprising that, in three of the cases examined in this volume (PS, PASOK and SAP) change occurred while they were in power. By contrast, radical changes occurred during the SPD's and the Labour Party's lengthy stints in opposition.

18 The example of PASOK is very illustrative in that respect: throughout the 1980s, Greece benefited from the CAP, while the government was often isolated on foreign policy issues.

19 The focus on 'bread and butter issues' and the perceived remoteness of the EU's central institutions contribute to this trend.

20 Nevertheless, two caveats are necessary here. First, this socialisation effect concerns primarily a 'softening' of the attitude vis-à-vis the principle of membership, which – as party and government officials have discovered – entails constraints as well as opportunities. Second, self-selection of the relevant political personnel might overstate the effect of socialisation. In other words, officials who were already (though implicitly) well disposed towards European integration might be more likely to participate in fora that eventually either enhance or reveal these predispositions.

21 The debates in the House of Commons on the Social Chapter in the early 1990s, when Labour was led by John Smith, offer a good example (Dimitrakopoulos 2009).

22 Comparing socialist parties on the basis of early data from the manifestos project, Featherstone concluded that there was no correlation between a socialist party's location on the left–right axis and its preferences for or against integration (1988, 307).

23 The PS much more so than PASOK.

24 However, the decision to adopt this paradigm (or at least tolerate it) was not the result of a systematic internal debate. Rather, it came from the top, i.e. the party leadership, without an explicit and systematic consideration of credible alternatives.

25 This is reminiscent of PASOK's preferences in the early stages of Greek membership, but (again like PASOK) it appears to have softened recently, as the SAP is now willing to accept the use of QMV in sensitive issues such as asylum and migration.

26 This is so despite the fact that France is a net contributor to, and Greece a net recipient from, the EU budget.

27 Indeed, it can be argued that, although social democrats who operate in the parties examined in this volume have often criticised aspects of European integration, they have been much less eager to ascribe to joint action at EU level successes that would otherwise have remained impossible to achieve.

28 This also indicates the limits of the obfuscation thesis (Bailey 2005). Given that none of their domestic achievements happened without a struggle that unfolded over time, it is unclear why this would not apply to the development of the EU.

29 The lowest score (15.7 per cent) among the parties examined here was that of New Labour, i.e. the party that did the most to espouse neo-liberalism.

30 Social democrats themselves appear to agree (albeit implicitly) with this argument. Indeed, meeting at the 8th Congress of the Party of European Socialists in Prague in December 2009, they pointed out that their defeat in the 2009 European elections stemmed in part from the fact that they were not successful 'at conveying the fact that the financial and economic crisis is fundamentally a failure of *conservative* ideology across the world' (Party of European Socialists 2009, 2).

31 They reportedly did so out of 'Iberian solidarity' (Jean Quatremer, *Les coulisses de Bruxelles* blog, 'Le socialisme ibérique soluble dans le nationalisme', posted on 17 September 2009).

32 The MEPs of the PS were also among the few social democrats who were consistent enough and voted against the second Barroso Commission (Jean Quatremer, *Les coulisses de Bruxelles* blog, 'Barroso II enfin en fonction', posted on 10 February 2010).

Bibliography

Andersson, Leif. 1996. *Beslut(s)fattarna: Socialdemokratiska riksdagsgruppen 100 år.* Stockholm: PM Bäckström Förlag.

Archibugi, Daniele. 2004. Cosmopolitan democracy and its critics: A review. *European Journal of International Relations* 10 (3): 437–73.

Aspinwall, Mark. 2000. Structuring Europe: Powersharing institutions and British preferences on European integration. *Political Studies* 48 (3): 415–42.

———. 2002. Preferring Europe: Ideology and national preferences on European integration. *European Union Politics* 3 (1): 81–111.

Aylott, Nicholas. 1997. Between Europe and unity: The Swedish social democrats. *West European Politics* 20 (2): 119–36.

———. 1999. *Swedish social democracy and European integration: The People's Home on the market.* Aldershot: Ashgate.

———. 2002. Let's discuss this later: Party responses to Euro-division in Scandinavia. *Party Politics* 8 (4): 441–61.

———. 2005. President Persson – How did Sweden get him? In *The presidentialization of politics: A comparative study of modern democracies*, edited by T. Poguntke and P. Webb, 176–98. Oxford: Oxford University Press.

———. 2007. A long, slow march to Europe: The Europeanization of Swedish political parties. In *The Europeanization of national political parties: Power and organizational adaptation*, edited by T. Poguntke, N. Aylott, E. Carter, R. Ladrech and K. R. Luther, 149–74. London: Routledge.

———, Laura Morales and Luis Ramiro. 2007. Some things change, a lot stays the same: comparing the country studies. In *The Europeanization of national political parties: Power and organizational adaptation*, edited by T. Poguntke, N. Aylott, E. Carter, R. Ladrech and K. R. Luther, 190–210. Abingdon: Routledge.

Bahr, Egon. 1996. *Zu meiner Zeit.* München: Beck.

Bailey, David. 2004. Legitimation through integration: Explaining the 'new' social democratic turn to Europe. Ph.D. diss., Government, London School of Economics and Political Science, University of London.

———. 2005. Obfuscation through integration: Legitimating 'new' social democracy in the European Union. *Journal of Common Market Studies* 43 (1): 13–35.

Baker, David, and David Seawright. 1998a. A 'rosy' map of Europe? Labour parliamentarians and European integration. In *Britain for and against Europe. British politics and the question of European integration*, edited by D. Baker and D. Seawright, 57–87. Oxford: Clarendon Press.

——, and David Seawright, eds. 1998b. *Britain for and against Europe*. Oxford: Clarendon Press.

Bauer, Otto. 2000. *The question of nationalities and social democracy*. Translated by J. O'Donnell. Minneapolis, MN: University of Minnesota Press.

Bealey, F., ed. 1980. *The social and political thought of the British Labour government*. London: Macmillan.

Beckett, Margaret. 2007. John Smith's European legacy. John Smith Memorial Lecture, 6 March.

Bergounioux, Alain. 2004. L'Europe et les socialistes: Une perspective historique. *La Recherche Socialiste* (28): 5–11.

——, Michel Destot and Catherine Tasca. 2007. Les socialistes et l'Europe: Le oui de la rénovation. *Libération*, 7 November, 28.

Bergquist, Mats. 1970. *Sverige och EEC: En statsvetenskaplig studie av fyra åsiktsriktningars syn på svensk marknadspolitik 1961–1962*. Lund Political Studies 11. Stockholm: P.A. Norstedt & Söners Förlag.

Berman, Sheri. 1998. *The social democratic moment: Ideas and politics in the making of interwar Europe*. Cambridge, MA: Harvard University Press.

——. 2001. Review article: Ideas, norms and culture in political analysis. *Comparative Politics* 33 (2): 231–50.

——. 2006. *The primacy of politics: Social democracy and the making of Europe's twentieth century*. Cambridge: Cambridge University Press.

——. 2010. The demise of social democracy: Rediscovering the goals that motivated the movement in the first place. Paper presented at the 17th International Conference of the Council for European Studies, 15–17 April in Montreal, Canada.

Bernstein, Eduard. [1899] 1969. *Die Voraussetzungen des Sozialismus und die Aufgaben der Sozialdemokratie*. Repr. Hamburg: Rowohlt.

Blair, Tony. 1997. The principles of a modern British foreign policy. Speech, Guildhall, London, 1 November.

——. 2000. Prime Minister's speech. Warsaw Stock Exchange, 6 October. www.guardian.co.uk/world/2003/may/30/eu.speeches

Blum, Léon. 1971. *A l'échelle humaine*. Paris: Gallimard.

Boyce, R.W.D. 1980. Britain's first 'no' to Europe: Britain and the Briand Plan, 1929–30. *European Studies Review* 10 (1): 17–45.

Broad, Roger. 2001. *Labour's European dilemmas: From Bevin to Blair*. Basingstoke: Palgrave.

Brown, Gordon. 2005. Speech given by the Chancellor of the Exchequer at the Mansion House, London, 22 June. www.hm-treasury.gov.uk/speech_chex_220605.htm.

——. 2007. Lord Mayor's Banquet Speech, London, 12 November. http://webarchive.nationalarchives.gov.uk/+/www.number10.gov.uk/Page13736.

Budge, Ian. 1994. A new spatial theory of party competition: Uncertainty, ideology and policy equilibria viewed comparatively and temporally. *British Journal of Political Science* 24 (4): 443–67.

——, Hans-Dieter Klingemann, Andrea Volkens, Judith Bara and Eric Tanenbaum. 2001. *Mapping policy preferences: estimates for parties, electors, and governments 1945–1998*. Oxford: Oxford University Press.

Buller, Jim. 2003. New Labour's foreign and defence policy: External support structures and domestic politics. In *New Labour in Government*, edited by S. Ludlam and M.J. Smith, 219–33. Basingstoke: Macmillan.

Bullock, Alan. 1983. *Ernest Bevin: Foreign Secretary*. New York: Norton.

Bulmer, Simon. 2000. European policy: Fresh start or false dawn? In *New Labour in power*, edited by D. Coates and P. Lawler, 240–53. Manchester: Manchester University Press.

——, Charlie Jeffery and William E. Paterson. 2000. *Germany's European diplomacy: Shaping the regional milieu*. Manchester: Manchester University Press.

Butler, David, and Uwe Kitzinger. 1976. *The 1975 referendum*. Basingstoke: Macmillan.

Byrd, Peter. 1975. The Labour Party and the European Community, 1970–75. *Journal of Common Market Studies* 13 (4): 469–83.

Cafruny, Alan W. 1997. Social democracy in one continent? Alternatives to a neoliberal Europe. In *Europe's ambiguous unity: Conflicts and consensus in the post-Maastricht era*, edited by A.W. Cafruny, C. Lankowski, 109–28. Boulder, CO: Lynne Rienner.

Camiller, Patrick. 1989. Beyond 1992: The Left and Europe. *New Left Review* (175): 5–17.

Camps, Miriam. 1964. *Britain and the European Community, 1955–1963*, Princeton: Princeton University Press.

——. 1966. *European unification in the Sixties: From the veto to the crisis*. New York: McGraw-Hill.

Carlsson, Ingvar. 1986. Speech at the government's lunch for Jacques Delors on 2 June 1986. Labour Movement Archives and Library, Ingvar Carlsson (2.1.1: 13).

——. 2003. *Så tänkte jag: Politik och dramatik*. Stockholm: Hjalmarson & Högberg.

Carter, Elisabeth, Kurt Richard Luther and Thomas Poguntke. 2007. European integration and party dynamics. In *The Europeanizatiom of national political parties: Power and organizational adaptation*, edited by T. Poguntke, N. Aylott, E. Carter, R. Ladrech and K.R. Luther, 1–27. Abingdon: Routledge.

Cassen, Bernard. 2002. Est-il encore utile de voter après le sommet de Barcelone? *Le Monde Diplomatique*, April, 4.

Clift, Ben. 2003. *French socialism in a global era: The political economy of the new social democracy in France*. London: Continuum.

Cook, R. 2004. *The point of departure: Diaries from the front bench*. London: Simon & Schuster.

Coufoudakis, Van. 1987. Greek foreign policy, 1945–85: Seeking independence in an interdependent world – problems and prospects. In *Political change in Greece: Before and after the colonels*, edited by K. Featherstone and D.K. Katsoudas, 230–52. London: Croom Helm.

Couloumbis, Theodore A. 1993. PASOK's foreign policies, 1981–89: Continuity or change? In *Greece, 1981–89: The populist decade*, edited by R. Clogg, 113–30. Basingstoke: Macmillan.

Criddle, Byron. 1969. *Socialists and European integration: A study of the French Socialist Party*. London: Routledge & Kegan Paul.

Crossman, R.H.S. 1963. British Labour looks at Europe. *Foreign Affairs* 41 (4): 732–43.

Daniels, Phil. 1998. From hostility to 'constructive engagement': The Europeanisation of the Labour Party. *West European Politics* 21 (1): 72–96.

Danielsson, Lars. 2007. *I skuggan av makten*. Stockholm: Bonniers.

Dehaene, Jean-Luc, Jacques Delors, Joschka Fischer, Felipe González, Pascal Lamy, Paavo Lipponen, Denis MacShane, Péter Medgyessy, John Monks, Tommaso Padoa-Schioppa and Romano Prodi. 2008. Un besoin d'Union face à la crise. *Le Monde*, 11 December.

Delaney, Erin. 2002. The Labour Party's changing relationship to Europe. *Journal of European Integration History* 8 (1): 121–38.

Delwit, Pascal. 1995. *Les partis socialistes et l'intégration européenne. Belgique, France, Grande-Bretagne.* Bruxelles: Editions de l'Université de Bruxelles.

Désir, Harlem, Marie-Noelle Lienemann and Philippe Marlière. 2001. Le vrai défi de la social-démocratie européenne. *Le Monde*, 16 March, 19.

DiMaggio, Paul J., and Walter W. Powell. 1991. The iron cage revisited: Institutional isomorphism and collective rationality in organizational fields. In *The new institutionalism in organizational analysis*, edited by W. Powell and P. DiMaggio, 63–82. Chicago: University of Chicago Press.

Dimitrakopoulos, Dionyssis G. 2005. Norms, interests and institutional change. *Political Studies* 53 (4): 676–93.

——. 2008a. Norms, strategies and political change: Explaining the establishment of the Convention on the Future of Europe. *European Journal of International Relations* 14 (2): 319–41.

——. 2008b. *The power of the centre: Central governments and the implementation of EU public policy in Greece, France and the UK*. Manchester: Manchester University Press.

——. 2009. Partisan Europe? Political parties and the implementation of EU policy. Paper presented at the 11th Biennial Conference of the European Union Studies Association, 23–5 April, in Marina del Rey, Los Angeles.

——, and Hussein Kassim. 2004a. Deciding the future of the European Union: Preference formation and treaty reform. *Comparative European Politics* 2 (3): 241–60.

——, and Hussein Kassim. 2004b. Preference formation and EU Treaty reform. *Comparative European Politics* 2 (3): 241–60.

——, and Hussein Kassim, eds. 2004c. Domestic preference formation and EU Treaty reform. Special issue, *Comparative European Politics* 2 (3).

Downs, Anthony. 1957. *An economic theory of democracy*. New York, NY: Harper & Row.

Dray, Julien, Arnaud Montebourg and Vincent Peillon. 2002. Un nouveau Parti Socialiste. *Libération*, 9 October, 5.

Druckman, James N., and Arthur Lupia. 2000. Preference formation. *Annual Review of Political Science* 3: 1–24.

Duhamel, Alain. 1998. *François Mitterrand: L'unité d'un homme*. Paris: Flammarion.

Duverger, Maurice. 1950. *L'influence des systèmes electoraux sur la vie politique*. Paris: Armand Colin.

——. 1951. *Les partis politiques*. Paris: Seuil.

ECJ. 2008a. Case C-438/05. Judgment of the Court (Grand Chamber) of 11 December 2007 (reference for a preliminary ruling from the Court of Appeal (Civil Division) – United Kingdom) International Transport Workers' Federation, Finnish Seamen's Union v Viking Line ABP, OÜ Viking Line Eesti. *Official Journal of the European Union*, C51: 11.

——. 2008b. Case C-341/05. Judgment of the Court (Grand Chamber) of 18 December 2007 (reference for a preliminary ruling from the Arbetsdomstolen – Sweden) Laval un Partneri Ltd v Svenska Byggnadsarbetareförbundet, Svenska Byggnadsarbetareförbundets avd. 1, Byggettan, Svenska Elektrikerförbundet. *Official Journal of the European Union*, C51: 9–10.

Eckstein, Gabriele, and Franz Urban Pappi. 1999. Die öffentliche Meinung zur europäischen Währungsunion bis 1998: Befund, geldpolitische Zusammenhänge und politische Führung in Deutschland. *Zeitschrift für Politik* 46 (3): 298–334.

Edinger, Lewis Joachim. 1965. *Kurt Schumacher: A study in personality and political behaviour*. Stanford: Stanford University Press.

Egle, Christoph, and Christian Henkes. 2004. Between tradition and new revisionism: The programmatic debate in the SPD. In *Reshaping Social Democracy: Labour and the SPD in the new century*, edited by S. Haseler and H. Meyer, 119–42. London: London Metropolitan University.

Ekengren, Ann-Marie. 2005. *Olof Palme och utrikespolitiken*. Umeå: Boréa.

Eley, Geoff. 2002. *Forging democracy: The history of the left in Europe, 1850–2000*. New York, NY: Oxford University Press.

Emmanuelli, Henri. 2008. Réponse à Jean-Marc Ayrault. Le Blog de Henri Emmanuelli, posted 10 January, www.henriemmanuelli.fr/spip.php?article262.

——, Alain Vidalies, Christian Bataille. 2000. Démocratie, égalité. *L'Hebdo des socialistes*. Congrès de Grenoble, 24–26 November. Paris: *Parti socialiste*.

Eriksson, Jonas. 2006. The pre-enlargement debate in Sweden. In *Freedom of movement for workers from Central and Eastern Europe: Experiences in Ireland and Sweden*, 17–28. SIEPS 2006: 5. Stockholm: Swedish Institute for European Policy Studies.

Erlander, Tage. 1962. Speech by the prime minister at the Conference of the Swedish Steel and Metalworkers' Union on 22 August 1961. In *Documents on Swedish foreign policy 1961*, 111–25. Stockholm: Norstedts.

Esping-Andersen, Gøsta. 1985. *Politics against markets: The social democratic road to power*. Princeton, NJ: Princeton University Press.

Eurobarometer. 2005. Standard survey – national report: United Kingdom. No. 64. Autumn 2005. Brussels: European Commission.

European Network of Social Democratic Foundations. 2008. Contribution to the PES consultation process for the 2009 European Elections Manifesto. ENSoF, July. www.fes-europe.eu/attachments/098_ENSoF%20Manifesto%202009%20booklet.pdf.

Fabius, Laurent. 2001. L'Europe du futur. *Commentaires* (94): 245–54.

Favier, Pierre, and Michel Martin-Roland. 1990. *La décennie Mitterrand. Vol. 1. Les ruptures*. Paris: Seuil.

Featherstone, Kevin. 1988. *Socialist parties and European integration: A comparative history*. Manchester: Manchester University Press.

——. 1994. Political parties. In *Greece and EC membership evaluated*, edited by P. Kazakos and P. Ioakimidis, 154–65. London: Pinter.

——. 2003. Greece and EMU: Between external empowerment and domestic vulnerability. *Journal of Common Market Studies* 41 (5): 923–40.

Ferenczi, Thomas. 2008. L'engagement européen du Parti socialiste français. *Le Monde*, 8 May, 2.

Fichtelius, Erik. 2007. *Aldrig ensam, alltid ensam – samtalen med Göran Persson 1996–2006*. Stockholm: Norstedts.

Fischer, Joschka. 2000. Vom Staatenverbund zur Föderation – Gedanken über die Finalität der europäischen Integration. Rede an der Humboldt-Universität zu Berlin, 12. Mai. www.auswaertiges-amt.de/diplo/de/Infoservice/Presse/Reden/Archiv/2000/000512-EuropaeischeIntegrationPDF.pdf.

Føllesdal, Andreas. 2003. Federalism. In *The Stanford encyclopedia of philosophy*, edited by E.N. Zalta (Winter 2003, online edition). http://plato.stanford.edu/archives/win2003/entries/federalism/.

Fondation Copernic. 2001. *Un social-libéralisme à la française? Regards critiques sur la politique économique et sociale de Lionel Jospin*. Paris: La Découverte.

Frank, Robert. 2005. La gauche et l'Europe. In *Histoire des Gauches en France*. *Vol. 2*, edited by J.-J. Becker and G. Candar, 452–71. Paris: La Découverte.

Frankel, Joseph. 1975. *British foreign policy, 1945–1973*. Oxford: Oxford University Press.

Frieden, Jeffry A. 1999. Actors and preferences in international relations. In *Strategic choice and international relations*, edited by David A. Lake and Robert Powell, 39–76. Princeton, NJ: Princeton University Press.

Friedrich, Paul. 1975. The SPD and the politics of Europe: From Willy Brandt to Helmut Schmidt. *Journal of Common Market Studies* 13 (4): 432–9.

Gabel, Matthew J., and Christopher M. Anderson. 2004. The structure of citizens' attitudes and the European political space. In *European integration and political conflict*, edited by G. Marks and Marco R. Steenbergen, 13–31. Cambridge: Cambridge University Press.

Gaffney, John. 1996a. Introduction. In *Political parties and the European Union*, edited by J. Gaffney, 1–30. London: Routledge.

———, ed. 1996b. *Political parties and the European Union*. London: Routledge.

Gamble, Andrew. 2003. *Between Europe and America. The future of British politics*, Basingstoke: Palgrave.

Gauche Socialiste. 2000. Attika: la motion. *L'Hebdo des socialistes*. Congrès de Grenoble, 24–6 November. Paris: *Parti socialiste*.

Gay, Peter. [1952] 1979. *The dilemma of democratic socialism: Eduard Bernstein's challenge to Marx*. New York, NY: Octagon Books. Originally published by Columbia University Press.

Généreux, Jacques. 2005. *Sens et conséquences du 'non' français*. Paris: Seuil.

George, Stephen. 1998. *An awkward partner: Britain in the European Community*. 3rd edn. Oxford: Oxford University Press.

George, Susan. 2004. *Another world is possible if . . .* London: Verso.

Gil, Ariane. 2008. Traité de Lisbonne: La position des socialistes. *L'Hebdo des socialistes*, 26 January, 10–11.

Giscard d'Estaing, Valéry. 2007. Traité européen: Les outils sont exactement les mêmes; seul l'ordre a été changé dans la boîte. *Le Monde*, 26 October, 21.

Glotz, Peter. 1985. *Manifest für eine neue Europäische Linke*. Berlin: Siedler.

Glyn, Andrew, ed. 2001. *Social democracy in neoliberal times: The left and economic policy since 1980*. Oxford: Oxford University Press.

Goldstein, Judith, and Robert O. Keohane. 1993. Ideas and foreign policy: An analytical framework. In *Ideas and foreign policy: Beliefs, institutions and political change*, edited by J. Goldstein and R. O. Keohane, 3–30. Ithaca, NY: Cornell University Press.

Gonzalez, Felipe, Lionel Jospin, Paavo Lipponen, Aleksander Kwasniewski, Gerhard Schröder, Constantinos Simitis, Mario Soares and Franz Vranitzky. 2009. A programme, a majority and a candidate to make a difference in the European Union: A declaration by personalities of the socialist and social democratic family. 3 June. www.costas-simitis.gr/content/158.

Gourevitch, Peter. 1986. *Politics in hard times: Comparative responses to international economic crises*. Ithaca, NY: Cornell University Press.

Griffiths, Richard T. 1993. European utopia or capitalist trap? The Socialist International and the question of Europe. In *Socialist parties and the question of Europe in the 1950s*, edited by R. T. Griffiths, 9–24. Leiden: E.J. Brill.

Guigou, Elisabeth. 2007. Oui au Traité de Lisbonne. *Libération*, 31 October, 5.

Gustavsson, Jakob. 1998. *The politics of foreign policy change: Explaining the Swedish reorientation on EC membership*. Lund: Lund University Press.

Guyomarch, Alain, Howard Machin and Ella Ritchie. 1998. *France in the European Union*. Basingstoke: Macmillan.

Haahr, Jens Henrik. 1993. *Looking to Europe: The EC policies of the British Labour Party and the Danish Social Democrats*. Aarhus: Aarhus University Press.

Haas, Ernst B. [1958] 2003. *The uniting of Europe: Political, social, and economic forces, 1950–1957*. Notre Dame, IN: University of Notre Dame Press. Originally published by Stanford University Press.

Halimi, Serge. 1993. *Sisyphe est fatigué. Les échecs de la gauche au pouvoir*. Paris: Robert Laffont.

Hall, Peter A. 1986. *Governing the economy: The politics of state intervention in Britain and France*. Cambridge: Polity.

———. 1993. Policy paradigms, social learning and the state: The case of economic policymaking in Britain. *Comparative Politics* 25 (3): 275–96.

Hanley, David. 1986. *Keeping left? CERES and the French Socialist Party*. Manchester: Manchester University Press.

Harlem Brundtland, Gro. 1999. *Dramatiska år: 1986–1996*. Stockholm: Norstedts.

Harmel, Robert, Uk Heo, Alexander Tan and Kenneth Janda. 1995. Performance, leadership, factions and party change: An empirical analysis. *West European Politics* 18 (1): 1–33.

Harrison, M. 1960. *Trade Unions and the Labour Party since 1945*. London: Allen & Unwin.

Hassapopoulos, Nikos. 2008. The litany of lost green programmes [in Greek]. *To Vima* (Athens), 30 November.

Hayward, J.E.S., ed. 1996. *Élitism, populism and European politics*. Oxford: Oxford University Press.

Heffernan, Richard, and Paul Webb. 2007. The British prime minister. Much more than 'first among equals'. In *The presidentialisation of politics: A comparative study of modern democracies*, edited by T. Poguntke and P. Webb, 26–62. Oxford: Oxford University Press.

Hellenic Government. 1982. Memorandum [in Greek]. March. Mimeo.

Hellenic Parliament. Various years. *Debates* [in Greek]. Athens: Hellenic Parliament.

Hellmann, Gunther. 2007. '. . . um diesen deutschen Weg zu Ende gehen zu können.' Die Renaissance machtpolitischer Selbstbehauptung in der zweiten Amtszeit der Regierung Schröder-Fischer. In *Ende des rot-grünen Projektes. Eine Bilanz der Regierung Schröder 2002–2005*, edited by Chr. Egle and R. Zohlnhöfer, 453–79. Wiesbaden: VS Verlag.

Hellström, Johan. 2008. Partisan responses to Europe: The role of ideology for national political parties' positions on European integration. *Journal of European Public Policy* 15 (2): 189–207.

Héritier, Adrianne. 1999. *Policy-making and diversity in Europe: Escape from deadlock*. Cambridge: Cambridge University Press.

Hettne, B., and F. Soderbaum. 2005. Civilian power or soft imperialism? The EU as a global actor and the role of interregionalism. *European Foreign Affairs Review* 10: 535–52.

Hill, R. 2001. *The Labour Party and economic strategy, 1979–1997: The long road back*. Basingstoke: Palgrave.

Hirst, Paul, and Graeme Thompson. 1999. *Globalisation in question*. 2nd edn. Cambridge: Polity.

Hix, Simon. 1999. Dimensions and alignments in European Union politics: Cognitive constraints and partisan responses. *European Journal of Political Research* 35 (1): 69–106.

——. 2008. *What's wrong with the European Union and how to fix it*. Cambridge: Polity.

HM Treasury. n.d. The UK government's policy on Economic and Monetary Union. http://webarchive.nationalarchives.gov.uk/+/www.hm-treasury.gov.uk/documents/international_issues/the_euro/euro_index_index.cfm.

Hohl, Thierry. 2008. *Les socialistes français et l'Europe. Documents et analyses*. Dijon: Editions Universitaires de Dijon.

Holden, Russell. 2002. *The making of New Labour's European policy*. Basingstoke: Palgrave.

Hollande, François. 2000. Ensemble, réussir aujourd'hui pour convaincre demain. *L'Hebdo des socialistes*. Congrès de Grenoble, 24–6 November. Paris: *Parti socialiste*.

——. 2005. Pour l'Europe. *La Revue Socialiste* (20): 4–5.

Hooghe, Liesbet, and Gary Marks. 1999. The making of a polity: The struggle over European integration. In *Continuity and change in contemporary capitalism*, edited by H. Kitschelt, P. Lange, G. Marks and J.D. Stephens, 70–97. Cambridge: Cambridge University Press.

——, Gary Marks and Carole J. Wilson. 2002. Does Left/Right structure party positions on European integration? *Comparative Political Studies* 35 (8): 965–89.

Howarth, David. 2002. The French state in the Euro zone: 'Modernization' and legitimizing dirigisme. In *European states and the Euro: Europeanization, variation and convergence*, edited by K. Dyson, 145–72, Oxford: Oxford University Press.

Howell, David. 1976. *British social democracy. A study in development and delay*. London: Croom Helm.

Hrbek, Rudolf. 1972. *Die SPD – Deutschland und Europa. Die Haltung der Sozialdemokratie zum Verhältnis von Deutschlandpolitik und West-Integration (1945–1957)*. Bonn: Europa Union Verlag.

——. 1993. The German Social Democratic Party. In *Socialist parties and the question of Europe in the 1950s*, edited by R.T. Griffith, 63–77. Leiden: Brill Academic Publishers.

Hughes, Colin, and Patrick Wintour. 1990. *Labour rebuilt. The new model party*. London: Fourth Estate.

Hugo, Victor. n.d. [1849]. Extraits du discours prononcé le 21 août 1849 lors du Congrès de la paix. Paris. www.lettres.net/hugo/texte03.htm.

Hyde-Price, Adrian, and Charlie Jeffery. 2001. Germany in the European Union: Constructing normality. *Journal of Common Market Studies* 39 (4): 689–717.

Ingebritsen, Christine. 1998. *The Nordic states and European unity*. Ithaca, NY: Cornell University Press.

Ioakimidis, Panagiotis. 1996. The participation of Greece in the intergovernmental institutions of the European Community/Union [in Greek]. In *Greece in the European Union: Assessment of the first fifteen years of membership – prospects*, edited by the European Movement – Hellenic Committee for European Union, 13–21. Athens: Papazissis.

ISTAME (The Andreas Papandreou Institute of Strategic and Development Studies). 2006. The EU for the 21st century Greece. Policy paper no. 6. Athens: ISTAME. www.istame.gr/files/pdf/euromellon.pdf.

——. 2007. Fifty years later: The EU for the 21st century world and Greece. Policy paper no. 16, April. Athens: ISTAME. www.istame.gr/files/pdf/50xronia.pdf.

——. 2009. For a democratic, social and influential Europe. Proposals for the 2009 European elections. Policy paper no. 21, January. Athens: ISTAME. www.istame. gr/files/pdf/keimenopolitikis21.pdf.

Jacob, Klaus, and Axel Volkery. 2007. Nichts Neues unter der Sonne? Zwischen Ideensuche und Entscheidungsblockade – die Umweltpolitik der Bundesregierung Schröder 2002–5. In *Ende des rot-grünen Projektes. Eine Bilanz der Regierung Schröder 2002–2005*, edited by Chr. Egle and R. Zohlnhöfer, 431–52. Wiesbaden: VS Verlag.

Jacobsson, Kerstin. 1997. *Så gott som demokrati: om demokratifrågan i EU-debatten.* Umeå: Boréa.

Jeffery, Charlie, and William E. Paterson. 2003. Germany and European integration: A shifting of tectonic plates. *West European Politics* 26 (4): 59–75.

Jennar, Marc Raoul. 2007. *Quelle Europe après le non?* Paris: Fayard.

Johansson, Karl Magnus. 1999. Tracing the employment title in the Amsterdam treaty: Uncovering transnational coalitions. *Journal of European Public Policy* 6 (1): 85–101.

——. 2002a. Another road to Maastricht: The Christian Democrat coalition and the quest for European Union. *Journal of Common Market Studies* 40 (5): 871–93.

——. 2002b. Party elites in multilevel Europe: The Christian Democrats and the Single European Act. *Party Politics* 8 (4): 423–39.

——. 2008. Chief executive organization and advisory arrangements for foreign affairs: The case of Sweden. *Cooperation and Conflict* 43 (3): 267–87.

——, and Anna-Carin Svensson. 2002. Sweden: Constrained but constructive? In *The Amsterdam Treaty: National preference formation, interstate bargaining and outcome*, edited by F. Laursen, 341–57. Odense: Odense University Press.

Johansson, Karl Magnus, and Tapio Raunio. 2001. Partisan responses to Europe: Comparing Finnish and Swedish political parties. *European Journal of Political Research* 39 (2): 225–49.

——, and Jonas Tallberg. 2010. Explaining chief executive empowerment: European Union summitry and domestic institutional change. *West European Politics* 33 (2): 208–36.

Jospin, Lionel. 2002. *My vision of Europe and globalization.* Cambridge: Polity.

Judt, Tony. 1996. *A grand illusion? An essay on Europe.* New York, NY: Hill and Wang.

Kassim, Hussein. 2008. A bid too far? New Labour and UK leadership of the European Union. In *Leaderless Europe*, edited by J.E.S. Hayward, 167–87. Oxford: Oxford University Press.

Katz, Richard S., and Peter Mair. 1995. Changing models of party organization and party democracy: The emergence of the cartel party. *Party Politics* 1 (1): 5–28.

Kazakos, Panos. 1987. Greece and the new European dynamics: The economic dimension [in Greek]. In *Greece in the EC: The first five years*, edited by P. Kazakos and C. Stephanou, 427–55. Athens: Ant. N. Sakkoulas.

——. 1994. Greece and the EC: A historical overview. In *Greece and EC membership evaluated*, edited by P. Kazakos and P. Ioakimidis, 13–23. London: Pinter.

Keßler, Ulrike. 2002. Deutsche Europapolitik unter Helmut Kohl. In *Deutsche Europapolitik von Konrad Adenauer bis Gerhard Schröder*, edited by G. Müller-Brandeck-Bocquet, N. Leuchtweis, U. Keßler and C. Schukraft, 115–66. Opladen: Leske & Budrich.

Kinnock, Neil. 1994. Reforming the Labour Party. *Contemporary Record* 8 (3): 535–54.

Kirchheimer, Otto. 1966. The transformation of Western European party systems. In *Political parties and political development*, edited by J. LaPalombara and M. Weiner, 177–200. Princeton, NJ: Princeton University Press.

Kite, Cynthia. 1996. *Scandinavia faces EU: Debates and decisions on membership 1961–1994*. Umeå: Umeå University/Department of Political Science.

Kitschelt, Herbert. 1994. *The transformation of European social democracy*. Cambridge: Cambridge University Press.

Knodt, Michèle, and Nicola Staeck. 1999. Shifting paradigms: Reflecting Germany's European policy. *European Integration Online Papers* 3 (3). http://eiop.or.at/eiop/texte/1999-003.htm.

Krasner, Stephen D. 1978. *Defending the national interest: Raw materials investments and U.S. foreign policy*. Princeton, NJ: Princeton University Press.

Krouwel, André. 2006. Party models. In *Handbook of party politics*, edited by R.S. Katz and W. Crotty, 249–69. London: Sage.

Labour Party. Various years. Manifestos. www.labour-party.org.uk/manifestos/.

Ladrech, Robert. 1993. Social democratic parties and EC integration: Transnational party responses to Europe 1992. *European Journal of Political Research* 24 (2): 195–210.

——. 2000. *Social democracy and the challenge of European Union*. Boulder, CO: Lynne Rienner.

——. 2002. Europeanization and political parties: Towards a framework for analysis. *Party Politics* 8 (4): 389–403.

——, and Philippe Marlière. 1999. The French Socialist Party. In *Social democratic parties in the European Union: History, organisation, policies*, edited by R. Ladrech and Ph. Marlière, 64–78. Basingstoke: Macmillan.

Laffan, Brigid. 2006. Getting to a European Constitution: From Fischer to the IGC. In *The making of a European Constitution*, edited by S. Puntscher Riekmann and W. Wessels, 68–89. Wiesbaden: VS Verlag.

Lafontaine, Oskar. 1999. *Das Herz schlägt links*. München: Econ.

——, and Dominique Strauss-Kahn. 1999. Europa – sozial und stark. *Die Zeit* 3/1999, 21 January.

Lake, David A., and Robert Powell. 1999. International relations: A strategic-choice approach. In *Strategic choice and international relations*, edited by D.A. Lake and R. Powell, 3–38. Princeton, NJ: Princeton University Press.

Landais, Benjamin, Aymeric Monville and Pierre Yaghlekdjian. 2008. *L'idéologie européenne*. Brussels: Aden.

Langdal, Fredrik. 2006. The Swedish debate on Turkey's prospect for EU membership. In *Turkey, Sweden and the European Union: Experiences and Expectations*, edited by SIEPS, 18–28. Stockholm: Swedish Institute for European Policy Studies.

Lees, Charles. 2002. 'Dark matter': Institutional constraints and the failure of party-based Euroscepticism in Germany. *Political Studies* 50 (2): 244–267.

Lemaire-Prosche, Geneviève. 1990. *Le PS et l'Europe*. Paris: PUF.

Leneveu, Claude, and Michel Vakaloulis. 1998. *Faire mouvement: novembre-décembre 1995*. Paris: PUF.

Leuchtweis, Nicole. 2002. Deutsche Europapolitik zwischen Aufbruchstimmung und Weltwirtschaftskrise: Willy Brandt und Helmut Schmidt. In *Deutsche Europapolitik von Konrad Adenauer bis Gerhard Schröder*, edited by G. Müller-Brandeck-Bocquet, N. Leuchtweis, U. Keßler and C. Schukraft, 63–113. Opladen: Leske & Budrich.

Levy, Jonah D. 2000. France: Directing adjustment? In *Welfare and work in the open economy, Vol. II*, edited by F.W. Scharpf and V.A. Schmidt, 308–50. Oxford: Oxford University Press.

Lewin, Leif. 2002. *Ideologi och strategi: Svensk politik under 130 år*. Stockholm: Norstedts Juridik.

——. 2004. Framing to persuade: Sweden's decision to join the European Union. *European Review* 12 (2): 127–41.

Lieber, Robert J. 1970. *British politics and European unity. Parties, elites, and pressure groups*. Berkeley, CA: University of California Press.

Lodge, Juliet. 1975. The organization and control of European integration in the Federal Republic of Germany. *Parliamentary Affairs* 28 (4): 416–30.

——. 1976. *The European policy of the SPD*. London: Sage.

Lordon, Frédéric. 2001. The logic and limits of *désinflation competitive*. In *Social democracy in neoliberal times: The left and economic policy since 1980*, edited by A. Glyn, 110–37. Oxford: Oxford University Press.

Loulis, John C. 1984. Papandreou's foreign policy. *Foreign Affairs* 63 (2): 375–91.

Ludlow, Peter. 1982. *The making of the European Monetary System: A case study of the politics of the European Community*. London: Butterworth Scientific.

Luif, Paul. 1995. *On the road to Brussels: The political dimension of Austria's, Finland's and Sweden's accession to the European Union*. Laxenburg: Austrian Institute for International Affairs.

Lundgren Rydén, Lizelotte. 2000. *Ett svenskt dilemma: Socialdemokraterna, Centern och EG-frågan 1957–1994*. Gothenburg: Gothenburg University, Department of History.

MacShane, Denis. 1988. *French lessons for Labour*. London: Fabian Society.

Mair, Peter. 1994. Party organizations: From civil society to the state. In *How parties organize: Change and adaptation in party organizations in western democracies*, edited by R.S. Katz and P. Mair, 1–22. London: Sage.

——. 2001. The limited impact of Europe on national party systems. In *Europeanised politics? European integration and national political systems*, edited by K.H. Goetz and S. Hix, 27–51. London: Frank Cass.

——. 2007. Political parties and party systems. In *Europeanization: new research agendas*, edited by P. Graziano and M.P. Vink, 154–66. Basingstoke: Palgrave.

af Malmborg, Mikael. 1994. *Den ståndaktiga nationalstaten: Sverige och den västeuropeiska integrationen 1945–59*. Lund: Lund University Press.

Mandelson, Peter, and Roger Liddle. 1996. *The Blair revolution*. London: Faber & Faber.

Maret, Jean, and Alain Houlou. 1990. *Histoire des socialistes. L'identité socialiste des utopistes à nos jours*. Paris: Pro-Edi.

Marks, Gary, and Carole J. Wilson. 2000. The past in the present: A cleavage theory of party response to European integration. *British Journal of Political Science* 30 (3): 433–59.

——, Carole J. Wilson and Leonard Ray. 2002. National political parties and European integration. *American Journal of Political Science* 46 (3): 585–94.

——, Liesbet Hooghe, Moira Nelson and Erica Edwards. 2006. Party competition and European integration in the East and West. *Comparative Political Studies* 39 (2): 155–75.

——, Liesbet Hooghe, Marco R. Steenbergen and Ryan Bakkera. 2007. Crossvalidating data on party positioning on European integration. *Electoral Studies* 26 (1): 23–38.

Marlière, Philippe. 1999. Introduction: European social democracy *in situ*. In *Social democratic parties in the European Union*, edited by R. Ladrech and P. Marlière, 1–15. Basingstoke: Macmillan.

——. 2001. Introduction. *Journal of Southern Europe and the Balkans* (special issue on social democracy in Southern Europe and the challenge of European integration) 3 (1): 5–9.

——. 2003. *La troisième voie dans l'impasse. Essais sur Tony Blair et le New Labour.* Paris: Syllepse.

——. 2007. De Lionel Jospin à Ségolène Royal: l'introuvable troisième voie du socialisme français. *Mouvements* (50): 14–23.

——. 2008. Référendum: assez de tartufferies! *L'Humanité*, 12 January, 10.

——. 2009. La cogestion néolibérale sanctionnée. *L'Humanité*, 17 June, 17.

May, James. 1975. Is there a European socialism? *Journal of Common Market Studies* 13 (4): 492–502.

McKenzie, R. 1963. *British political parties*. London: Heinemann.

Mélenchon, Jean-Luc. 2007. *En quête de gauche*. Paris: Balland.

——. 2008a. Le vote de Versailles: la honte! Le Blog de Jean-Luc Mélenchon, 4 February, www.jean-luc-melenchon.fr/?p = 555.

——. 2008b. Discours au meeting de lancement du Parti de Gauche. Le Blog de Jean-Luc Mélenchon, 29 November, www.jean-luc-melenchon.fr/?p = 649.

Menon, Anand. 2004. Britain and the Convention on the future of Europe. *International Affairs* 79 (5): 963–78.

Merkel, Wolfgang, and Tobias Ostheim. 2004a. Grenzen und Chancen sozialdemokratischer Politik im Handlungsraum Europa. In *Gesellschaft mit beschränkter Hoffnung. Reformfähigkeit und die Möglichkeit rationaler Politik*, edited by P. Stykow and J. Beyer, 145–74. Wiesbaden: VS Verlag.

——, and Tobias Ostheim. 2004b. Policy making in the European Union: Is there a social democratic space? Discussion paper. Bonn: Friedrich Ebert Stiftung. www.fes.de/europolity/finalversionmerk.PDF.

Messmer, William B. 2003. Taming Labour's MEPs. *Party Politics* 9 (2): 201–18.

Meyer, Thomas. 1997. The transformation of German social democracy. In *Looking left. Socialism in Europe after the Cold War*, edited by D. Sassoon, 124–42. New York: I.B. Tauris.

——. 2007. Die blockierte Partei – Regierungspraxis und Programmdiskussion der SPD 2002–5. In *Ende des rot-grünen Projektes. Eine Bilanz der Regierung Schröder 2002–2005*, edited by Chr. Egle and R. Zohlnhöfer, 83–97. Wiesbaden: VS Verlag.

Michels, Robert. [1911] 1989. *Zur Soziologie des Parteiwesens in der modernen Demokratie. Untersuchungen über die oligarchischen Tendenzen des Gruppenlebens.* 4th edn. Stuttgart: Kröner.

Miles, Lee. 1997. *Sweden and European integration*. Aldershot: Ashgate.

——, ed. 2000. *Sweden and the European Union evaluated*. London: Continuum.

——. 2005. *Fusing with Europe? Sweden in the European Union.* Aldershot: Ashgate.

Milward, Alan S. 1992. *The European rescue of the nation state*. London: Routledge.

Minkin, L. 1980. *The Labour Party conference*. Manchester: Manchester University Press.

Minkin, Lewis. 1991. *The contentious alliance. Trade unions and the Labour Party*. Edinburgh: Edinburgh University Press.

Mitterrand, François. 1969. *Ma part de vérité*. Paris: Fayard.

——. 1988. La lettre à tous les Français. www.psinfo.net/entretiens/mitterrand/1988lettre.html.

Moeller, Richard. 1996. The German social democrats. In *Political parties and the European Union*, edited by J. Gaffney, 33–52. London: Routledge.

Montebourg, Arnaud, and Paul, Christian. 2002. Elargissement de l'Europe: nous exigeons un référendum. *Le Monde*, 20 September, 19.

Moravcsik, Andrew. 1993. Preferences and power in the European Community: A liberal intergovernmentalist approach. *Journal of Common Market Studies* 31 (4): 473–524.

——. 1994. *Why the European Community strengthens the state: Domestic politics and international cooperation*. Center for European Studies Working Paper Series # 52. Cambridge MA: Center for European Studies, Harvard University.

——. 1997. Taking preferences seriously: A liberal theory of international politics. *International Organization* 51 (4): 513–53.

——. 1998. *The choice for Europe: Social purpose and state power from Messina to Maastricht*. Ithaca, NY: Cornell University Press.

Moschonas, Gerassimos. 2002. *In the name of social democracy. The great transformation, 1945 to the present*. London: Verso.

——. 2007. PASOK and the French socialists: Image of a new social democracy [in Greek]. *Ta Nea* (Athens), 27 March. http://ta-nea.dolnet.gr/print_article.php?e=A&f=18798&m=N06&aa=2.

Moscovici, Pierre. 2004. Comment sortir de la crise européenne? *La Revue Socialiste* (15–16): 78–83.

——. 2007. *L'Europe est morte, vive l'Europe!* Paris: Perrin.

——, and Bernard Poignant. 2007. Oui, malgré tout au mini traité européen. *Le Monde*, 24 October, 21.

Mouzelis, Nikos, and George Pagoulatos. 2002. *Civil society and citizenship in post-war Greece*. Discussion paper. Athens: AUEB. www.aueb.gr/deos/papers/Mouzelis-Pagoulatos-AUEB-Discussion-Paper1.pdf.

Mullen, Andrew. 2007. *The British Left's 'great debate' on Europe*. London: Continuum.

Muller, Pierre. 1995. Les politiques publiques comme construction d'un rapport au monde. In *La construction du sens dans les politiques publiques: Débats autour de la notion de référentiel*, edited by A. Faure, G. Pollet and Ph. Warin, 153–79. Paris: L'Harmattan.

Müller-Brandeck-Bocquet, Gisela. 2002. Deutsche Leadership in der Europäischen Union? Die Europapolitik der rot-grünen Bundesregierung 1998–2002. In *Deutsche Europapolitik von Konrad Adenauer bis Gerhard Schröder*, edited by G. Müller-Brandeck-Bocquet, N. Leuchtweis, U. Keßler and C. Schukraft, 167–220. Opladen: Leske & Budrich.

——. 2006. Europapolitik als Staatsraison. In *Regieren in der Bundesrepublik Deutschland*, edited by M.G. Schmidt and R. Zohlnhöfer, 456–78. Wiesbaden: VS Verlag.

218 Bibliography

——, Nicole Leuchtweis, Ulrike Keßler and Corina Schukraft, eds. 2002. *Deutsche Europapolitik von Konrad Adenauer bis Gerhard Schröder*. Opladen: Leske & Budrich.

Nairn, Tom. 1972. The Left against Europe? *New Left Review* (I/75): 5–120.

Newman. Michael. 1983. *Socialism and European unity: The dilemma of the Left in Britain and France*. London: Junction Books.

Niedermayer, Oskar. 2005. Die Wahl zum Europäischen Parlament vom 13. Juni 2004 in Deutschland: Ein schwarzer Tag für die SPD. *Zeitschrift für Parlamentsfragen* 36 (1): 3–19.

Nordlinger, Eric A. 1981. *On the autonomy of the democratic state*. Cambridge, MA: Harvard University Press.

Notermans, Ton, ed. 2001a. *Social democracy and monetary union*. Oxford: Berghahn.

——. 2001b. Introduction. In *Social democracy and monetary union*, edited by T. Notermans, 1–19. Oxford: Berghahn.

——. 2001c. The German social democrats and monetary union. In *Social democracy and monetary union*, edited by T. Notermans, 71–96. Oxford: Berghahn.

O'Donnell, Clara Marina, and Richard G. Whitman. 2007. European policy under Gordon Brown: Perspectives on a future Prime Minister. *International Affairs* 83 (1): 253–72.

Office Universitaire de Recherche Socialiste. n.d. *L'Europe vue par 3 socialistes: Léon Blum, Guy Mollet, François Mitterrand. La construction européenne vue par trois socialistes français, 1948–1995*. www.lours.org/default.asp?pid = 372.

Oscarsson, Henrik, and Sören Holmberg. 2006. *Europaval*. Göteborg: Statsvetenskapliga institutionen.

Ostheim, Tobias. 2003. Praxis und Rhetorik deutscher Europapolitik. In *Das rot-grüne Projekt. Eine Bilanz der Regierung Schröder 1998–2002*, edited by Chr. Egle, T. Ostheim and R. Zohlnhöfer, 351–80. Wiesbaden: VS Verlag.

——. 2006. Europa als Handlungsraum sozialdemokratischer Politik. In *Die Reformfähigkeit der Sozialdemokratie. Herausforderungen und Bilanz der Regierungspolitik in Westeuropa*, edited by W. Merkel, Chr. Egle, Chr. Henkes, T. Ostheim and A. Petring, 407–55. Wiesbaden: VS Verlag.

——. 2007. Einsamkeit durch Zweisamkeit? Die Europapolitik der zweiten Regierung Schröder. In *Ende des rot-grünen Projektes. Eine Bilanz der Regierung Schröder 2002–2005*, edited by Chr. Egle and R. Zohlnhöfer, 480–510. Wiesbaden: VS Verlag.

Owen, David. 1992. *Time to declare*. Harmondsworth: Penguin.

Padgett, Stephen, and William E. Patterson. 1991. *A history of social democracy in postwar Europe*. Harlow: Longman.

Palme, Olof. 1981. Sverige vid sidan av EG. Speech in Lund, Sweden, 9 November. Labour Movement Archives and Library, Olof Palme (2.4: 98) www.olofpalme.org.

Pangalos, Theodoros. 2003. The unfortunate end of the Presidency [in Greek]. *To Vima tis Kiriakis* (Athens), 8 June, A22.

——. 2004. Not a club of like-minded people [in Greek]. *Eleftherotypia* (Athens), 5 September, 26.

Papandreou, George A. 2005. Speech delivered at the European Socialist Party meeting, Vienna, 24 June. www.papandreou.gr/papandreou/content/Document. aspx?d=6&rd=7739474&f=1359&rf=1307755822&m=5509&rm=935734&l=2.

——. 2006a. Press conference, Athens, 31 January. www.papandreou.gr/papandreou/ content/Document.aspx?d=6&rd=7739474&f=1361&rf=1293666608&m=6685& rm=9352203&l=2.

——. 2006b. New challenges for Greece in the 21st century. Speech delivered at the meeting of PASOK MEPs with foreign ambassadors based in Greece. Athens, 31 June. www.papandreou.gr/papandreou/content/Document.aspx?d=6&rd=77394 74&f=1359&rf=1307755822&m=7244&rm=23694652&l=2.

——. 2006c. Speech delivered at the 7th PES Congress. Porto, 8 December. www. papandreou.gr/papandreou/content/Document.aspx?d=6&rd=7739474&f=1359&rf= 1307755822&m=7969&rm=22115334&l=2.

——. 2006d. *Constructing a progressive future for the 21st century. Italianieuropei. Bimestrale del riformismo italiano.* 22 September. www.papandreou.gr/papandreou/ content/Document.aspx?d=6&rd=7739474&f=1360&rf=1307380017&m=7629& rm=18244664&l=2.

——. 2006e. Speech delivered at the Economist conference. Athens, 28 June. www.papandreou.gr/papandreou/content/Document.aspx?d=6&rd=7739474&f= 1359&rf=1307755822&m=7239&rm=8693235&l=2.

——. 2006f. Seven proposals for the new Socialist International [in Greek]. Interview, *Ethnos tis Kiriakis* (Athens), 22 January. www.papandreou.gr/papandreou/content/ Document.aspx?d=6&rd=7739474&f=1361&rf=1293666608&m=6645&rm=18637 094&l=2.

——. 2007a. Speech delivered at the plenary session of the Socialist Group in the European Parliament. Brussels, 31 January. www.papandreou.gr/papandreou/content/ Document.aspx?d=6&rd=7739474&f=1359&rf=1307755822&m=8277&rm=2417 2300&l=2.

——. 2007b. I shall govern with the people, for the people and the homeland [in Greek]. Speech delivered at the meeting of PASOK's National Council. Athens, 3 March. www.papandreou.gr/papandreou/content/Document.aspx?d=6&rd=7739474&f= 1359&rf=1307755822&m=8380&rm=21187798&l=2.

——. 2007c. Speech delivered at the 33rd congress of the General Confederation of Greek Workers. Athens, 16 March. www.papandreou.gr/papandreou/content/ Document.aspx?d=6&rd=7739474&f=1359&rf=1307755822&m=8459&rm=18052 987&l=2.

——. 2007d. Statement on the occasion of the 50th anniversary of the signing of the Treaty of Rome [in Greek]. Athens, 25 March. www.papandreou.gr/papandreou/ content/Document.aspx?d=-1&rd=0&f=1354&rf=1290836267&m=8526&rm= 18317281&l=2.

——. 2008a. The crisis is an opportunity to bring up our values. Address by George Papandreou, president of PASOK and president of the Socialist International, at the meeting of the Council of the European Socialist Party in Madrid, 1 December. www.papandreou.gr/papandreou/content/Document.aspx?d=6&rd=7739474&f= 1359&rf=1307755822&m=11700&rm=11847678&l=1.

——. 2008b. Solving this financial crisis is a political matter. Speech at the conference on 'The financial crisis, the international security and the new economic architecture', New York, 14 November. www.papandreou.gr/papandreou/content/ Document.aspx?d=6&rd=7739474&f=1359&rf=1307755822&m=11628&rm=1776 7209&l=1.

——. 2009a. Speaking notes for the meeting of the electoral strategy committee for the 2009 European elections [in Greek]. www.pasok.gr/portal/resource/contentObject/ id/4b2343b9-be06–4cb9-a5cc-ea91e6878f04.

——. 2009b. Political system and identity [in Greek]. Speech, Old Parliament building, Athens, 6 April. www.papandreou.gr/papandreou/content/Document.aspx?d=6&rd= 7739474&f=1359&rf=1307755822&m=12056&rm=15590832&l=2.

——. 2009c. We are voting on Europe; We are deciding on Greece [in Greek]. Speech at an election rally, Patra, 17 May. www.papandreou.gr/papandreou/content/Document.aspx?d=6&rd=7739474&f=1359&rf=1307755822&m=12246&rm=9354925&l=2.

Pappamikail, Peter Brown. 1998. Britain viewed from Europe. In *Britain for and against Europe. British politics and the question of European integration*, edited by D. Baker and D. Seawright, 206–21. Oxford: Clarendon Press.

Pappas, Tassos. 2008. Strangers in the same family [in Greek]. *Eleftherotypia* (Athens), 16 June.

Parti Socialiste. 1972. *Changer la vie. Programme de gouvernement du Parti Socialiste.* Paris: Flammarion.

——. 1980. *Projet socialiste pour la France des années 80.* Paris: Club Socialiste du Livre.

——. 1996. Convention Nationale. Mondialisation, Europe, France. *Vendredi* (276): 22–31.

——. 2006. *Projet socialiste pour la France.* Paris: *Parti socialiste.*

——. 2008. Déclaration de principes du Parti socialiste. *L'Hebdo des socialistes* (494): 20.

——. 2009. Donner une nouvelle direction à l'Europe. *L'Hebdo des socialistes* (521): 6–15.

Party of European Socialists. 2009. A new direction for progressive societies: A new way forward, a stronger PES. Resolution No. 2 adopted by the 8th PES congress. Prague, 7–8 December.

Passas, Argyris G. 2008. National parliaments and their influence on the European Union's political system: The case of the Hellenic Parliament [in Greek]. In *Greece in the European Union: Past, present and future*, edited by N. Maravegias, 330–52. Athens: Themelio.

PASOK. 1976. *Greece and the Common Market* [in Greek]. Athens: PASOK.

——. 2004a. Programmatic statement [in Greek]. Athens: PASOK. www.pasok.gr/portal/gr/128/8608/3/1/showdoc.html.

——. 2004b. PASOK's government programme, 2004–8 [in Greek]. Athens: PASOK. www.pasok.gr/portal/gr/000F4240/Data/2004.pdf

——. 2004c. 2004 European Elections manifesto [in Greek]. 3 May. Athens: PASOK. www.pasok.gr/portal/gr/eu_el/5000576/11432/1/7/1/showdoc.html.

——. 2004d. Final results of the election for the leadership of the party [in Greek]. 9 February. www.pasok.gr/portal/gr/3/8796/7/print/135/1/showdoc.html.

——. 2005. Political declaration on the occasion of the party congress [in Greek]. 3 March. Athens: PASOK. www.pasok.gr/portal/gr/7osyn/179/21605/7/7/1/showdoc2.html.

——. 2007. Programmatic framework – proposals for dialogue [in Greek]. March. Athens: PASOK. http://programma.pasok.gr/wp-content/uploads/PROGRAMMA/programma_pasok.pdf.

Pateras, Michael G. 1984. From association to accession: Changing attitudes of Greek political parties towards Greek relations with the European Communities, 1957–75. Ph.D. diss., London School of Economics and Political Science, University of London.

Paterson, William E. 1974. *The SPD and European integration.* Westmead: Saxon House.

——. 1975. The SPD after Brandt's fall – change or continuity? *Government and Opposition* 10 (2): 167–88.

——, Penny Henson and Peter Shipley. 1995. *The European policies of Labour and the Conservative Party in Great Britain*. Interne Studien Nr 109/1995. Sankt Augustin: Konrad-Adenauer-Stiftung.

——, and James Sloam. 2006. Is the Left alright? The SPD and the renewal of European social democracy. *German Politics* 15 (3): 233–48.

Peillon, Vincent. 2004. Enfin dépasser nos contradictions. *La Revue Socialiste* (15–16): 84–89.

——, David Assouline, Jacques Bascou, Geneviève Gaillard, Jean Gaubert, Jean Guérard, Christian Martin, Béatrice Patrie, Gilbert Roger, Claude Saulnier, Pascal Terrasse and Jean-Jacques Thomas. 2007. Pourquoi les nonistes du PS votent oui au nouveau traité. *Libération*, 5 November, 20.

Persson, Göran. 2001. *European challenges: A Swedish perspective*. Speech delivered at Humboldt University, Berlin, 18 October. www.whi-berlin.de/documents/HRE-Persson.pdf.

——. 2004. Speech delivered at the SAP Conference. 16–18 April, Stockholm. www.socialdemokraterna.se/Templates/Page – 6854.aspx.

——. 2007. *Min väg, mina val*. Stockholm: Bonniers.

Peston, Robert. 2005. *Brown's Britain*. London: Short Books.

Pierson, Paul. 1993. When effect becomes cause: Policy feedback and political change. *World Politics* 45 (4): 595–628.

Pivert, Marceau. 1948. Le socialisme fera l'Europe. *La Revue Socialiste* (June–July): 110–26.

Poguntke, Thomas, and Paul Webb. 2005a. The presidentialization of politics in democratic societies: A framework for analysis. In *The presidentialization of politics: A comparative study of modern democracies*, edited by T. Poguntke and P. Webb, 1–25. Oxford: Oxford University Press.

——, and Paul Webb, eds. 2005b. *The presidentialization of politics: A comparative study of modern democracies*. Oxford: Oxford University Press.

Poguntke, Thomas, Nicholas Aylott, Elisabeth Carter, Robert Ladrech and Kurt Richard Luther, eds. 2007. *The Europeanization of national political parties: Power and organizational adaptation*. Abingdon: Routledge.

Pop, Valentina. 2009. EU socialists disagree with early choice of Commission chief, *EUObserver*, 30 March, http://euobserver.com/883/27868.

Poulantzas, Nicos. 1968. *Pouvoir politique et classes sociales*. Paris: François Maspero.

Przeworski, Adam. 1985. *Capitalism and social democracy*. Cambridge, UK: Cambridge University Press.

PS/SPD. 2007. Déclaration commune sur l'avenir de l'Europe. http://international.parti-socialiste.fr/files/brochure_ps_spd.pdf (accessed 6 June 2007).

Quatremer, Jean. Les coulisses de Bruxelles blog. http://bruxelles.blogs.liberation.fr/coulisses/.

Quilliot, Roger. 1963. Rénovation et regroupement. *La Revue Socialiste* (March): 67–79.

Radice, Giles. 1992. *Offshore: Britain and the European idea*. London: I.B. Tauris.

Raunio, Tapio. 2002. Why European integration increases leadership autonomy within political parties. *Party Politics* 8 (4): 405–22.

Rawnsley, Andrew. 2000. *Servants of the people. The inside story of New Labour*. London: Hamish Hamilton.

Ray, Leonard. 1999. Measuring party orientations towards European integration: Results from an expert survey. *European Journal of Political Research* 36 (6): 283–306.

——. 2003. When parties matter: The conditional influence of party positions on voter opinions about European integration. *Journal of Politics* 65 (4): 978–94.

Reinhardt, Nickolas. 1997. A turning point in the German EMU debate: The Baden-Württemberg regional election of March 1996. *German Politics* 6 (1): 77–99.

Rimbert, Pierre. 1948. Révolution directoriale et socialisme. *La Revue Socialiste* (June–July): 78–92.

Robins, L.J. 1979. *The reluctant party: Labour and the EEC, 1961–1975*. Ormskirk: G.W. & A. Hesketh.

Rohrschneider, Robert, and Stephen Whitefield. 2007. Representation in new democracies: Party stances on European integration in post-communist Eastern Europe. *Journal of Politics* 69 (4): 1133–46.

——, and Stephen Whitefield. 2010. Consistent choice sets? The stances of political parties towards European integration in ten Central East European democracies, 2003–7. *Journal of European Public Policy* 17 (1): 55–75.

Rosamond, Ben. 1993. National labour organizations and European integration: British trade unions and '1992'. *Political Studies* 41 (3): 420–34.

Ross, George. 1992. Confronting the new Europe. *New Left Review* (191): 49–68.

——. 1995. *Jacques Delors and European integration*. Cambridge: Polity.

——. 1998a. *French social democracy and EMU*. ARENA Working Paper no. 19. Oslo: ARENA.

——. 1998b. The Euro, the French model of society and French politics. *French Politics and Society* 16 (4): 1–16.

Rothstein, Bo. 1996. *The social democratic state: The Swedish model and the bureaucratic problem of social reforms*. Pittsburgh: University of Pittsburgh Press.

Royal, Ségolène. 2007a. Lettre à la Ligue des Droits de l'Homme. www.ldh-france. org/actu_derniereheure.cfm?idactu=1441.

——. 2007b. Pacte présidentiel. www.desirsdavenir.org/actions/telecharge_pacte.php.

Ruin, Olof. 2002. *Sveriges statsminister och EU: Ett halvår i centrum*. Stockholm: Hjalmarson & Högberg.

Russell, Meg. 2005. *Building New Labour. The politics of party organization*. Basingstoke: Palgrave.

Salesse, Yves. 2004. *Manifeste pour une autre Europe*. Paris: Le Félin.

SAP. 2005. A just world is possible – The Swedish Social Democratic Party's international policy programme adopted by the 35th ordinary party congress. www.socialdemokraterna.se/upload/Internationellt/Other%20Languages/Internation ellt%20Program%20English.pdf (accessed 7 June 2007).

Sapir, Jacques. 2006. *La fin de l'eurolibéralisme*. Paris: Seuil.

Sassoon, Donald. 1996. *One hundred years of socialism: The West European Left in the twentieth century*. London: Fontana.

Scharpf, Fritz. 1999. *Governing in Europe: Effective and democratic?* Oxford: Oxford University Press.

Schattschneider, E.E. 1960. *The semisovereign people: A realist's view of democracy in America*. New York: Holt, Rinehart and Winston.

Schmidt, Helmut. 1990. *Die Deutschen und ihre Nachbarn. Menschen und Mächte, Band II*. Berlin: Siedler.

Seyd, Patrick. 1987. *The rise and fall of the Labour Left*. Basingstoke: Macmillan.

Shaw, Eric. 1996. *The Labour Party since 1945: Old Labour, New Labour*. Oxford: Blackwell.

———. 2007. *Losing Labour's soul? New Labour and the Blair government*. London: Routledge.

Simitis, Costas. 1995. *For a strong society, for a strong Greece* [in Greek]. Athens: Plethron.

———. 2002a. *For a powerful Greece in Europe and the world* [in Greek]. Athens: Kastaniotis.

———. 2002b. *For a powerful, modern and democratic Greece* [in Greek]. Athens: Kastaniotis.

———. 2002c. *For a socially just and economically powerful Greece* [in Greek]. Athens: Kastaniotis.

———. 2005. *Policy and politics for a creative Greece, 1996–2004* [in Greek]. Athens: Polis.

———. 2007a. *Objectives, strategy and prospects: Texts, 2000–2006* [in Greek]. Athens: Polis.

———. 2007b. The EU risks remaining a mere market for the powerful [in Greek]. Interview, *Ethnos tis Kiriakis* (Athens), 18 March. www.ethnos.gr/article.asp?catid= 5347&subid=2&PubID=98312&word=%D3%E7%EC%DF%F4%E7%F2#.

———. 2008. Why we must change our policy. *To Vima tis Kiriakis*, 17 February.

Sjöblom, Gunnar. 1968. *Party strategies in a multiparty system*. Lund: Studentlitteratur.

Sloam, James. 2003. 'Responsibility for Europe': The EU policy of the German Social Democrats since unification. *German Politics* 12 (1): 59–78.

———. 2005. *The European policy of the German Social Democrats: interpreting a changing world*. Basingstoke: Palgrave Macmillan.

Smith, Julie. 2005. A missed opportunity? New Labour's European policy 1997–2005. *International Affairs* 81 (4): 703–21.

———, and Mariana Tsatsas. 2002. *The new bilateralism. The UK's relations within the EU*. London: The Royal Institute of International Affairs.

Smith, M.J. 1994. Neil Kinnock and the modernisation of the Labour Party. *Contemporary British History* 8 (3): 555-66.

Socialdemokraterna. 2000. *S-politik i EU*. Stockholm: Socialdemokraterna.

———. 2004. European Parliament election manifesto. Stockholm: Socialdemokraterna.

———. 2006. Election Manifesto. Stockholm: Socialdemokraterna.

———. 2007. Party Conference, 17–18 March. Stockholm: Socialdemokraterna.

———. 2008. Socialdemokraternas valplattform inför valet till Europaparlamentet 2009. Stockholm: Socialdemokraterna.

———. Activity reports 1989–2004. Stockholm: Socialdemokraterna.

Soudais, Michel. 2007. Le retour des oui-oui socialistes. *Politis*, 6 November, www.pour-politis.org/spip.php?article401.

———. 2009. Europe libérale: le simplisme du PS. *Politis*, 1 March, www.pour-politis.org/spip.php?article694.

SPD. 1959. *Grundsatzprogramm der Sozialdemokratischen Partei Deutschlands*. Beschlossen vom Außerordentlichen Parteitag der Sozialdemokratischen Partei Deutschlands in Bad Godesberg vom 13. bis 15. November 1959. http://library.fes.de/pdf-files/bibliothek/retro-scans/fa-57721.pdf.

———. 2001. Leitantrag 'Verantwortung für Europa'. In *Parteitag der SPD in Nürnberg, 19. bis 22. November 2001: Beschlüsse*, edited by SPD–Parteivorstand, 42–55. Berlin.

———. 2007. *Soziale Demokratie im 21. Jahrhundert*. Party programme adopted at the Hamburg party conference, 28 October. Berlin: SPD.

Spourdalakis, M. 1998. From the 'protest movement' to the 'new PASOK' [in Greek]. In *PASOK: Party, state, society*, edited by M. Spourdalakis, 15–74. Athens: Patakis.

Steenbergen, Marco, and David Scott. 2004. Contesting Europe? The salience of European integration as a party issue. In *European integration and political conflict*, edited by G. Marks and M. Steenbergen, 165–94. Cambridge: Cambridge University Press.

Steinmo, Sven, Kathleen Thelen and Frank Longstreth, eds. 1992. *Structuring politics: Historical institutionalism in comparative politics*. Cambridge, UK: Cambridge University Press.

Stephens, Philip. 2005. Britain and Europe: An unforgettable past and an unavoidable future. *Political Quarterly* 76 (1): 12–21.

Stjernø, Steinar. 2004. *Solidarity in Europe: The history of an idea*. Cambridge: Cambridge University Press.

Stråth, Bo. 1992. *Folkhemmet mot Europa: Ett historiskt perspektiv på 90-talet*. Stockholm: Tiden.

Stroh, Astrid. 2004. *Die SPD im europäischen Einigungsprozeß: Organisation und innerparteiliche Willensbildung in der Europapolitik von 1979 bis 1998*. Hamburg: Verlag Dr. Kovač.

Strøm, Kaare. 1990. A behavioural theory of competitive political parties. *American Journal of Political Science* 34 (2): 565–98.

———, Ian Budge and Michael J. Laver. 1994. Constraints on cabinet formation in parliamentary democracies. *American Journal of Political Science* 38 (2): 303–35.

———, and Wolfgang Müller. 1999. Political parties and hard choices. In *Policy, office or votes? How political parties in Western Europe make hard decisions*, edited by W.C. Müller and K. Strøm, 1–35. Cambridge: Cambridge University Press.

Stuart, Mark. 2005. *John Smith: A life*. London: Politico's.

Svåsand, Lars, and Ulf Lindström. 1996. Scandinavian political parties and the European Union. In *Political parties and the European Union*, edited by J. Gaffney, 205–20. London: Routledge.

Swedish Government. 2000. Promemoria till EU-nämnden inför nästa regeringskonferens. Stockholm: Swedish Government.

———. 2002. EU:s framtidsfrågor. Official Letter to the Parliament from the Government. Stockholm: Swedish Parliament.

Swedish Parliament. 2002. EU:s framtidsfrågor. Report from the Swedish Parliament. Stockholm: Swedish Parliament.

Taggart, Paul. 1998. A touchstone of dissent: Euroscepticism in contemporary Western European party systems. *European Journal of Political Research* 33 (3): 363–88.

———. 2000. *Populism*. Buckingham: Open University Press.

———, and Aleks Szczerbiak, eds. 2008a. *Opposing Europe? The comparative party politics of Euroscepticism. Vol. 1: Case studies and country surveys*. Oxford: Oxford University Press.

———, and Aleks Szczerbiak, eds. 2008b. *Opposing Europe? The comparative party politics of Euroscepticism. Vol. 2: Comparative and theoretical perspectives*. Oxford: Oxford University Press.

Tartakowsky, Danielle. 1972. Guerre Froide et Troisième Force, 1947–54. In *La 4e République: La France de 1945 à 1958*, edited by H. Claude, D. Tartakowsky, E. Mignot and R. Leroy, 48–64. Paris: Editions Sociales.

Taylor, Paul. 1975. The politics of the European Communities: the confederal phase. *World Politics* 27 (3): 336–60.

Thielemann, Eiko R. 2004. Dividing competences: Germany's vision(s) for Europe's federal future. *Comparative European Politics* 2 (3): 358–74.

Tilly, Charles. 1984. *Big structures, large processes, huge comparisons.* New York: Russell Sage Foundation.

Trägårdh, Lars. 2002. Sweden and the EU: Welfare state nationalism and the spectre of 'Europe'. In *European integration and national identity: The challenge of the Nordic states*, edited by L. Hansen and O. Wæver, 130–81. London: Routledge.

Tsakalotos, Euclid. 2001. The political economy of social democratic economic policies: The PASOK experiment in Greece. In *Social democracy in neoliberal times: The Left and economic policy since 1980*, edited by A. Glyn, 138–72. Oxford: Oxford University Press.

Tsardanidis, Charalambos. 1998. Foreign policy, 1990–97 [in Greek]. In *PASOK: Party, state, society*, edited by M. Spourdalakis, 295–318. Athens: Patakis.

Tsebelis, George. 2002. *Veto players: How political institutions work.* Princeton, NJ: Princeton University Press.

Tsoukalas, Constantine. 1969. *The Greek tragedy.* London: Penguin.

Varfis, Grigoris. n.d. Note on the memorandum of the Hellenic government [in Greek]. Mimeo.

Venizelos, Evagelos. 2006. *Two words: Left – Right in our era* [in Greek] Athens: Polis.

Verney, Susannah. 1987. Greece and the European Community. In *Political change in Greece: Before and after the colonels*, edited by K. Featherstone and D.K. Katsoudas, 253–70. London: Croom Helm.

———. 1990. To be or not to be within the European Community: The party debate and democratic consolidation in Greece. In *Securing democracy: Political parties and democratic consolidation in southern Europe*, edited by G. Pridham, 203–23. London: Routledge.

———. 1994. Panacea or plague: Greek political parties and accession to the European Community, 1974–79. Ph.D. diss., History, King's College, University of London.

Vertovec, Steven, and Robin Cohen. 2003. *Conceiving cosmopolitanism: Theory, context, and practice.* Oxford: Oxford University Press.

Volkens, Andrea. 2001. Quantifying the election programmes: Coding procedures and controls. In *Mapping policy preferences. Estimates for parties, electors, and governments, 1945–1998*, edited by I. Budge, H.-D. Klingemann, A. Volkens, J. Bara and E. Tanenbaum, 93–109. Oxford: Oxford University Press.

Wagner, Markus. 2008. Debating Europe in the French Socialist Party: the 2004 internal referendum on the EU Constitution. *French Politics* 6 (3): 257–79.

Waterfield, Bruno 2007. EU polls would be lost, says Nicolas Sarkozy. *Daily Telegraph*, 15 November, 17.

Wehner, Herbert. 1960. Rede im Deutschen Bundestag am 30.06.1960. *Bundestags-Plenarprotokolle.* 3. Wahlperiode, 122. Sitzung, 7052–61.

Westberg, Jacob. 2003. *Den nationella drömträdgården: Den stora berättelsen om den egna nationen i svensk och brittisk Europadebatt.* Stockholm: Stockholm University/Department of Political Science.

Westlake, Martin. 2001. *Kinnock: The biography.* London: Little, Brown & Co.

Wheare, K.C. 1946. *Federal government.* London: Oxford University Press for the Royal Institute of International Affairs.

Whiteley, Paul. 1983. *The Labour Party in crisis*. London: Methuen.

Wickham-Jones, Mark. 1996. *Economic strategy and the Labour Party*. Basingstoke: Macmillan.

Wildavsky, Aaron. 1987. Choosing preferences by constructing institutions: A cultural theory of preference formation. *American Political Science Review* 81 (1): 3–21.

Windrich, Elaine. 1952. *British Labour's foreign policy*. Stanford, CA: Stanford University Press.

Young, Hugo. 1998. *This blessed plot. Britain and Europe from Churchill to Blair*. Basingstoke: Macmillan.

Young, John W. 1984. *Britain, France and the unity of Europe 1945–51*. Leicester: Leicester University Press.

——. 1993. *Britain and European Unity, 1945–92*. Basingstoke: Macmillan.

Zeigler, Philip. 1993. *Wilson: The authorised life*. 2nd edn. London: Weidenfeld & Nicolson.

Zohlnhöfer, Reimut, and Christoph Egle. 2007. Einleitung: Der Episode zweiter Teil – ein Überblick über die 15. Legislaturperiode. In *Ende des rot-grünen Projektes. Eine Bilanz der Regierung Schröder 2002–2005*, edited by Chr. Egle and R. Zohlnhöfer, 11–25. Wiesbaden: VS Verlag.

Index

Page references to illustrations are given in *italic* type.

For Product Safety Concerns and Information please contact our EU
representative GPSR@taylorandfrancis.com
Taylor & Francis Verlag GmbH, Kaufingerstraße 24, 80331 München, Germany

www.ingramcontent.com/pod-product-compliance
Lightning Source LLC
Chambersburg PA
CBHW050419280326
41932CB00013BA/1926

9 781138 996212